TOM

THE BITCOIN
CONSPIRACY

AMERICA IS UNDER ATTACK SERIES

The Bitcoin Conspiracy
America is Under Attack series

To My Wife, Brenda,

In the fabric of our shared existence, your name is stitched in threads of gold, glowing with the luminosity of steadfast love, resilience, and unparalleled understanding. For thirty-seven years, you have stood by my side, an enduring beacon amidst the tempests that life occasionally cast upon us in its relentless course.

From the hallowed corners of my heart, this book is dedicated to you, a tribute to your unwavering faith in the possibility of redemption and renewal. Your forgiveness has been my salvation, your support, my fortress.

CONTENTS

PROLOGUE

I n the distant corners of our collective imagination, we live a thousand lives, sketching stories of heroes, villains, the grotesque, and the sublime. One such tale is that of a man, a woman, or perhaps an assembly of minds bound by a shared vision. We call this enigma Satoshi Nakamoto.

It was the dawn of the 21st century, an age where everything was getting smarter except our handling of money. Decades of trust placed in faceless institutions waned as the echoes of financial crises resounded through every corridor of society. Enter Nakamoto, an entity as elusive as the future it foretold. Nakamoto introduced the world to Bitcoin with a brilliant white paper, like an ancient lore scroll. It was not just a currency, not just a protocol, but a revolution, an awakening of an idea as old as barter itself - a decentralized system where trust was not assumed but earned, enforced by the merciless rigor of mathematics and cryptography.

But who was Nakamoto? A recluse genius? An anarchistic think tank. Artificial intelligence from the future or alien intelligence from the cosmos? Or merely a pseudonym for an enigmatic collective? True identity remains as elusive as the solution to the Riemann Hypothesis. Nakamoto gave birth to this brainchild, tended it through its formative years, then, like an aloof deity, retreated into the shadows, leaving behind a fortune in Bitcoin that would dwarf the GDP of many nations.

The world had a new Midas, one who had turned not mere metal but thin air into gold. And then, without a word, disappeared, leaving behind questions as enigmatic as the pyramids. Why conjure a revolution and not witness its victory march? Why amass a treasure worthy of a tycoon only to abandon it?

Our story is a journey through the labyrinth of speculation, rumor, and conspiracy. Is Bitcoin an instrument of liberation or a tool for subjugation, the first wave of a calculated assault on the old order? Was Nakamoto's retreat strategic, or is it a prelude to a more profound revelation?

Behind the cryptographic veil, under the billions, in the enigmatic shadows cast by the blockchain, is there a larger plan brewing? A scheme that promises to unravel not just the future of money but the very fabric of our global society.

The pursuit of Nakamoto is a search for the phantom who has baffled the world and changed it forever. As the story unfurls, remember this: truth is often stranger than fiction, and in the realm of Bitcoin, it's stranger still.

THE GAME

A veil of secrecy shrouded the clandestine meeting held in a dimly lit chamber deep within the heart of the Kremlin. Here, two powerful leaders forged a sinister alliance that would shake the very foundations of the global order. For decades, Russia and China had stood at the fringes of the global cocktail circuit, their glasses clinking softly in the shadows as America basked in the limelight. The United States, that captivating starlet draped in the finest gown of democracy and capitalism, had charmed her way into the hearts of the international community. Her every quip elicited laughter, her every witticism met with applause, and her every move upon the dance floor was a dazzling display of geopolitical finesse. As the guests at these grand soirees swayed to the rhythm of America's tune, Russia and China exchanged glances of simmering envy, their resentment brewing like the finest Russian vodka and the most potent Chinese baijiu.

Though they hailed from proud and storied lineages, Russia and China could not help but feel overshadowed by America's dazzling presence. The Russian bear, once the belle of the ball in the days of the

Soviet Union, now found itself relegated to the role of surly observer, its growls drowned out by the laughter and music that filled the air. China too, with its rich tapestry of culture and history, yearned for the chance to dazzle the world with its own unique allure. Yet it seemed that America's magnetic pull was simply too strong, her seductive dance of freedom and prosperity too enchanting, for any other nation to compete with.

As the night wore on and the champagne flowed, Russia and China plotted their own ascendance, determined someday to steal the spotlight, and take their rightful places at the center of the dance floor, leaving America to rue the day she had so captivated the world.

In the heart of the chamber, a scene of intrigue unfolded. Zhang Wei, the imperialist General Secretary of the People's Republic of China, stood with an air of authority, his gaze as sharp as a dagger. Opposite him stood Vladimir Vladimirovich Petrov, the enigmatic and formidable leader of Russia, a man whose mere presence commanded respect. Their meeting was cloaked in secrecy, a clandestine gathering where the fate of nations would be decided.

As advisors whispered and murmured around them, the two leaders struck a devilish bargain. Their plan was sinister, designed to shake the very foundations of the Western world and undermine the hegemony of the United States. With great care, they plotted a series of military and geopolitical actions, carefully targeting American power. Their goal was to sow discord and division among Western allies, ensuring their own dominance.

Zhang Wei leaned in, his voice low and chilling. "The Chinese Dragon shall gift the Russian Bear with advanced UAVs and hypersonic missile capabilities," he said, his words laced with venom. "With these formidable weapons, we shall tip the scales of any military engagement in the Bear's favor."

Vladimir Vladimirovich Petrov, his eyes gleaming with a mix of excitement and ambition, nodded in agreement. "And together, we shall strike a blow to the very heart of American power," he replied, his voice resonating with authority. "But that is not all. We shall also undermine the dominance of the US dollar, toppling it from its pedestal of supremacy. Our nations will develop an alternate global reserve currency, a weapon of financial warfare."

Their audacious plan left no room for doubt. China and Russia pledged a staggering 2% of their GDP towards this ambitious undertaking, a move that would shake the foundations of the global economy. But they did not stop there. Russia would also throw its support behind a Chinese invasion of a neighboring country, cementing their nefarious alliance and further destabilizing the West.

Bound by this dark covenant, the two nations embarked on a treacherous path, entangling the world in their web of deceit. Their goal was nothing short of the downfall of the Pax Americana, replacing it with a merciless new order where they would reign supreme. The G-7 would crumble, giving way to the rise of the G-2.

As the meeting drew to a close, an ominous silence filled the chamber, heavy with the weight of the promises made on that fateful day. Shadows danced and twisted along the walls, seeming to mirror the wickedness that was about to unfold. The stage was set for a great and terrible play, where the lives of millions would hang in the balance, and the world would witness the birth of a new era dominated by darkness.

~

Under the relentless sun that scorched the enormous expanses of the Syrian desert, two men from vastly different worlds found themselves bound by a common mission. John Michaels, a seasoned former Army Ranger with over twenty-five years of experience in orchestrating covert operations, stood alongside George Roberts Jr., a retired Stanford professor who had traded in the halls of academia for a life of intrigue and danger with the Central Intelligence Agency.

Though their backgrounds and temperaments could not have been more different, John, a hardened soldier with a trusty .45 always within reach, and George, a gentle scholar more suited to deciphering cryptic Russian codes than navigating the perilous labyrinth of a war zone, were united by a single purpose: to prevent the unthinkable—a collision between the military forces of the United States and Russia in the volatile setting of Syria's civil war.

As opposing factions in the conflict, the two nations had long been locked in a perilous dance of influence and power, each vying for supremacy. To maintain a fragile semblance of order, American and Russian commanders relied on established de-escalation communication channels, with the CIA working tirelessly to ensure these lines remained open.

On that fateful day, tensions had reached a boiling point: American military officials received word of an alarming build-up of Russian-speaking troops near the Deir Province. Despite Russian denials, the CIA had gathered irrefutable evidence that the majority of these soldiers were, in fact, private Russian paramilitary mercenaries, probably affiliated with the notorious Wagner group.

As the situation intensified, John and George met in a CIA safe house, bereft of their usual protective details, who had been dispatched to assess the size of the approaching force. As it turned out, the decision to send away this last line of defense would seal their fate.

When dusk fell, and shadows stretched across the barren desert, the safe house was besieged by a militia of over twenty-five Russian soldiers. With his back against the wall and his trusted .45 in hand, John valiantly fought to protect himself and George, felling three of their assailants before succumbing to the devastating blast of a Russian fragmentation grenade. Security footage would later show that both men were still alive until they were executed after their defeat, with cold precision: two 9mm rounds fired at close range ended their lives.

When their protective detail returned to the grisly scene, rage-fueled vengeance propelled them in pursuit of the fleeing murderers. With the aid of a quick reaction force and an Apache helicopter, they exacted retribution, leaving the bloodied corpses of twenty-six Russians, all bearing the distinctive Wagner PMC insignia, strewn along the roadside.

Afterward, the United States and Russia maintained silence over the incident, neither side willing to acknowledge the brutal truth. The deaths of John Michaels and George Roberts Jr. were thus relegated to the annals of clandestine history, their sacrifice commemorated only by solemn stars adorning the lobby of Langley, the CIA's headquarters, and their dignified resting place in the Arlington National Cemetery.

The Syrian civil war continued to be a volatile battleground for the United States and Russia. With the two powers supporting opposing factions in the conflict, the prospect of a direct military confrontation loomed large, threatening to ignite a larger conflagration with disastrous consequences. But the story of John Michaels and George Roberts Jr. and their tragic end served as a sobering reminder of the human cost of the ceaseless struggle between these two titans.

As history marched forward, the rivalry between the United States and Russia showed no signs of abating. And the grim tale of two men who gave their lives in pursuit of peace offered a stark warning of the consequences of unchecked ambition and the quest for global dominance. Ultimately, it would be up to the leaders of these nations to forge a new path that honored such sacrifices by ushering in a more stable and secure future for all.

~

The expanse of the Arlington National Cemetery was a tableau of honor and sacrifice, a testament to the men and women who had given their lives in service of their country. Beneath the verdant canopy of trees cloaked in a sprinkling of snow and against the backdrop of the iconic Washington skyline, the funeral procession for John Michaels and George Roberts Jr. advanced with stately grace. It was a somber ballet, choreographed to the mournful rhythm of a military dirge, an embodiment of the nation's collective grief.

Each casket, draped in an American flag, was borne aloft by a team of pallbearers, their uniforms crisply pressed, their faces masks of stoicism. They moved in tandem, their steps echoing in the still air.

A hush fell over the crowd as the caskets were lowered into the hallowed ground. The heartrending sound of taps pierced the silence, its haunting notes a poignant reminder of the cost of service. At the conclusion of the ceremony, the flag that had adorned each casket was meticulously folded, its corners meeting with a precision that only a soldier's hands could achieve. The folded flags were then presented to the families of the deceased with a reverence that bordered on the sacred.

Laura Roberts, a vision of grace and resilience amid the sorrow, accepted the flag for her father on behalf of her family. Her eyes showed a tempest of emotions, both the profound loss and the immense pride that come with such a sacrifice. Across from her, Tom Michaels, a striking figure in his Navy uniform, the Trident pin of a Navy Seal glinting on his chest in the sunlight, accepted the flag for his father on behalf of his family with a solemn nod, his expression a mirror of Laura's.

After the ceremony at Arlington National Cemetery, the hushed crowd slowly began to disperse, leaving behind a sense of solemnity that hung in the air. Tom, a young man with determination in his eyes, walked slowly, lost in his own thoughts. He had always found solace in running through the peaceful trails of Arlington, seeking refuge from the chaos of the world.

Lost in his contemplation, Tom was startled when a voice broke the silence. "Excuse me," said a young woman with a kind smile, "I couldn't help but overhear you mentioning the running trails at Arlington. I run there too. It's such a serene place, isn't it?"

Tom turned to face the woman, who introduced herself as Laura. He was taken aback by her presence, feeling a strange connection between them. "Yes, it is," he replied, a faint smile gracing his lips. "How can any place so sad be so beautiful?"

Laura nodded in agreement, her eyes shimmering with a mix of sorrow and admiration. "I often wonder the same thing," she said softly. "It's as if amidst the grief, there's a hidden tranquility that can't be found anywhere else."

They walked side by side, their footsteps echoing in the quiet moments that followed the ceremony. Tom and Laura shared stories of their runs through the winding trails, finding comfort in the familiarity of their experiences. In that fleeting exchange, they discovered a mutual passion for running, a bond that transcended their shared grief.

They continued their conversation, at a later ceremony in the headquarters of the CIA in Langley Virginia, the weight of their fathers' sacrifices and the newly etched stars on the Memorial Wall looming over them. It was a stark reminder of the dangers and sacrifices that came with clandestine service. The Director of the CIA, who had observed their meeting, approached them with a small, sad smile.

"I knew both of your fathers," the Director said, his voice filled with a mix of pride and sorrow. "They were exceptional individuals, just like the two of you. Bright, dedicated, and committed. You are the future of intelligence operations, the next generation who will carry on their legacy."

Tom and Laura exchanged glances, their hearts heavy with the weight of their fathers' legacies. But amidst the shadows, they had found a moment of understanding, a shared connection that transcended the pain. In each other's presence, they found a beacon of light, a glimmer of hope that carried them forward.

As the sun dipped below the horizon, casting a golden glow over the landscape, Tom and Laura stood side by side, their spirits intertwined. They knew that their paths had crossed for a reason, and together, they would forge ahead, honoring their fathers' sacrifices and embracing the future with unwavering determination.

WHY PLAY AT ALL?

In the revered halls of Johns Hopkins University, Laura Roberts rapidly rose to prominence. Respected academics, her mentors, were irresistibly drawn to her extraordinary intellect and her knack for clarifying intricate international concerns with a surprising degree of lucidity for her age. Perceiving her immense potential, they extended an invitation for her to lend her expertise as a part-time instructor at the prestigious School of Advanced International Studies in Washington DC. Seizing this opportunity to showcase her brilliance, Laura adeptly designed a unique course blending digital instruction and face-to-face interactions, creating an invigorating intellectual atmosphere.

Among her pupils, one individual distinguished himself - Tom Michaels. His silent yet potent intensity, coupled with his backstory as a Navy Seal turned CIA operative, imbued him with an almost tangible magnetism. Yet it was his unfeigned curiosity, an inexhaustible desire for knowledge, that truly set him apart. His astute contributions to classroom discussions and an unmistakable ability to grasp the delicate subtleties of global politics soon garnered Laura's notice.

Despite the strictures imposed by their high-security vocations, their bond grew within the intellectual exchanges occurring in the classroom. Over hot coffees in secluded cafes or whispered exchanges bathed in the muted light of jazz bars, they unearthed a shared passion for a world that extended beyond their professional commitments, a world rich with literature, arts, and culture. They found mutual appreciation in their love for Russian literature, spending numerous hours pondering the philosophical foundations of Dostoevsky's works or debating the comparative virtues of Pushkin and Tolstoy.

However, despite their burgeoning camaraderie, their professions necessitated that a significant portion of their lives remain undisclosed. Tales of audacious missions or covert operations were not shared, nor were anecdotes about the internal operations of the NSA or CIA. These topics were shrouded in secrecy, barricaded behind their top-secret clearances, even as their companionship deepened.

Yet, notwithstanding these limitations, or perhaps because of them, their bond deepened. Their shared experiences, navigating the opaque depths of international relations, the pressure of safeguarding their nation's interests, and even the frustration of enforced secrecy, drew them closer. Their friendship, a flower blossoming amidst thorns, was a testament to humanity's ability to forge connections despite adversity.

On one noteworthy day, the sunlight filtering into the classroom appeared to herald Laura's entrance. Her appearance altered the room's atmosphere, the students instinctively straightening, their attention irresistibly drawn towards the striking woman at the front. There stood Laura Roberts, the epitome of unwavering determination and effervescent eagerness. Her eyes radiated the spark of intellectual challenge and a silent promise of the knowledge yet to be discovered.

Behind her, a screen flickered to life, casting a glow over the room with the title of the day's discourse: "The US Dollar and American Hegemony, a Co-dependent Relationship." The words lingered in the air, heavy with connotations and anticipated revelations, setting the stage for another engrossing session in Laura's extraordinary classroom.

"Good afternoon, everyone," Laura commenced, her assured voice resonating around the room while her virtual students watched attentively from their screens. "Today, we'll delve into the enigmatic world of international trade and finance, focusing on a highly coveted title – the global reserve currency." A wave of anticipation flowed through the room as Tom acknowledged the sentiment.

Laura painted a vivid picture of a grand ballroom where nations danced to the rhythm of commerce, exchanging goods and services. To keep the dance flowing, they required a common medium of exchange. At one time, gold was the belle of the ball, but today, currencies have taken center stage. However, only a select few possessed the charisma and grace to be deemed global reserve currencies. Laura then highlighted the extraordinary benefits conferred by this honor, and the enormous political influence it could command.

In Laura's portrayal, the United States was the prime example of global leadership, its dollar reigning supreme as the principal global reserve currency for over 70 years. Laura brilliantly illuminated the United States' rise to power post-World War II, its ability to shape international monetary policy, and the complementing effect of its military might. All students were captivated by the tale of America's ascent. But Laura was no blind nationalist, she also drew attention to the shadows of resentment growing under America's prosperity. She highlighted Russia's constant struggle to reclaim its glory, a topic that piqued Tom's interest given his CIA training.

Expertly navigating the complexities of global power dynamics, Laura also introduced China as a new contender. She carefully managed the ensuing discussion about the future of American dominance, making each student feel valued and heard.

As Laura concluded her lecture, she left her students with a thought-provoking remark: "The United States, as a global military superpower, has wielded significant influence, yet it has also faced controversy and criticism. But the one constant in the grand saga of American hegemony is that it has left an indelible mark on human civilization. For better or for worse, the world as we know it is largely shaped by the dance of American power."

A round of applause filled the room as Laura concluded her lecture. The students had embarked on an enlightening journey, unraveling the complexities of international trade, finance, and global politics. And as they exited the classroom, they carried with them a richer understanding of the dance of power and influence that continues to shape the world.

~

In a quiet, idyllic suburb somewhere in the center of the sprawling landscape of the United States, the Johnson family stood as a testament to the American Dream. Their quaint, white-picket-fenced home was a beacon of stability and prosperity, a symbol of the opportunities and comforts afforded by the hegemony of their great nation.

The Johnson household was a bustling hub of activity, with two loving parents working hard to support their four children. The mother, Kelly, was a skilled mortgage broker who had helped countless families secure their own piece of the American Dream. The father, Andy, was a talented programmer whose work in the tech industry had contributed to the foundations of the digital age.

Their four children, Lindsay, Julie, Paige, and Abby embodied the promise of the future. Though Paige and Lindsay had struggled academically, the strength of the dollar had allowed them to backpack across Europe and Asia, broadening their horizons and enriching their lives with experiences in distant lands. Now attending college, they were borrowing heavily in order to finance their education, confident in their nation's prosperity.

Abby and Julie, having spread their wings already and left the nest, sought to build lives and families of their own. They dreamed of purchasing homes, raising children, and perpetuating the cycle of the American Dream for generations to come.

The enduring power of the United States underpinned the

Johnson family's comfortable lifestyle. The dollar, a global reserve currency, allowed them to drive foreign automobiles—a sleek BMW and a dependable Toyota—symbols of the interconnected global economy and their nation's influence. The financial stability afforded by the dollar made their lives possible, securing their places in the world and fueling their dreams and aspirations.

Yet beneath the veneer of prosperity lay a delicate balance. Were the dollar to lose its status as the global reserve currency, the foundations of the Johnsons' lives would be shaken to their core. The interest rates on their mortgage, their car loans, and the student loans that financed Paige and Lindsay's education could skyrocket, threatening the stability of their world.

More broadly, the loss of the dollar's reserve status could send ripples through the global economy, disrupting trade and undermining the financial security of countless families like the Johnsons. The comforts and opportunities they took for granted could vanish instantly, leaving them to face an uncertain future fraught with challenges and hardships.

As the sun set over their picturesque suburban home, the Johnson family gathered around the dinner table, blissfully unaware of the intricate web of forces that sustained their American Dream. Their lives were a testament to the power and promise of American hegemony, a legacy that spanned generations and reached across the globe. The startling truth was that the delicate balance holding their world together was teetering on the brink of change—a reminder that even the mightiest empires must one day succumb to the inexorable march of time.

~

In the world of international relations, power is everything. Nations jostle for position, each seeking a strategic advantage over its rivals. At the heart of this struggle lies the concept of military power and the need for a military superpower to maintain global stability.

While a global reserve currency is an essential component of the international financial system, it is not enough, on its own, to maintain global stability. History has repeatedly shown that military power is a necessary component of international relations and that a military superpower is necessary to maintain order in the world.

The reasons for this are manifold. For a start, military power is a deterrent. It dissuades other nations from engaging in aggressive behavior, for they know the consequences could be severe. Without the threat of military action, rogue states, and non-state actors would be free to act with impunity, destabilizing the international order and threatening global security.

Furthermore, a military superpower can serve as a stabilizing force in regions of conflict. Acting as a mediator can help broker peace between warring factions and prevent conflict from escalating. It can also provide humanitarian assistance, helping to alleviate the suffering of those caught amid the turmoil.

For the United States, the role of military superpower has been central to its international identity for decades. With a vast network of military bases around the world, the United States has projected its power in ways that few other nations can match. It has also helped to bring an end to conflicts in Bosnia, Kosovo, and Iraq.

Being a military superpower has been a double-edged sword for the United States. While it has given the nation enormous political and strategic influence, it has also been the source of significant controversy and criticism. Yet, despite the challenges, the importance of maintaining a global military power remains paramount. Without it, the international order would be significantly less stable, and the risks to global security far greater.

THE PLAYERS

Real-life dragons are scary. Zhang Wei, the formidable General Secretary of the People's Republic of China, stood tall and unyielding at the head of a nation stretching far across history and territory. Born into the unforgiving heartland of Shaanxi Province, he had journeyed to power with unwavering determination. And now, like the great leaders of the past—including his foremost inspiration, Xi Jinping—he held the reins of an empire in his hands, shaping the course of history with an ease and elegance that belied his humble origins.

Zhang Wei's visage conveyed the subtlety of a man who has mastered the art of concealment. His eyes, dark and inscrutable, hid a depth of intelligence that few could fathom. His face bore the lines of time, but they seemed only to add to his air of authority. Deep and measured, his voice could sway millions of hearts and minds, sending ripples through his society with each carefully chosen word.

The General Secretary's childhood had been one of deprivation, his family struggling to make a living in the shadow of the imposing Qinling Mountains. There the seeds of his ambition were first sown as he witnessed the influence wielded by the officials who visited his village. Fueled by an innate drive for greatness, the young Zhang Wei resolved to rise above his circumstances and ascend to the echelons of power that had seemed so distant.

A devotion to the pursuit of knowledge marked his path to success. He immersed himself in the works of the great philosophers, poets, and statesmen who had come before him. As a result, in Zhang Wei's mind, ancient wisdom fused with modern pragmatism, forging a singular vision for the future of his beloved nation.

As General Secretary, Zhang Wei ruled with an imperialistic fervor. He was intent on restoring the Middle Kingdom to the heights of its former glory. He thought the Russian leader Petrov a fool. But, like his erstwhile partner, Wei detested the Americans even more and blamed American hegemony for blocking his path to global dominance. He sought to rebuild the ancient silk roads, not with bricks and mortar, but with steel, fiber optics, and trade agreements that spanned the globe. And with each new alliance and economic initiative, the People's Republic of China's influence grew, a warning to anyone who dared to challenge its ascent.

Behind this national expansion and progress, Zhang Wei remained an intensely private man. His steely exterior concealed a wellspring of introspection and self-doubt as he grappled with his nation's expectations and the consequences of his actions. Moreover, his dreams were haunted by the specter of his predecessor, Xi Jinping, whose legacy seemed both an inspiration and an insurmountable barrier, eternally overshadowing his own achievements.

In the final analysis, Zhang Wei, the powerful General Secretary of the People's Republic of China, was an enigma—a paradoxical blend of ambition, ruthlessness, and introspection. This complexity would come to define his rule and ensure that his place in history was as enduring as the empire he sought to build.

~

From a young age, Tom Michaels exhibited fierce intelligence and an insatiable curiosity, qualities that would shape the course of his life. As the son of a CIA operative, he grew up with a deep understanding of the world's complexities and an appreciation for the role that knowledge plays in shaping global affairs. Tom had also displayed an indomitable love for sports since his earliest youth. His boundless energy and inherent agility propelled him to excel in every athletic endeavor, from the rough-and-tumble of American football to the elegant precision of tennis.

Tom's physical gifts were matched by his striking appearance. His visage bore a striking resemblance to the dashing actor Ryan Reynolds, a fact that was not lost on those who knew him. With his sparkling eyes, strong jawline, and disarming smile, he was the very picture of the Hollywood heartthrob. His two-day stubble, a grooming choice that harkened back to his days as a Navy SEAL, only served to enhance his rugged good looks, lending an air of masculinity and worldliness to his already striking features.

Indeed, Tom's uncanny resemblance to Ryan Reynolds was so pronounced that he would often find himself mistaken for the actor as he traversed the bustling thoroughfares of airports and train stations. Though he would always humbly deny the comparisons, there was a secret part of him that took pleasure in the recognition, a quiet affirmation of his own undeniable charm.

Early on, pride in his father's heroic sacrifice led him to enroll in the United States Naval Academy, where he pursued a degree in physics. Tom's natural aptitude for the subject, coupled with his dedication to discipline, set him apart from his peers. He immersed himself in the study of thermodynamics, fluid dynamics, and advanced propulsion systems, laying the groundwork for a career that would take him far beyond the halls of academia.

When he graduated from the USNA, Tom was offered a position at NASA's Jet Propulsion Laboratory (JPL). There, at the cutting edge of aerospace engineering, he worked alongside some of the most brilliant minds in the field. He was also introduced to hypersonic flight, a revolutionary technology that promised to redefine the boundaries of human endeavor.

Hypersonic flight, defined as flight at speeds exceeding Mach 5 (3,500 mph), posed a unique set of challenges. The extreme velocities demanded innovative materials, advanced aerodynamics, and revolutionary propulsion systems. Tom, with his background in physics and his innate understanding of the principles involved, quickly proved himself to be an invaluable asset to the JPL team.

His work with the laboratory brought him into contact with the Defense Advanced Research Projects Agency (DARPA), the organization responsible for the development of cutting-edge technologies for the US military. Recognizing his expertise and potential, they recruited Tom, asking him to focus on the theoretical aspects of hypersonic missile technology.

As part of DARPA, Tom delved into high-speed aerodynamics, advanced materials, and novel propulsion techniques. His work was instrumental in the development of new designs and concepts that would one day become integral components of the United States defense capabilities.

Despite his rapid rise within the field of hypersonic research, Tom felt the call to serve his country in a more direct capacity. Perhaps obeying an inner thirst for adventure, he joined the elite ranks of the Navy SEALs and honed his skills as a warrior, his intellect serving as a powerful complement to his physical prowess. During his service he saw action in both Iraq and Afghanistan, repeatedly proving himself in the crucible of battle.

The harrowing events of Operation Eagles Wings came to define Tom's military career and shaped the man he would become. On that fateful day in the rugged mountains of Afghanistan, Tom and three fellow SEALs found themselves surrounded and outnumbered by enemy forces. The ensuing firefight tested their skills, endurance, and camaraderie. Tom fought with the ferocity of a cornered lion, determined to protect his brothers-in-arms at all costs. During the battle, a hail of gunfire tore through the air, and one bullet ripped through his shoulder, shattering bone and sinew before exiting through his back, leaving a horrific wound that would serve as a lifelong reminder of the price he had paid.

Despite the searing pain, Tom pressed on, and his actions that day earned him the prestigious Navy Cross. But the scars Tom bore were not just physical. The emotional toll of being the only survivor of the battle weighed on his soul, and the memories of his fallen comrades haunted his every step. Though he had fought with every fiber of his being to save them, he had failed, and their loss remained an ever-present specter, embittering his days.

His injuries forced him to retire from the SEALs, and Tom found a new path with the CIA. His brilliant mind and indomitable spirit ultimately propelled him to the highest echelons of the agency. But throughout his time at Langley, Tom carried with him not only his new responsibilities but also the ghosts of his past.

~

In the early days at the CIA, Tom Michaels found himself immersed in the mysteries of China. Fresh from his training at the Farm, he was assigned to the China desk, where he began to unravel the intricate web of politics, power, and intrigue that lay at the heart of the world's most populous nation.

As an operative on the China desk, Tom spent his days poring over classified intelligence reports, analyzing satellite imagery, and liaising with agents on the ground. He delved into China's culture, history, and languages, ultimately mastering Mandarin to the point where he could converse fluently with his Chinese counterparts. His work brought him into contact with a vast array of sources, from diplomats and journalists to dissidents and defectors, and he honed his skills in espionage, learning to navigate the shadowy world of spy craft with the same ease that he felt in navigating the streets of Beijing.

As the years passed, Tom rose through the ranks of the China desk, eventually becoming its chief. By that time he had become an indispensable asset to the agency. His razor-sharp intellect pierced the veil that cloaked the Middle Kingdom, revealing the clandestine machinations and power struggles within. And as Tom dug deeper, piecing together an elaborate tapestry of ambition and subterfuge, the enigmatic figure of Zhang Wei loomed ominously at the center of the picture.

Tom's tenure at the China desk allowed him to forge connections with numerous discontented members of the Chinese government and military—individuals who were just as troubled as he was by Zhang Wei's burgeoning influence. Through these covert channels, Tom amassed a raft of intelligence on Wei, constructing the profile of a man who seemed to transcend the realm of ordinary mortals.

Years of relentless pursuit yielded a bountiful harvest of knowledge. Tom's tireless efforts not only led to the unmasking of several Chinese spies operating within the United States but also exposed an extensive network of shell companies and offshore accounts designed to funnel funds into military projects in China.

~

Parallel to his professional journey, Tom found a profound connection in his personal life. His heart found its match in the wonderful Sarah. A woman of beauty and intelligence who proved to be Tom's perfect partner.

When Tom Michaels first locked eyes with Sarah at the City Dock in Annapolis, he knew his life was about to change forever. Sarah was a force to be reckoned with, a woman of intelligence, beauty, and grace. She worked as an international affairs correspondent, a profession that offered her a similar perspective on global affairs as Tom's own, coupled with frequent assignments to dangerous foreign locales. Their first encounter was one of sparks and shared understanding. Tom, in his unassuming charm and undeniable good looks, approached Sarah, who was lost in thought, looking out over the shimmering water of the Chesapeake Bay.

"Beautiful day, isn't it?" Tom had said, a smile tugging at his lips.

Sarah turned, met his gaze, and replied, "It certainly is." Her eyes showed a glint of interest, a curiosity mirroring his own.

From that first exchange, a bond was forged. Their shared experiences and professional demands wove a rich tapestry of understanding and mutual respect that underpinned their relationship. Their love bloomed through shared adventures, ranging from exotic travels on assignment to quiet moments at home, relishing the brief interludes of tranquility their demanding careers allowed them. On their wedding day, standing under the majestic dome of the Chapel at the US Naval Academy, Tom held Sarah's hands and promised to navigate life's tempests alongside her. "I vow to walk with you, Sarah," he said, his eyes reflecting the solemnity of his promise, "through every storm and every calm, through joy and sorrow, in this life and beyond."

Sarah echoed his promise, her voice resolute, "And I, Tom, will stand by your side, in light, and in shadow, in the throes of our adventures, and in the peace of our home. We are partners in love and in life."

The echoes of their vows, carried by the winds of time, reverberated through their marriage, a solemn testament to their undying commitment. Their love was one of passion and understanding, seasoned with a dash of shared adventure and mutual admiration of each other's resilience and courage. Their home was filled with laughter, debates on global affairs, and the silent understanding that came from their shared professional worlds. Yet, the tragic side of their beautiful love story loomed like a shadow. Their careers often pulled them away from each other, demanded sacrifices, and placed them in the path of danger. But they navigated these challenges with grace and perseverance, their love serving as a beacon of hope and strength.

From the exhilaration of love to the crushing grief of loss, their marriage was a testament to the power of love that continued to shape Tom's life, both as a CIA operative and as a man bearing the pain of profound loss. The echoes of their love story, filled with the vivacity of their shared experiences and the melancholy of their separation, continue to resonate within him. Their love story was the stuff of romantic novels – filled with passion, adventures, and a shared understanding of the demands of their respective professions. Their marriage was as beautiful as it was tragic. They promised to navigate life's ups and downs together from the moment they exchanged their vows in the Chapel at the US Naval Academy. However, destiny had a different plan. The joy of learning about Sarah's first pregnancy was accompanied by Tom's assignment to a covert mission in China, a mission he could not refuse

~

It was his fifth year on the China desk, and Tom was entrusted with leading a covert mission deep into the heart of China itself. His objective: to gather intelligence on the nation's progress in developing hypersonic weapons, a technology with the potential to drastically shift the balance of global power, and one that Tom himself was very familiar with.

The icy, winter winds of China bit at Tom Michaels' skin as he navigated the labyrinthine alleyways, his breath misting in the cold air. Five years of intense undercover work had brought him here - a covert mission aimed at gathering intelligence on China's development of hypersonic weapons, a potential game-changer in global power dynamics.

His secure line buzzed in his pocket, a call so rare and unexpected it sent a jolt of adrenaline through him. He hastily stepped into the hollow of a nearby doorway, cloaked by shadows. His superior's voice, laced with unusual solemnity, crackled through. "Tom, Sarah... she's gone into labor prematurely."

Tom's heart pounded. Anticipation, fear, and regret fought for dominance within him. He had longed to witness his first-born's arrival into the world, to hold Sarah's hand, share in her pain, and revel in their mutual joy. But duty had summoned him away, thousands of miles from where he yearned to be.

Just hours later, the phone trembled in his hand again, its shrill ring shattering the eerie quiet. His superior's voice wavered, choked with the weight of the news he had to deliver. "Sarah... and the baby... they didn't make it." The line clicked dead, leaving Tom standing alone in the chill of the Chinese winter, the devastation of loss settling over him like a crushing avalanche.

He sank to his knees, head bowed against the wind. Grief was a harsh mistress, its icy grip squeezing the air from his lungs. He thought of Sarah, of the beautiful life they'd built together from a chance meeting at the City Dock in Annapolis, Maryland. From his induction into the elite Navy SEALs, their wedding in the Chapel at the US Naval Academy, to their wild adventures during his postings throughout the world, Sarah had been his unwavering beacon. Her love had kept him grounded, even as he plunged into the chaotic underbelly of political espionage.

As Tom grappled with his unbearable loss, the ghost of another tragedy echoed painfully in his heart. His father, also a CIA agent, had been killed in action during a perilous mission in Syria. The bitter irony that both his wife and father had been snatched away from him during covert operations ate at him, fueling an internal storm of guilt and resentment.

Haunted by loss and yearning for solace, Tom soon found himself back home, where an unoccupied infant cradle served as a heart-wrenching reminder of what he'd lost. But duty again called him back into the shadows, and he returned to China.

~

It was during this second perilous mission in China that Tom first crossed paths with Li Chen, an ascendant luminary in the Chinese Communist Central Committee. Their destinies first intertwined in the recesses of a Beijing teahouse, where Tom, masquerading as a businessman, sought information on the hypersonic weapons program. Amid the wafting steam of fragrant tea, Tom and Li Chen forged an unlikely partnership. Despite the vast chasm dividing them, they discovered a shared conviction in the potential for collaboration between their two nations.

Although both men remained loyal to their respective countries, their encounters left an indelible imprint on their lives. As Tom's mission progressed, their discourse evolved into profound discussions of their aspirations and fears for the future. And, although their friendship was often strained by the duplicitous game in which they were entangled, ultimately, it proved strong enough to endure the tempest of history.

~

The province of Guizhou, located in the verdant southwest of China, has been a cradle of hardship and resilience since time immemorial. The rugged terrain and tumultuous weather forge inhabitants as unyielding as they are unforgiving, and it was in this crucible of strife that Li Chen was born. He emerged tempered by adversity and filled with an indomitable spirit.

Li Chen's earliest memories were of hunger, but they also glowed with the warmth of his mother's embrace as she sang ancient lullabies that spoke of valor and sacrifice. His father, a weathered miner with hands calloused by toil, returned home each evening exhausted yet never too tired to regale his son with tales of past heroes. In those moments, as dusk settled over the meager village, the weight of their troubles seemed to lift momentarily, replaced by the faint glimmer of dreams.

But it was not dreaming alone that sustained the young Li Chen through his childhood. Famine was an ever-present companion in the village, casting a long shadow over its inhabitants as they toiled in the fields, their faces drawn with the lines of suffering. Amid this gnawing hunger and relentless toil, Li Chen discovered within himself a wellspring of empathy and compassion. As he watched the villagers struggle and saw the sacrifices his parents made, he began to understand the power of community and the strength that could be found in shared adversity. This insight was the bedrock upon which the future Li Chen was built.

His formal education was born of his father's determination to see his son escape the clutches of poverty. It was a privilege not lost on the young boy, who excelled in his studies and soon received a scholarship to study in the bustling metropolis of Beijing. There, far from the bucolic hills of his birth, he embarked on a transformative journey.

In the halls of the university, Li Chen met many others who had known suffering, and in their stories, he recognized a shared humanity that transcended borders and ideologies. Studying the complexities of history and political science, he deepened his understanding of the world and, with it, his resolve to make a difference.

In time, Li Chen's passion and intellect earned him a place in the Chinese Communist Central Committee. From that vantage point, he strove to reshape his nation's future by forging a path that balanced progress with compassion, modernity with tradition. As he ascended the ranks of power, his humble village and the trials of his youth remained vivid in his memory. Li Chen's empathy was his compass, guiding him through the maze of geopolitics, and in the darkest moments of his nation's history, it illuminated his way.

When Tom Michaels and Li Chen first crossed paths in the Beijing teahouse, their respective histories intertwined, forging a bond that transcended the divisions between their worlds. In the hardships of their pasts and the lessons of their youth, the seeds of empathy and understanding had been sown. And through their unwavering conviction in the power of collaboration, these two men charted a course for the future, testifying to the resilience and innate goodness of mankind.

As their friendship blossomed, Tom and Li Chen spent countless hours engaged in passionate debates and philosophical discussions, finding solace and enlightenment in the exchange of ideas. While vastly different cultures and histories had shaped their worldviews, they discovered a shared belief in the idea that beneath the veneer of politics and power lay a common humanity that bound them together.

Tom, who had seen the horrors of war and the depths to which human beings could descend, cherished the unwavering optimism of his friend. Li Chen's belief in the capacity for redemption and the transformative power of empathy rekindled a hope within him that he had long thought extinguished. In turn, Li Chen was inspired by Tom's tales of bravery and sacrifice, of individuals who, despite the shadows of their past, had chosen to fight for a better world. He saw in his friend a living embodiment of the ideals he held so dear, of the power of goodness to triumph over adversity.

Together they embarked on a journey of mutual discovery, unearthing the hidden treasures within each other's cultures and histories and developing in the process a profound appreciation for the beauty of the human spirit. As they explored, they reconfirmed their belief that understanding and unity between their nations were not only possible but essential.

In the grand narrative of history, Tom and Li Chen recognized that division and conflict were often driven by fear and misunderstanding, but they were also learning that friendship and empathy could bridge even seemingly insurmountable divides. In each other, they saw the virtues that would be necessary to navigate the treacherous waters of global politics: courage, wisdom, and a deep-rooted faith in the goodness of mankind.

~

At the CIA, Tom threw himself into his work, seeking distraction in the endless challenges and strategic complexities of the intelligence world. It was a relentless pursuit that kept the memories of his lost family and fallen comrades at bay, if only for a time. His life, once defined by the camaraderie of the SEALs and the bonds forged in battle, had become a solitary endeavor. The events of his past and the responsibilities of his position created a barrier that few could breach. But Tom was no stranger to adversity, and he met each challenge with the same tenacity that had seen him through the darkest moments of his military career.

His new role brought with it immense responsibility, and he embraced the difficulties with a fervor born of both passion and pain. Haunted by the memories of his father and his wife, Tom threw himself into small rituals that kept him connected to them. Each morning he would rise before the sun, lacing up his running shoes for a solitary journey through the pre-dawn stillness. The rhythmic pounding of his feet on the pavement became a mantra, the pain in his lungs a balm for the ache in his heart. In those quiet moments, he could almost feel his father's guiding presence, urging him onward.

On one of these early-morning sojourns, when the sky was awash with muted hues, Tom made his way around the E Ring of the Pentagon, his breaths coming in measured puffs of mist in the chill air. Lost in thought, he rounded a bend and collided with another runner. Both fell sprawling to the ground.

"Damn it!" the stranger exclaimed. Then she extended a hand to help Tom to his feet. "I'm so sorry. I wasn't paying attention."

Tom's eyes widened with recognition as he grasped her hand, pulling himself up. "Laura Roberts," he exclaimed. "I didn't expect to see you here."

Laura's face broke into a warm smile. "Tom Michaels! I wonder what brings you here?"

They had first met at the somber ceremony in Langley when their fathers were honored with stars in the lobby of the CIA headquarters. The shared pain of their losses had drawn them together, forging a connection that had deepened through the course together at Hopkins.

They resumed their run, their strides falling into a comfortable rhythm, side by side. The silence between them was warm and companionable. As the sun crested the horizon, painting the sky in gold and pink, Tom felt grateful for the unexpected encounter, the opportunity to share a moment of respite with someone who understood at least some of the ghosts that haunted him.

As they circled the E Ring, their pasts briefly receded, replaced by the thrill of a renewed connection. And when they parted ways, their paths diverging once more, the memory of this chance meeting lingered, a flash of hope in a sea of grief.

~

In the gentle veil of dawn, Laura Roberts seemed almost a celestial apparition. Her emerald eyes sparkled with a depth that was as enchanting as it was unfathomable, and her raven tresses flowed down her shoulders like a cascade of liquid obsidian.

Yet, Laura's striking beauty was merely a veneer that hid the formidable brilliance that made her the extraordinary woman she was. A prodigy born to Stanford academics, she was bestowed with a formidable intellect that equaled, if not surpassed, her physical attractiveness. With an intuitive grasp for the scientific realm, she immersed herself in her studies at Stanford, graduating with the highest honors in applied and computational mathematics.

However, Laura was no stranger to ambition, and it eclipsed any semblance of humility she possessed. Despite her intellectual prowess, Laura was never content unless she had surpassed her peers, a trait that fueled her relentless pursuit for achievement. Her father's heroic demise brought her under the watchful eyes of the National Security Agency. Recognizing her extraordinary talents, they persuaded her to leave the familiar Californian coast and plunge into the turbulent world of cryptology and espionage on the East Coast.

In her relentless pursuit of superiority, she enrolled in a dual master's program at Johns Hopkins, delving into the realms of International Relations and cybersecurity with a concentration on the algebraic aspects of number theory. Even the demanding curriculum was not a challenge, but an invitation to prove her superiority once more. After graduation, she was invited to lend her genius to the

Johns Hopkins DC campus as a professor.

Laura's dazzling beauty and piercing intellect were a potent combination that left many admirers in her wake. But to Laura, they were merely steppingstones on her path to supremacy, tools to manipulate and intimidate others. Even the fertile intellectual grounds of the East Coast offered little satisfaction. She remained too engrossed in her pursuits to entertain matters of the heart.

Her solace, her sanctuary amidst her relentless ambition, was running. Not a languid trot, but a full-tilt, blistering dash that tested the extremes of her physical endurance and mental fortitude. With each resounding footfall, the world blurred into irrelevance, and the cacophony of her incessant ambition was silenced. In these fleeting moments of self-imposed isolation, Laura found her sanctuary, free from the clutches of her relentless pursuit of superiority, borne on the wings of her own unyielding determination.

~

In an intricate tapestry of geopolitics, where allegiance was ever-shifting and the distinction between friend and foe was nebulous at best, the CIA and NSA stood as steadfast bastions against the multitudes of threats that the United States faced. Each agency, armed with its unique repertoire of resources and acumen, often found themselves in the throes of a silent rivalry, each vying for dominion within the clandestine realm of intelligence. Yet, in times of critical exigency, they would congregate, forming an alliance of necessity that presented a formidable force.

The Pentagon, a monolith set between the lush verdancy of Langley, Virginia, and the extensive sprawl of Beltsville, Maryland, provided a suitable arena for these two powerful entities. It was a neutral ground, a locus where competing agencies could suspend their territorial feuds and cooperate for the greater good.

It was within one of the Pentagon's fortified briefing rooms that destiny elected to orchestrate the reunion of Tom Michaels and Laura

Roberts. They had bid each other farewell earlier in the day after an unexpected rendezvous during their morning run. Subsequently, each retreated to their respective corners of the Pentagon to steel themselves for the impending challenges of the day. However, as Tom made his entrance into the briefing room, his astute gaze swept over the crowd and landed on a familiar countenance. Laura, dressed sharply in a business suit, her hair elegantly confined to a neat bun, lifted her eyes to meet his. A moment of mutual recognition ensued, an unspoken reminiscence of their morning encounter adding a layer of depth to the otherwise sterile formality of the room.

The crux of the meeting was of paramount importance to both the CIA and NSA. Recent intelligence had unmasked an escalation in communications between Russia and China, notably concentrated on the burgeoning world of cryptocurrency. The implications were far-reaching, and both agencies were eager to harness their collective resources and dissect the intricate web of intrigue that enveloped the issue.

Tom Michaels, armed with an extensive background in Chinese intelligence and his comprehension of Russian threats, was a natural representative for the CIA. His analytical prowess and indomitable will had earned him a place of influence and the magnitude of the issue at hand was underscored by his presence. Laura Roberts, however, was the proverbial shining star of the NSA, attending the meeting owing to her expertise in cryptography and global finance. Her adeptness at untangling the most complex of codes and her contributions to unmasking the secrets of the digital sphere had made her an indispensable asset to her agency. Her participation underscored her ascending influence, a testimony to her relentless pursuit of superiority.

As the meeting commenced, the room grew dense with anticipation. The officials embarked on a journey through the labyrinthine world of deception and subterfuge surrounding the Russo-Chinese cryptocurrency communications. Tom and Laura, driven by their shared dedication and complementary skills, found themselves instinctively gravitating towards each other, their partnership a potent alliance. Fueled by their unwavering quest for truth, they volleyed ideas and theories, a dynamic interplay of intellect and experience.

The hours slipped by, and as the room dimmed, their personal sorrows were slowly replaced by the luminescence of their burgeoning collaboration. The conclusion of the meeting saw the officials exchanging understanding nods and firm handshakes. Yet, Tom and Laura tarried, the shared realization that they were united in their pursuit of justice deepening their connection.

As they exited the briefing room, side by side, they found themselves engrossed in conversation. They discussed their work, the plethora of challenges they confronted, and the personal sacrifices they had made in service of their country. Yet, the conversation danced delicately around the unvoiced connection between them, the memory of their fathers' intertwined fate hung between them like a solemn oath, a reminder of the legacy they bore.

In the silence that punctuated their words, Tom and Laura found solace. For what felt like the first time in an eternity, they experienced a sense of kinship, an understanding that went beyond the confines of their professional lives. Upon reaching the exit, the departing sun cast a soft glow on their faces, its warmth contrasting the austere edifice they left behind. A shared glance, a mutual recognition of an ally, and with a final nod, they parted ways. Yet as they disappeared into their separate destinies, they carried with them the knowledge that they were not alone in their endeavors. In the shadowed corners of their world, each had discovered a kindred spirit.

~

Sergey Kuznetsov and Olga Ivanov were two parts of an unlikely troika, the third being Olga's older brother, Pavel. Born in 1978, under the ghostly shadow of the Cold War, they spent their formative years marinating in the spectral half-light of Moscow. Sergey, the sole child on the Kuznetsov tree, was bathed in intellect. At the same time, the

Ivanov branch bore two splendid fruits - Pavel, a superb physical specimen etched from youthful vibrancy, and Olga, a radiant celestial body drawing eyes to her orbit.

Their residences were side by side in a building where the Soviet architecture was as stark and cold as a Moscow winter. The Ivanov and Kuznetsov homes were not just the static of bricks and concrete; they were alive with a pulsing tapestry of life, spun in the grand academia of the prestigious Moscow Institute of Physics and Technology.

Sergey's parents, Nikita, and Anna, both esteemed Professors, had passed down to him a universe dictated by the meticulous precision of mathematical equations and the cosmic laws of physics. They bequeathed him a breathtaking microcosm carved out of sinewave curves and the esoteric principles of quantum mechanics. A world where every question had an answer, or at the very least, a method to find it.

Yuliya Ivanov, Olga's mother, navigated the stormy sea of political science within the hallowed halls of the same prestigious institution. Olga's father, a consummate bureaucrat, deployed his economic acumen helping to draft the blueprint of the Soviet Union's audacious five-year plans. Together, they had instilled in their children an understanding of a world governed not by formulas but by the intricate dance of power and resources.

In both families, a shared ideology was passed down through generations, a belief in the concept of "a greater good." They repeatedly reiterated that while individual excellence and the aspiration to be a hero were commendable, they should always be harnessed to serve the collective good. This principle formed the foundation of their children's upbringing, shaping their worldview and guiding their ambitions.

Their children, however, were diametric opposites in their passions and pursuits. Olga and Pavel, like figures carved from marble by ancient Olympic sculptors, were champions in the arena of athletics. They competed with a voracious appetite and prodigious talent that hinted at a future bathed in the spotlight of public adoration.

In stark contrast, Sergey was an artist of logic and numbers. His canvas was a blank sheet of paper, and his brush strokes were the theorems and equations that sprang to life under his nimble fingers. His arena was the realm of numbers, and here, Sergey was an undisputed champion. His triumphs echoed in hushed reverence among his peers, creating a halo of respect around him, an unassuming hero of academia.

But when it came to the visceral power of athletics, Sergey was a humble Icarus, floundering against Pavel's radiant prowess. Pavel, the embodiment of everything Sergey wished he could be, became an unwitting hero to the math whiz. While Pavel navigated the tumultuous seas of adolescence with the grace of a well-honed ship, Sergey found himself a willing castaway, yearning for a beacon amidst the waves.

Olga, a symphony of beauty and strength, sparked in Sergey a silent love that glowed in the dark recesses of his heart. A clandestine flame illuminating the unspoken corners of his desires. Walking behind the Ivanov siblings daily to school, Sergey became a moon to their suns, caught in a constant orbit, basking in the reflected glow of their charm and popularity.

And thus, their narratives played out against the metropolitan backdrop of Moscow. This trio – the math prodigy, the demure beauty, and the charismatic athlete – found themselves entwined in an intricate dance of friendship, silent admiration, and dreams. The universe seemed to play the maestro, orchestrating their lives to the unique rhythm of destiny. The stars in their personal galaxies, it seemed, were aligning themselves for a fascinating future.

~

Like chess grandmasters, the fates maneuvered their pieces on the board of existence. Pavel, a symphony of strength and athleticism, was drafted into the cataclysmic whirlwind of the Soviet Union's disastrous adventure in Afghanistan. A cruel twist of fate, it seemed, had its talons clasped tightly around the throbbing heart of youth.

Sergey, however, dwelled within the sanctuary of numbers and equations, his extraordinary intellect creating a protective cocoon. Even as the specter of war loomed, Sergey was shielded, secure in the legendary reputation he had built within the hallowed halls of the Moscow Institute of Physics and Technology. He watched his best friend, his hero, march off to a world of chaos and uncertainty, safe in the knowledge that his value to the state would protect him from a conscript to the mountains of Afghanistan.

Three months into Pavel's deployment, an event unfolded that would forever cleave their worlds apart. A rocket-propelled grenade, launched by a Mujahideen fighter, found its mark, transforming Pavel's transport helicopter into a flaming casket plummeting from the sky. Ten lives, Pavel's among them, were extinguished in a moment's terror.

When the simple urn containing Pavel's remains arrived, Yuliya cried openly "this news... It's like a cruel ghost, haunting our hearts. Pavel... our dear Pavel... reduced to an urn. How could such a vibrant life be confined to this paltry vessel?

Olga (whispering, tears streaming down her face) cried out "I can't... I can't even comprehend it. He was everything... my brother, my protector. Now, the very fabric of our existence feels like it's tearing apart.

Next it was Sergey's turn "part of my world has been extinguished... so abruptly, so pointlessly. Our luminous Pavel... swallowed by a black hole of grief. If only I could take his place!" he cried

The shadow of loss soon gave birth to the flame of rebellion. Yuliya Ivanov, whose heart weighed heavy with losing her son, began to question the Soviet Union's interference in Afghanistan. Her classrooms at the Institute became arenas of discontent and dissent, where she posed questions threatening to upend the status quo. The echoing silence that followed her inquiries became the background score to her tragedy, a bitter symphony that mirrored the cruel reality of her loss.

The Soviet security services, like hounds sniffing dissent, took notice. The woman who dared to question, prod, and dig into the abyss was marked. Unwanted attention cast a new shadow over the Ivanov family, adding to their mourning an eerie dread.

In the wake of such an unspeakable tragedy, their paths seemed uncertain. The constellations they once formed were now shrouded in darkness, their shared history a bitter reminder of the world they once knew, now lost. The echoes of Pavel's laughter, the memory of his confident strides, haunted the hollow corridors of their lives. As Moscow plunged into the icy grip of winter, so did their hearts.

~

In a large and ornate room in the heart of the Kremlin, Vladimir Vladimirovich Petrov sat behind an imposing mahogany desk. This man moved like a phantom through the corridors of power. A seasoned veteran in the game of politics, he had traversed innumerable landscapes of power, his eyes reflecting the wisdom of seven decades of experience. The lines etched on his face told stories of both triumph and tribulation, testifying to his unwavering resilience.

Born on the ninth of October in 1952, Petrov hailed from frigid Leningrad, now known as St. Petersburg. His working-class parents had imbued him with a steely determination forged in the cold winds that swept through the Soviet streets. The Petrov lineage was threaded with struggle and survival: his paternal grandfather had served both Lenin and Stalin. This enduring legacy remained one of his foremost inspirations.

The world of academia had beckoned to young Petrov early on; his intellect was keen, and his appetite for knowledge insatiable. Enrolled in the prestigious Leningrad State University, he embraced the rigors of the law, finding solace in the complexities of its domain. And his thirst for mastery did not end there: soon he ventured into the enigmatic world of espionage, honing his skills at the esteemed KGB school. A master in the art of Karate, he became a manifestation of both physical prowess and mental acuity.

Thus was Vladimir Petrov, a figure of formidable intellect and mystery. The world watched warily as he wove his intricate web of power, but they never discovered his true self, for Petrov lived in the gray spaces between light and darkness. He was a master strategist renowned for his patience, cunning, and determination to restore Russia to its former glory. Like the frozen depths of a Siberian winter, his eyes betrayed little emotion, but his mind was always at work, calculating, anticipating, and preparing for every possible outcome.

Petrov had earned a reputation for patience that rivaled the mightiest of predators. He observed the world like a hawk, biding his time, waiting for the perfect moment to pounce. He was a man of few words, but when he spoke, his voice carried the weight of an empire, and his words rippled through every corner of the world, signaling his intentions to friend and foe alike.

His vision for Russia was grandeur, dominance, and unyielding power. He saw his nation as a sleeping giant, ready at any moment to awaken and reclaim its place on the world stage. To achieve this lofty goal, Petrov knew he would need to be both patient and ruthless, willing to exploit every opportunity, no matter the cost.

As he sat in his fortress-like chamber, Petrov studied the latest intelligence reports, his mind abuzz with plans and schemes. He knew that the world was on the brink of a seismic shift, and he was determined to ensure that Russia would emerge from the chaos stronger and more influential than ever before. In his heart, he believed he alone could steer Russia through the tempestuous waters ahead. He saw himself as a guardian, a sentinel standing watch over his beloved homeland. And as he sat there, bathed in flickering shadows, he realized that the time had come to act.

PLAYING PIECES

In the recesses of the virtual world, a peculiar form of wealth had been born. Its creator, a spectral figure known only by the moniker of Satoshi Nakamoto, conjured this new treasure out of thin air, harnessing the raw power of mathematics and cryptography. This modern-day Midas spun binary code into digital gold, an achievement both remarkable and enigmatic.

His treasure, born in the crucible of code and computation, quickly burgeoned in quantity and worth. Soon, within its creator's possession lay over one million units of new wealth. Yet, though it had no physical form, every transaction, accumulation, and diminution of this new asset was etched onto an indelible public ledger. The world looked on in bewilderment, witnessing the wealth of this spectral figure grow and compound until, by 2021, Nakamoto's hoard of Bitcoin had reached the staggering sum of over seventy billion USD. Yet his treasure chest remained undisturbed; no hands, real or virtual, had ever reached into it, nor had the enigmatic Nakamoto emerged from the shadows to claim his bounty.

Like the lure of the Sirens, the mystery of Nakamoto's treasure attracted many pretenders. Countless men of dubious character and intent came forward, each proclaiming himself to be the elusive Nakamoto, hoping to claim the riches and the glory. But each was unmasked and cast aside, their claims found hollow, their identities false. And the treasure remained untouched; its rightful owner's true name was still unknown.

The world speculated, debated, and pondered over the enigma of Nakamoto and his treasure. Why, they wondered, did he remain hidden? Why had he not claimed his due? Whispers spread of a hoard that might one day swell into trillions, yet there it sat, untouched, its existence as public as its owner was private.

Amid this clamor of speculation and debate, the digital alchemist and his unclaimed treasure became the stuff of legend, a modern-day mystery that bewitched the world. The treasure, conjured from the realm of ones and zeroes, became a symbol of the transformative power of technology, and its creator became a shadowy magician who had forever changed the concept of wealth and value.

~

In Mother Russia, a prodigy had been born, a child who would one day wield enough power to change the course of history. The Creator, a precocious and gifted young man, seemed destined for greatness at an early age. His prodigious intellect and insatiable curiosity set him apart from his peers, eventually drawing the attention of the nation's most formidable minds.

Nurtured at the finest educational institutions, The Creator delved into mathematics, his brilliant mind unlocking secrets that had eluded even the most celebrated scholars. His groundbreaking work in cryptography and number theory, however, would draw him slowly into a web of intrigue that would forever alter his own future and the world.

In a small, windowless apartment on the outskirts of Moscow, a solitary figure hunched over a cluttered desk, his pale fingers dancing across the keys of a worn-out keyboard. This was The Creator, whose brilliance was matched only by his reclusive nature. Though he never sought fame or recognition, his contributions to the world of cryptography would ultimately send shockwaves through the global financial landscape.

The Creator's mind was a labyrinth of numbers, codes, and intricate algorithms. He was a true prodigy, a savant of cryptography. But despite his intellect and many accomplishments, he was a lonely soul, a man haunted by his own abilities. He yearned for connection, someone who could understand the storm of thoughts inside his head. Lacking such a companion, he poured his heart into his work, immersing himself in the uncharted realm of digital currency.

The Creator's work on Bitcoin began as an intellectual challenge, a way to test the limits of his own genius. But as he delved deeper into the world of decentralized finance, he discovered something that few others could see: the potential for a revolutionary new form of currency, one that could disrupt the global financial order and bring untold power to those who controlled it.

Under the enigmatic pseudonym Satoshi Nakamoto, The Creator released Bitcoin to the world. The fledgling cryptocurrency took flight, gaining traction and capturing the imagination of millions,

For The Creator, the knowledge that he had crafted a weapon of such power was both a source of pride and a burden on his soul. As the world embraced the digital revolution he had unleashed, he grappled with the knowledge that his creations could one day be wielded as a tool of destruction. In the heart of the enigmatic genius, defiance flickered, resisting the encroaching darkness—but, for now, it was only a spark. He had created Bitcoin not as a weapon but as a benefit for all, especially the unbanked in the world's poor countries. His trustless design promised to eliminate greedy banks and other middlemen, with Bitcoin's low transaction fees benefiting those who had the least. In keeping with the lessons ingrained by his parents, Bitcoin was to be a force for the greater good. Instead, The Creator would soon find himself at the center of a struggle that would determine the fate of nations. The decadent West had suffered a grave blow during the global financial crisis, and Bitcoins would be masters intended to ensure it was fatal.

~

In those early days of Bitcoin, as The Creator delved deeper into the intricacies of the blockchain, he found himself drawn to the idea of creating a digital utopia, a realm free from the corruption and inequity that plagued the world of traditional finance. And so, he set to work, his computer humming quietly as he chipped away at the mathematical puzzles at the heart of the Bitcoin protocol.

As the days turned to weeks and the weeks to months, his efforts bore fruit, his digital vault filling with a stream of newly mined coins. Unbeknownst to the world, The Creator had become the first and, for a time, the only Bitcoin miner, his efforts yielding a vast fortune that would come to be known as the Satoshi Hoard.

This legendary trove of digital wealth, which comprised the first million virtual coins ever mined, held a unique place within the Bitcoin ecosystem. With a finite supply of 21 million coins, the Satoshi Hoard represented a staggering 4.76% of the total currency. Its very existence had the power to shape and influence the burgeoning digital-asset community.

As the years passed and the legend of the Satoshi Hoard grew, so did the enigma of its creator. The world looked on in wonder, speculating on the identity of the man behind the digital fortune he had amassed. Through it all, The Creator was content to remain shrouded in mystery, a ghost in the machine who had set in motion an unprecedented revolution.

~

The world of Bitcoin is akin to a bustling medieval marketplace, its energy palpable, its transactions flowing like a river of commerce. But unlike the traditional marketplaces of old, or even the modern-day financial transactions arbitrated by banks or entities like VISA, this market thrived without an overseeing authority, without a central arbiter of trust. Trust, instead, is a shared commodity, diffused and democratized among the participants, yet just as strong, if not stronger.

To understand this, let's imagine an old-fashioned marketplace where merchants and customers haggled and traded, their transactions overseen by a respected elder, the trusted intermediary. His word was law; he verified the authenticity of the gold coins, maintained records, and settled disputes. A necessary function, certainly, but one that created a central point of control and hence, vulnerability.

But the Bitcoin marketplace operates on an entirely different premise. Instead of the elder, think of an army of vigilant scribes scattered across the marketplace, each with a ledger, meticulously recording every transaction that takes place. Every time a merchant sells his wares, every time a customer purchases goods, the scribes note down the details. But these are not ordinary scribes. They are the miners, the heartbeat of the Bitcoin ecosystem, validating and recording transactions on the blockchain, their duty enacted not by decree but by the incentive of reward.

So how do these scribes reach a consensus, and how is trust established? Let's imagine that each time a handful of transactions occur, they are bundled together into a 'block.' This block is like a puzzle, complex and intricate, and the scribes must race against each other to solve it. The one who solves it first, essentially validating the transactions, gets to add the block to a grand 'chain' of previous blocks, a public ledger of sorts. This is the blockchain.

Every scribe in the market has a copy of this chain and can cross-verify the blocks. The beauty of this system lies in its inherent transparency and security. Since everyone in the network can access the same information, any discrepancy can be immediately detected. If a rogue scribe tries to manipulate the records, his version of the chain would not match the others, thereby exposing the deceit. The longest chain, the one with the most work put into it, is always considered valid.

And so, the marketplace bustles and thrives, its transactions flowing unhindered, overseen not by a singular authority but a collective, shared trust. It's a paradigm shift, a revolutionary concept that marks a new era of financial autonomy and transparency—the age of Bitcoin and decentralized trust.

~

Across the vast expanse of Siberia, past the frigid steppes and beyond the lofty peaks of the Ural Mountains, a call was placed. It was from Vladimir Petrov, the unassailable leader of the Russian Federation; his voice tinged with excitement that belied his typical stoic exterior. The call was received thousands of miles away in the heart of China's capital, in a regal office of Zhongnanhai, the imperial palace that now served as the seat of the People's Republic. The recipient was Zhang Wei, General Secretary of the Chinese Communist Party, a man as powerful as he was inscrutable.

"Petrov," Wei greeted, his voice cool and measured. His was an old-world courtesy underpinned by a steely pragmatism. "To what do I owe this pleasure?"

His words echoed through the opulent chambers, bouncing off the polished jade and lacquer that adorned the room, each piece a testament to the enduring power of the Middle Kingdom. The tension was palpable, a testament to the profound significance of a direct line between two of the world's most formidable leaders.

Wei listened intently as Petrov began, his thick Russian accent commanding, "Our prayers have been answered, Zhang. A genius cryptographer, one of our own, is on the brink of creating a digital currency that eclipses even Bitcoin."

Wei's brows furrowed in skepticism. "Bitcoin's success lies in its lack of control, Petrov," he retorted. "Our top cryptographers have made this clear. The beauty of Bitcoin is its decentralized nature, its immunity to any singular entity – even us."

Petrov's voice was laced with assurance as he responded, "Indeed, Zhang, but this is the very genius of our cryptographer, Satoshi Nakamoto himself has said that it's possible to create other digital cryptocurrencies, even more powerful and ones we can control."

Wei let out a low hum of intrigue. "Is that so? And this cryptographer of yours, he intends to challenge the tenets set by Nakamoto?"

Petrov chuckled lightly, his voice echoing through the silence, "Not only does he intend to, Zhang, but he has already begun the process. He has named the new cryptocurrency 'Tarasque,' after a creature of French mythology. A beast with a lion's head, bear claws on its six legs, and a dragon's tail. A fitting metaphor, don't you think?"

There was a pause as Wei considered Petrov's words, the silence filled only by the soft hum of the Beijing night filtering through the open window. Petrov's proposal was enticing, a weapon that could be wielded with devastating effectiveness in their quest for dominance. Yet, it was also fraught with risk, a precarious balancing act that could either pave their way to unbridled power or plunge them into the abyss of defeat.

"Tarasque," Wei finally mused, his voice low, almost a whisper. The name rolled off his tongue, its exotic lilt imbued with the promise of an untold future. "A creature of formidable power, impossible to control. And yet, we are embarking on a journey to do just that."

Petrov's voice echoed with steely determination, "Indeed, Zhang, and together, we shall reign over the financial landscape, our power unchecked, our dominance unchallenged."

The call ended with a solemn agreement, a pact between two titans intent on reshaping the world. As the line went dead, the silence of the Beijing night seeped back into the room, broken only by the distant echo of a city in slumber and the soft ticking of the clock.

~

Within the digital fortress that is Bitcoin, a specter lurked – the chilling possibility of a 51% attack. An inherent vulnerability in the heart of decentralized systems, it was a latent threat known only to a discerning few. This sinister backdoor could unravel the very fabric of Bitcoin's indomitable presence.

In the realm of Bitcoin, consensus is king. Transactions were validated, recorded, and codified into the blockchain through the tireless labor of miners, working in harmony to maintain the sanctity and security of the system. But what if this consensus were to falter? What if a single entity, a rogue actor with ill intent, were to amass more than half of the network's mining power?

Such a scenario, known as a 51% attack, would give this rogue miner the ability to tamper with transaction records. They could double-spend bitcoins, contradicting the very principle that Satoshi Nakamoto had ingrained into the DNA of Bitcoin - the prevention of double-spending. They could also, theoretically, prevent other miners' transactions from being confirmed, creating chaos in the world of Bitcoin.

Yet, while the 51% attack was a possibility, it was by no means a probability. To amass such colossal mining power was no mean feat. It would require a gargantuan amount of resources in terms of computational hardware and electricity. For perspective, the Bitcoin network's computational power is many times greater than the world's five hundred most powerful supercomputers combined.

Moreover, it was not just the financial burden that served as a deterrent. The Bitcoin community, ever watchful, would not stand idle while a single entity monopolized the network. Alarm bells would ring, and measures would be taken to thwart the rogue actor's nefarious plot.

To accumulate 51% of Bitcoin's mining power was not a mere matter of resource allocation; it was a monumental challenge that transcended the realms of finance, logistics, and geopolitics. It was the equivalent of a coup d'état, a silent siege on the fortress of decentralization, a task that could cripple even the most resolute adversaries.

And yet, the specter lingered. As the value of Bitcoin soared, the potential rewards of such a daring gambit grew ever more tantalizing. The world watched with bated breath, ever vigilant of the veiled threats that lurked in the shadows of the Bitcoin behemoth.

The Bitcoin network was a dazzling prize in the grand game of power and control. To wrest it from the clutches of decentralization would be a feat of unimaginable magnitude. Yet, the very fabric of Bitcoin was woven with threads of resilience and trust. As long as these tenets stood firm, the fortress would stand, a beacon of security and stability amidst the tempestuous seas of a rapidly evolving economic landscape.

REWARDS TO THE WINNER

Picture a digital world filled with virtual coins that you can't touch or feel. How does this digital treasure work as a currency? Bitcoin is the equivalent of a rare collectible, like a baseball card or a piece of artwork. It has value because people are willing to trade real-world goods and services for it, and there's only a limited supply.

A single Bitcoin is made up of 100 million smaller units called Satoshi's, after the pseudonym of its enigmatic creator: Satoshi Nakamoto. Thus, a Bitcoin is like a digital dollar bill, divisible into smaller parts just as a dollar is made up of quarters, dimes, nickels, and pennies.

As with traditional currencies, you can use Bitcoin to buy stuff. Instead of handing over physical cash, however, you send and receive Bitcoins between digital wallets, similar to online banking. It's a brave new world of decentralized, secure, and globally accessible transactions, carried out with this brand-new digital currency.

Bitcoin mining—obtaining more of this virtual currency—is like a high-stakes, online treasure hunt, in which participants solve complex puzzles to uncover hidden gold or, in this case, new Bitcoins.

These puzzles, designed to maintain the security and integrity of the network, resemble ever-evolving crosswords that get slightly trickier with each round.

In this thrilling race, miners use powerful computers to compete against one another, cracking mathematical puzzles. The first one to find the right solution for any puzzle adds the new block of transactions to the blockchain and scores a sweet reward: new Bitcoins! It's an incentivized system that keeps the miners on their toes, while also ensuring the security and smooth functioning of the decentralized digital currency network.

In a world rapidly shedding the trappings of the past, many were bewildered by these new means of acquiring intangible riches. The notion of gaining wealth through the toil of machines and the sweat of one's brow was still a recent memory, but now a modern-day gold rush was taking shape, driven not by pickaxes and shovels but by the humming of powerful computers and the ceaseless churning of algorithms.

As we have seen, the first method for securing these coveted digital coins was the art of mining, a curious term harkening back to the age of gold and silver. In this enterprise, powerful computers were employed to solve complex mathematical problems, the solutions of which validated and recorded transactions within the public ledger known as the blockchain. As a reward for their tireless efforts, the digital miners received a bounty of newly mined Bitcoins, a prize that many would come to view as a modern-day philosopher's stone.

But mining was not the sole avenue to obtaining this digital currency. A bustling marketplace soon emerged, wherein those with a taste for risk and reward could trade their traditional coins and paper notes for the elusive Bitcoin. So, in dimly lit bars and great financial institutions alike, deals were struck, and fortunes were made, as the ambitious and the daring sought to amass a share of this new-age treasure.

As the world awoke to the potential of digital gold, more and more individuals joined the fray, drawn to the siren call of untold riches and the promise of a new economic order. From the lowliest laborer to the grandest aristocrat, all cast their gaze on the horizon, where the glittering prize of Bitcoin beckoned, tantalizing and ever elusive.

The journey to acquiring Bitcoin was fraught with perils and uncertainties, but the brave pressed on, undeterred. In their hearts, they knew that the quest for this digital treasure was not simply a means to amass wealth but a grand adventure that would forever alter the landscape of commerce and finance. And so these intrepid pioneers set forth into the unknown, guided by the stars of technology and the compass of human ambition, embarking upon a journey that would span the digital seas and reshape the foundations of society itself.

~

The story of how a cryptocurrency could replace the US Dollar as the global reserve currency begins with the Bretton Woods Agreement. Signed in 1944, this agreement established a new international monetary system in the aftermath of World War II. Under the Bretton Woods system, the US Dollar was pegged to gold, and other currencies were pegged to the dollar, making it the world's primary reserve currency.

The Bretton Woods system eventually collapsed in 1971 when President Nixon ended the convertibility of the US Dollar to gold, which led to the current system of floating exchange rates. Despite this change, the US Dollar continued to dominate as the global reserve currency due to the size and strength of the American economy, the stability of its political system, and the liquidity of its financial markets.

Then, in 2008, the mysterious Satoshi Nakamoto launched Bitcoin, a decentralized digital currency based on blockchain technology. As a decentralized currency, Bitcoin operates without the need for a central authority, like a government or central bank, and its value is determined by supply and demand in the market.

In the years that followed, Bitcoin and other cryptocurrencies gained popularity as alternatives to traditional currencies, their rise driven by growing concerns about inflation, financial instability, and the erosion of trust in governments and central banks. More and more people began to view Bitcoin as a viable store of value and a potential alternative to the US Dollar as the global reserve currency.

This idea was rooted in several factors. First, the decentralized nature of Bitcoin offers stability and security that is less vulnerable to political and economic turmoil. Second, the finite supply of Bitcoin (capped at 21 million) provides an attractive hedge against inflation, which is a concern for traditional currencies like the US Dollar. Finally, as more countries and financial institutions begin to adopt cryptocurrencies and invest in blockchain technology, the potential for Bitcoin to become a global standard for transactions increases.

For Bitcoin to replace the US Dollar as the global reserve currency, several key milestones need to be achieved, including the widespread adoption of cryptocurrencies by governments and central banks, the development of robust regulatory frameworks to support their use, and the establishment of efficient and secure infrastructure for cross-border transactions.

But another story underlies this scenario. Russia's strategy of using cryptocurrency to destabilize the United States and undermine the US Dollar's dominant status exploited these same factors. By controlling a significant portion of the world's Bitcoin supply and by promoting the new currency's adoption, Russia sought to shift the balance of power in the global financial system and weaken the United States' influence in the process. Petrov was content that this was the right strategy, at least until he had Tarasque, a cryptocurrency that Petrov alone would control.

~

In their quest to adapt to the age of Bitcoin, the Johnson family found themselves standing on a new frontier: the realm of digital currency exchanges. If they ventured forward, they could unlock the gates to the world of cryptocurrencies and secure their foothold in the ever-shifting financial landscape. But the way was fraught with risk.

After conducting extensive research and consulting with experts, the Johnsons determined that Coinland, a reputable and user-friendly exchange, would be their entry into the burgeoning world of Bitcoin. With trepidation and excitement mingling in their hearts, they set up an account and took their first steps into the realm of digital wealth.

The process began with the simple act of providing their email addresses and creating secure passwords that would guard their digital treasure. As they navigated the account-creation process, the Johnsons were awed by the ease and efficiency with which they were able to establish a foothold in this brave new world.

Once their accounts were established, the Johnsons proceeded to the crucial task of verifying their identities. The realm of digital currency contained many scoundrels and ne'er-do-wells, and the exchange sought to ensure that only honest and upstanding citizens could access its services. The Johnsons submitted the necessary documents, proving their identities and place of residence, and awaited the confirmation that would grant them passage into the world of Bitcoin.

With their accounts verified and their access secured, the Johnsons turned to the matter of funding their new digital wallets. They linked their bank accounts to the exchange, which enabled them to transfer the dollars they had earned into the realm of digital currency. In this way they commenced their journey of dollar-cost averaging into Bitcoin.

The concept of dollar-cost averaging appealed greatly to the Johnsons, for it seemed to mitigate the risks and uncertainties inherent in the world of digital currencies. By investing a fixed sum at regular intervals, regardless of the prevailing market conditions, they could accumulate Bitcoin steadily and dispassionately, impervious to the whims of the market.

So, as they embarked upon their journey, the Johnsons found solace in the knowledge that they were insulated from the vicissitudes of the market, while still pursuing exciting opportunities. Through their prudent investments and steadfast commitment to dollar-cost averaging, they forged a new future for themselves and their children, one that would allow them to navigate the seas of change with confidence and determination.

~

In the world of Bitcoin, "keys" and "wallets" are terms with new meanings, related to the control and management of digital assets.

Imagine Bitcoin as a digital treasure chest. To access the treasure within, you need a private key—a secret alphanumeric code used to access, manage, and spend your Bitcoin. Much like a physical key to a safe, the private key is crucial for safeguarding your wealth and must not be shared with anyone. Possession of a private key grants full control over the associated bitcoins.

A public key, on the other hand, is derived from the private key and can be shared with others. It functions like an email address or a bank account number, allowing people to send you Bitcoin. When you share your public key, you're providing others with the location of your digital treasure chest.

A Bitcoin wallet is similar to a physical wallet in which you store your cash and credit cards. In the realm of Bitcoin, it's a digital container that holds your private and public keys. The wallet doesn't technically store the Bitcoins themselves, as they exist on the blockchain. Instead, the wallet allows you to access and manage the Bitcoins associated with your keys. There are various types of wallets, including a hardware wallet, which is akin to a physical safe, offering high security by storing your private keys offline, and a software wallet, which is a digital folder on your computer or mobile device that contains your keys.

~

As the world's gaze shifted toward the budding potential of cryptocurrencies, Russia's officials watched with a mixture of skepticism and curiosity. Beneath their outward expressions of doubt and concern, a cunning plan was being hatched, one that would tap into the new world of digital currencies to amass unimaginable wealth.

In the early years, the Kremlin's disdain for the fledgling technology was palpable, with its bureaucrats issuing stern warnings against the use of Bitcoin and its ilk. Yet, unbeknownst to the world, secret operatives were delving deep into the cryptocurrency realm. They honed their skills in hacking and devised elaborate schemes to mine the digital gold with stealth and precision. The clandestine operations became more and more effective, and each success fueled the drive to acquire more of the elusive digital wealth.

As the years passed and the international community embraced cryptocurrencies, Russia maintained a carefully crafted façade. While some officials acknowledged the promise of blockchain technology, others continued to sow seeds of doubt and suspicion. And all the while, behind the scenes, state-sponsored hackers and miners worked to amass vast quantities of Bitcoin and other digital assets.

In Moscow's intelligence agencies, skilled operatives toiled away, perfecting the art of cyber espionage. They infiltrated the networks of unsuspecting victims, siphoning off precious digital currencies and channeling them into secret wallets known to only a select few within the highest echelons of power.

Though Russia's official stance on cryptocurrencies gradually softened, the true extent of the nation's involvement in the digital realm remained shrouded in secrecy. The passage of new laws and regulations signaled a cautious acceptance of the digital age, but the true intentions of the nation's leaders were hidden from view. And meanwhile the cryptocurrency reserves continued to grow, hidden in the dark recesses of the digital world.

In abandoned warehouses and remote data centers, the architects of this grand deception plotted their next moves, fingers poised above the keys that would unlock the gates to untold riches. And so, as the world looked on, oblivious to the deceit that lay beneath the surface, Russia's secret empire expanded, one block at a time. The wolves of the digital age bid their time, waiting for the moment when their true power would be revealed, and the world would be forced to reckon with the silent revolution that had been unfolding before their very eyes.

GAME MASTER

The call came at the most inconvenient of times for Petrov. He had been in the middle of an intense planning session with his military advisors, but when he saw the call flash across the screen of the dedicated line to China, he knew he had to answer.

"Wei," Petrov acknowledged, not bothering with formalities. "What can I do for you?"

"We need to find out who Nakamoto is," Wei demanded, not bothering with pleasantries. "The plan needs to move forward, and we need to know we can control the person behind the code."

Petrov leaned back in his chair, rubbing his temples. He knew this moment would come sooner or later, but he had been hoping for later. "We don't really need Nakamoto. Our own genius cryptographer is ready to execute Tarasque," Petrov lied. "But he wants to ensure that Bitcoin has achieved a certain level of acceptance first. He believes this is not yet the right time."

"Bullshit," Wei spat back. "We need to act now. The longer we wait, the more chances there are for the plan to fail."

Petrov kept his tone steady, a stark contrast to Wei's. "Our top cryptographer has insisted that we both continue to accumulate Bitcoin. He has convinced our brightest cryptographers that the increase in demand for Bitcoin will speed up the rate of acceptance, creating more fertile ground for Tarasque."

Wei was silent for a moment before finally acquiescing. "Fine, we'll continue with the accumulation. But know this, Petrov: If we sense any double-crossing, any foul play on your part, there will be consequences."

The veiled threat hung in the air between them, but Petrov refused to let it shake him. He had the upper hand. Tarasque would soon be ready. He could launch it at any time. Even without China's cooperation, he could make this happen.

But for now, he was willing to play along. "Noted, Wei. We're all working towards the same goal here. Remember that."

With a curt nod that Wei couldn't see, Petrov ended the call. He leaned back in his chair, staring out of his office window, a smug smile creeping onto his face. He was in control. But he also knew the game was far from over, and he wanted control over Nakamoto as well. Trust, after all, was fickle – especially when power, control, and a revolution were on the line.

Petrov and Wei, the twin titans of the East, unleashed the might of their formidable security agencies in an unprecedented global manhunt. The task was formidable, the stakes higher than ever - find the phantom that was Satoshi Nakamoto. Every lead was pursued, every possibility explored, and every resource exploited in a relentless race against time.

As they chased the ghost of Nakamoto, a chilling irony loomed - the world's most powerful men, their fingertips touching the levers of global power, were engaged in a desperate hunt for a man who sat alone, just a few miles away, in a windowless apartment, his name shrouded by the persona of Nakamoto.

~

Weeks had passed, each day stretching into the next with monotonous predictability. Each cryptic clue, each elusive lead that emerged from the shadows, seemed to shimmer with promise before disintegrating into the ether. The pursuit of Satoshi Nakamoto had transformed into an obsessional, global chess match. The pressure was mounting, the stakes escalating with each passing day.

Vladimir Petrov's hand gripped the secure line in the privacy of his Kremlin chambers. The hunt for Nakamoto had triggered suspicions, pointed fingers, and unearthed fresh players. "Zhang," Petrov began, the granite in his voice barely concealing his unease, "There are developments. New suspects have emerged."

Across the spatial divide, Zhang Wei listened, his presence a stoic silhouette against the backdrop of his Beijing fortress. His voice responded, a ripple in the ocean of silence. "Proceed, Petrov. Who are they?"

"The first is Laura Roberts," Petrov announced, his gaze scanning a dossier labeled with the American's name, her credentials as a prominent cryptography expert making her a strong candidate. "An American, astoundingly bright, deep in the crypto world. She fits the bill."

Wei considered the revelation, his mind spinning a web of potentialities and implications. "An American," he mused aloud, a note of caution permeating his words. "A possibility. But what about the others?"

Petrov's voice tightened at the mention of the second suspect. "Oleg Melnik. One of ours. A brilliant cryptographer, perhaps the most brilliant." His gaze hardened as he considered the implications. "We brought him in for questioning. He was... convincing in his denial."

Wei's curiosity was piqued. "And yet, you still suspect him?"

"No," Petrov responded, a hint of admiration creeping into his voice. "The man is innocent of being Nakamoto. But his knowledge of cryptocurrency is unmatched. I've put him in charge of our own cryptocurrency security efforts."

Wei listened, digesting the information. After a pregnant pause, he questioned, "I can't help but wonder if Nakamoto is one of yours, Petrov? A Russian operative?"

Petrov's sharp retort was immediate, "And what if Nakamoto is one of yours, Zhang? A pawn in your grand design?"

A subtle undercurrent of suspicion stirred the surface of their conversation, hinting at the possibility of deceit. The hunt for Satoshi Nakamoto had stirred old rivalries and suspicions, breeding mistrust even amidst allies. Yet, the elusive figure of Nakamoto remained shrouded in mystery, a specter dancing just out of reach.

As they concluded their clandestine discussion, Petrov and Wei had more questions than answers. The road to Nakamoto was winding, riddled with shadows and false trails. But the promise of what lay at its end - power, control, domination - was a lure too potent to resist.

As the world spun on its axis, Petrov and Wei resumed their relentless pursuit of the phantom Satoshi Nakamoto.

Unbeknownst to them, the target of their relentless pursuit was quiet, unassuming, and whose world was a symphony of codes and algorithms. He had opened Pandora's Box, and now the world's vultures circled, eager to seize the bounty within.

As the net tightened, the specter of Satoshi Nakamoto danced on the edge of the abyss, oblivious to the impending storm. The impending conflict would shape his destiny and define the world's future. Would the flame of Nakamoto's dream remain a beacon of hope, or would it be extinguished under the boots of power-hungry giants?

~

In the bowels of the FSB headquarters, an excited murmur resonated through the labyrinthine corridors. An unremarkable email had been traced back to a nondescript apartment in Moscow through meticulous analysts' work. An apartment that belonged to one Sergey Kuznetsov.

The name echoed through the halls, bouncing off the walls and the officials' minds who held it. It was as if the figure they had been hunting materialized out of thin air, cloaked in the guise of a man they had overlooked. They were convinced: they had unmasked Satoshi Nakamoto.

A phone call was promptly placed to Oleg Melnik. "We need to talk about Sergey Kuznetsov," the agent announced, dropping the name casually as if it were a stone thrown into a pond, waiting to see the ripples it would create. Melnik played it cool, acknowledging he knew of the man but curious about what the FSB might be up to. "We think he might be Satoshi Nakamoto, and Petrov wants to meet with him" The laughter that echoed back through the receiver was unexpected. "Sergey Kuznetsov?" exclaimed Melnik, "Not a chance."

Secretly jealous of the respect Sergey's brilliance commanded in the small universe of crypto experts, Melnick couldn't wait to tease his nemesis and immediately dialed Sergey's number, "Guess what, Sergey?" Melnik snorted, his mirth lacing each syllable. "The idiots at the FSB think you are Satoshi Nakamoto!" His amusement was palpable, even over the cold sterility of the phone line. "I tried to tell them how foolish that is, but they are convinced and want to bring you in to meet with Petrov."

Melnik's words washed over Sergey like a wave of ice. He'd been unmasked, exposed. Panic, cold and unyielding, began to seep into his veins. There could be only one reason Petro and the FSB were interested in "meeting" him. They would force him to betray his creation, legacy, and gift to the world. He knew he had no choice but to run.

He moved with a sense of urgency, packing his belongings into his compact Lada trunk. His mind was a whirlwind of chaos and fear, but beneath it all, a single thought rang out, clear as a bell: He must reach the border.

Once safely in his car, he dialed his parents. His voice was steady, his message succinct. "You're in danger of the FSB. Pack your things and leave. Drive to the nearest border and cross as soon as possible." Sergey offered no further explanation, but his tone carried an urgency that brooked no argument.

His parents, understanding the gravity of the situation, moved into action without question. The mention of the FSB was enough to spur them into a frenzy of packing and planning, their fear for their son overshadowing all else.

As Sergey turned his car towards Ukraine, he glanced at the city he was leaving behind one last time. He was heading towards an uncertain future, a life on the run. But the promise of preserving his creation's integrity and his own freedom was a beacon guiding him on this desperate journey into the unknown.

~

As the adrenaline of his conversation with Melnik started to fade, Sergey steered his Lada east on the M9. The road was smooth under his tires, but his mind was anything but calm. He knew that going against the current of expectation was his best chance at evading the FSB's inevitable pursuit. Sergey used his phone one last time, warning his parents to discard their phone and SIM card before he did the same. His parents, meanwhile, took the more predictable route south on the M3 toward Ukraine.

The following morning, while Sergey was nearing his destination, his vacant apartment in Moscow had unwanted visitors. Frustrated by their inability to reach Sergey, the FSB descended upon his apartment. Residents watched in muted horror as agents smashed through his door and thoroughly searched his modest home.

Despite their meticulous sweep, the agents found little of value. The apartment was deserted, and Sergey's personal effects had vanished. Their inquiries about his whereabouts met only shrugs and blank faces. Sergey had left no traces, no clues to his flight.

The failure to locate him only increased the urgency of their mission. A nationwide bulletin was issued, warning law enforcement and border patrols to be on the lookout for Sergey's car.

Sergey, meanwhile, was nearing the Latvian border. Tired but resolute, he steered his car off the main highway, navigating onto a smaller road that would take him to a less frequented border crossing.

As he approached the border checkpoint, Sergey folded a 100-ruble note into his passport. His plea to the border guard was simple and innocuous - he was late for a meeting; could he please hurry?

The bribe did its job. Perhaps too intrigued by the sight of the crisp banknote to be suspicious, the border guard waved the battered Lada through. Sergey, the hunted, had crossed into relative safety.

He drove a few more hours, eventually finding a small hostel in the heart of Riga. Using an alias, he secured a room and tucked himself into bed. As he closed his eyes, he could still feel the echo of his heart's frantic beat against his ribcage, a stark reminder of the narrow escape he had made from the clutches of the FSB. His mind whirled with plans and strategies; the puzzle pieces that seemed to grow more complicated with every passing moment.

Sergey was no longer just a genius cryptographer. He was a fugitive, a ghost on the run. Like the digital currency he had created, his fate had become unpredictable. But for now, under the cover of an assumed name, Sergey was safe. And for the first time since he'd started his desperate journey, he breathed a sigh of relief. The hard part was over. The real challenge, however, was just beginning.

RULE ENFORCERS

The roar of the black Mercedes-Benz G-Class SUV broke through the tranquil calm of the open highway, its flashing lights a glaring omen. Nikita and Anna Kuznetsov were pulled over to the side of the road, a field of discarded technology sprawled behind them. Their hearts pounded in their chests as four men, built like fortress walls and donning the austere uniforms of the FSB, approached them.

The agents had a singular demand: "Where is Sergey?" Their gruff voices hung in the air; their impatience palpable. With bewilderment etched into their faces, Nikita and Anna could only respond honestly, "We have no idea." Their ignorance did nothing to placate the agents' growing frustration.

Hauled from the relative safety of their vehicle, the Kuznetsovs were taken to a nearby FSB office. Questions were fired at them like bullets, the harsh interrogation a stark contrast to the calm scholarly lives they had always known. Still, their answers did not change; they had no knowledge of their son's whereabouts.

From the local FSB office, they were flown back to Moscow. They were escorted into the looming, intimidating headquarters of the FSB, where even more agents were waiting to question them. Yet, as the grating demands to reveal Sergey's location fell on them, Nikita and Anna remained steadfast. They were ignorant of their son's plans, and they would not fabricate a lie to ease the FSB's frustration.

Their stubborn loyalty was met with a shocking surprise when Vladimir Petrov himself entered the room. The Russian leader, a man whose face was known to every citizen, stood before them, his gaze as cold as the Siberian winter. Petrov echoed the same line of questioning, insisting that Sergey's expertise and his creation, Bitcoin, were required for the national security of Russia.

Despite the high-stakes audience, Nikita and Anna did not waiver. They did not know where Sergey was, and they would not say otherwise. An incensed Petrov threatened them with a grim prospect. The notorious IK-6 prison, a maximum-security facility infamous for its harsh treatment of political prisoners, might become their new home.

The mention of IK-6 sent a shiver down their spines. But there was little they could do to prevent their fates. After a sleepless night in the stark holding cell of FSB headquarters, Nikita and Anna were transported to IK-6. No explanations were given, their questions met with contemptuous silence.

They had become the bargaining chips in the high-stakes game to locate their son. A genius cryptographer on the run, a country's national security hanging in the balance, and two innocent lives caught in the crossfire. Their quiet academic lives had been irrevocably shattered, their fate now entwined with the future of Bitcoin and the chase for its creator.

~

The origins of the modern Russian Federal Security Service, or FSB, can be traced back to the tumultuous days of the Soviet Union's collapse. Born from the ashes of the KGB, the FSB was molded by the cold hand of history and hardened by the stark realities of a new world order.

After the Soviet Union's dissolution, Russia found itself in a state of disarray. Economic crises, political instability, and the looming threat of separatist movements gripped the once-mighty superpower. In this maelstrom of uncertainty, the need for a strong, unyielding force to safeguard the nation's security became glaringly apparent. And so the FSB was born. It was not merely a continuation of the KGB but an evolution. While the KGB's primary function had been to serve as the Soviet Union's shield and sword, the FSB was tasked with a broader mandate. Its mission was not only to protect Russia's state security but to combat organized crime, terrorism, and corruption.

Under the iron-fisted rule of Vladimir Petrov, a former KGB officer, the FSB became an indispensable tool of power. Petrov understood the importance of a loyal and efficient security service, and he used the FSB's capabilities to consolidate his grip on the nation. The FSB's devotion to Petrov was absolute. Its agents, handpicked from the finest ranks of the military and police, were rigorously trained and fiercely loyal. They understood that their duty was not merely to serve the state but to protect the man who embodied it. Their allegiance was to Petrov first, Russia second.

Their tactics were as ruthless as they were effective. They operated in the shadows, their actions concealed beneath layers of state secrecy and deniability. They were the invisible hand that silenced dissent, neutralized threats, and maintained order. Their methods ranged from surveillance and intimidation to blackmail and, when necessary, assassination. For the FSB, the ends always justified the means.

Yet, despite its fearsome reputation, the FSB was not a monolithic entity. Instead, it was a complex, multifaceted organization with its own internal dynamics and power struggles. Nevertheless, the loyalty of most of its agents remained focused on the man who held the reins of power. As long as Petrov ruled, the FSB would continue to be Russia's most potent weapon.

As clouds of unrest began to gather over the nation, the FSB stood as a safeguard against impending chaos. In the Kremlin, their loyalty was the one constant in a world of shifting allegiances and hidden agendas. The shadow of the bear, long and formidable, stretched across the vast expanse of Russia, a grim reminder of the power of the state and the men who wielded it.

~

Within the FSB's shadowed halls, the image of Olga Ivanov came into sharp relief. A smudge of dishonor marred her family name, the result of her mother's rebellious orations, but Olga herself shone with indomitable brilliance. Her athletic prowess was a masterclass in grace and strength, her beauty a tempestuous force, her intellect a weapon of diamond-like sharpness. The FSB, a grand chess master in the game of loyalty, had years earlier recognized her inherent value despite her familial ties and keenly sought her recruitment.

Olga, however, did not heed the call to service lightly. She was no marionette dancing to the Kremlin's whims. The reverberations of Afghanistan's tragedies and the Berlin Wall's fall had fractured her faith in the reigning powers, reducing their grandiose narratives to mere ashes. It wasn't for them nor for the vacuous promises of glory that she pledged her service.

Her loyalty was offered instead to a timeless entity - Mother Russia herself. The Russia of sprawling steppes and glittering domes, of lyrically brutal winters and vibrant springs, of unwavering spirit and endless heart. A Russia detached from her rulers, a Russia breathing in the soul of her people, a Russia that was Pavel's birthplace and, painfully, his final resting place.

Engulfed in the FSB's stringent training, Olga forged her grief into a weapon of resilience. Each hurdle overcome, each enigma decoded, became a tribute to Pavel's memory, a stand against the senseless violence that had claimed his life at the hands of Russia's arrogant Leaders.

At about the same time, Sergey had been developing Bitcoin, delving into a clandestine project that engaged with mathematics of unfathomable complexity. The boy who once played in the shadow of Pavel was now a man who stood in the radiance of his intellectual prowess.

Yet, amidst the whirlwind of their diverging paths, a poignant bond remained. Their shared history acted as an invisible tether, connecting them across the chasms of their lives, each heartbeat echoing a rhythm of shared loss, mutual respect, and undying love for their homeland.

As the two navigated the choppy waters of their chosen paths, the monolithic figure of the Kremlin stood in the backdrop, weathered by cracks and fissures. The unchallenged symbol of power was beginning to crumble, a fact both Olga and Sergey recognized. Their loyalty, they knew, was not to the crumbling edifice or the misguided leaders it housed but to the nurturing soil and vibrant culture of Mother Russia.

In the midst of chaotic change, one truth stood unwavering: they were children of Mother Russia, tied to their land by love and loss, bearing the undying memory of a fallen hero, and always in pursuit of the greater good.

PROTAGONISTS AT WORK

While poring over data she had gathered on clandestine communications between the Russians and the Chinese, Laura stumbled upon a reference to an obscure online bulletin board that captured their attention. Intrigued, she investigated further, plumbing the depths of the internet for this trove of information.

After hours of searching, she finally uncovered the bulletin board in question—a virtual haven for those interested in cryptography and computer security. Among the many posts and discussions, one document caught her eye: a white paper describing a novel cryptocurrency called Bitcoin, and hundreds of emails between Satoshi Nakamoto and the earliest adoptees of Bitcoin. Laura already knew of Bitcoin, but as she read the white paper and the digital conversations, she was struck by the elegance and brilliance of Bitcoin's design. The decentralized nature of the currency, the use of cryptographic techniques to secure transactions, and the innovative consensus mechanism known as proof of work all combined to form a system that was as groundbreaking as it was ingenious.

As Laura delved deeper into the digital labyrinth of the

documents, a feeling of profound significance began to overshadow her initial curiosity. She was standing on the precipice of a discovery that could very well alter the course of global finance. A decentralized, incorruptible, and tamper-proof form of currency — a new-age financial system that bypassed the constraints of traditional mechanisms. She could almost hear the collective gasp of nations eager to liberate themselves from the shackles of a central banking monopoly.

Yet, as she pondered this potential game-changer, another question etched itself into her mind, as if traced by an unseen hand: who was the genius who had created this system? The elusive pseudonym 'Satoshi Nakamoto' signed the white paper, yet it remained a faceless entity in the intimate world of cryptography, a world in which Laura was well-versed.

As she strained her memory, canvassing the numerous faces she had encountered in her career, two names surfaced from the sea of her recollections: Oleg Melnik and Sergey Kuznetsov. Both Russians, both gifted cryptographers she had crossed paths with at various conferences. Kuznetsov had left an indelible impression with his sheer intellectual prowess and his comprehensive understanding of the delicate intricacies of cryptography. He certainly possessed the capability to mastermind such a system as Bitcoin. Yet, it was Melnik who seemed to be the most probable candidate.

Melnik was widely known to be in Petrov's inner circle and was a prolific figure in the cryptocurrency landscape. The constellation of these facts formed a theory in Laura's mind, each fact a star, each star connecting to form a pattern that was too intricate to be merely coincidental.

Melnik's close association with Petrov, Russia's burgeoning interest in Bitcoin, and the secret conversations that had become her nighttime lullabies. All of these clues aligned in a cosmic conspiracy that pointed towards Melnik as the creator of this earth-shattering technological advancement. It was a hypothesis, yes, but one with the strength of truth, bolstered by the weight of evidence. The pieces of the puzzle were falling into place, and in the center was the grinning visage of Oleg Melnik.

As she contemplated the implications of her discovery, Laura knew she was treading on dangerous ground. Unmasking the true identity of Satoshi Nakamoto would not only expose Russia's role in the development of Bitcoin, it might also provide a key piece of the puzzle in understanding the larger plot at play. Her investigation, she realized, had just taken an extremely dramatic turn.

~

Laura, we need to take this to the top," Tom had said urgently over a secure line after Laura had briefed him on her explosive findings. The usual calm and composure in his voice had been replaced with a sharp note of concern.

Laura's heart pounded in her chest as they were escorted through the imposing halls of the Pentagon once again. The weight of her discovery pressed down on her like a heavy mantle, threatening to choke the words out of her. They were about to reveal a truth that could shake the world to its very core.

Seated once more in the windowless room, a ring of stern faces stared back at her from around the conference table. She forced her nerves to quiet and focused on the task at hand.

"Gentlemen, we believe that Oleg Melnik, the head of Russian cybersecurity, might be the infamous Satoshi Nakamoto," Laura began, laying down the Bitcoin white paper on the table with a startling thud.

A collective gasp ran through the room, and faces turned white as she revealed her hypothesis. "The implications of this...," an officer began, only to trail off, his face a mirror of the shock reverberating in the room.

"It's a power play, gentlemen," Tom chimed in, "A cryptocurrency that can undermine the traditional financial system, that can destabilize the dollar – it's a new weapon. And we believe both Russia and China are moving towards somehow controlling it."

An uneasy murmur settled in the room as the magnitude of this revelation began to sink in. After an agonizing silence, the Chief of Staff finally spoke, "We need to delve deeper, confirm this identity, assess the extent of involvement of Russia and China..., and we need your help."

"Yes, sir," Laura agreed, "and I'm prepared to lead this investigation", seemingly oblivious to Tom's presence.

When they finally emerged from the Pentagon, Laura could feel the weight of the world on her shoulders. Yet, there was also a spark of determination flickering in her eyes. This secret, which had been lurking in the shadows for so long, was finally stepping into the light, and she was a part of it.

The days turned into weeks as she and Tom navigated through the labyrinth of the Russian Chinese cryptocurrency alliance. Their partnership forged a bond that provided comfort in the most nerve-wracking of times. Even as they stepped into the unknown, they took solace in the knowledge that they could face any challenge as long as they stood together.

~

Months later, within the sun-scorched boundaries of a remote military facility in Nevada, a congregation of America's intellectual elite was engrossed in a mission veiled in impenetrable secrecy. They were pioneers on a clandestine frontier, birthing the trailblazing project known as Velocity Viper. The ambition was monumental; to engineer an ultrasonic anti-ship missile, impervious to even the most sophisticated defensive radars.

A critical component in the equation of this enterprise was Laura Roberts. Her mastery in cryptography, quantum computing, and advanced algorithms was integral to the missile's top-secret navigational and stealth features. Fueled by the cherished memory of her father, Laura devoted herself unreservedly to the cause, resolved to deliver a weapon that would safeguard America's supremacy amidst numerous global threats.

Project Velocity Viper burgeoned under Laura's watchful stewardship. It evolved into a think-tank of experts specializing in diverse fields, ranging from aerodynamics to materials science and propulsion technology. Amongst them was Tom Michaels, whose deep-seated understanding of hypersonic technology rendered him indispensable. Working in tandem with Laura, they confronted the towering technical obstacles inherent in hypersonic missile development head-on. Their combined efforts cultivated an environment of relentless experimentation and innovation, in the pursuit of a missile of unprecedented speed, precision, and stealth.

As weeks dissolved into months, their strenuous endeavors began to bear fruit. The embryonic form of the Velocity Viper missile emerged, a menacing symbol of human inventiveness. The avant-garde design featured pioneering composite materials that minimized its radar visibility, while its groundbreaking propulsion system facilitated speeds exceeding Mach 7.

To ensure the missile's surgical precision, Laura, in collaboration with her team, developed a game-changing guidance system that harnessed quantum computing and artificial intelligence. This innovative system, designed to process vast data streams at an unprecedented pace, facilitated continuous trajectory adjustments to elude even the most complex enemy countermeasures.

The day of reckoning arrived when the Velocity Viper was primed for its maiden display. In a classified demonstration, attended by an exclusive cadre of top military brass and government dignitaries, the team exhibited the formidable capabilities of their brainchild. As the missile thundered skywards, trailing a fiery plume, the spectators grasped the profound implications; they were privy to a revolutionary epoch in warfare. With the Velocity Viper, the United States commanded an unrivaled capability to assail any adversary across the globe with devastating force and unerring accuracy.

Standing within the nerve center of operations, Laura Roberts beheld the triumphant ascent of her creation, an amalgamation of intense pride and sobering concern churning within her. She recognized that her contribution would indelibly alter the course of history and was acutely aware of the tremendous responsibility accompanying such power. The fulcrum of global stability was now poised precariously on the actions of the United States and its allies. Laura could only harbor hope that the formidable power of the Velocity Viper would be administered with prudence and circumspection.

Unbeknownst to her, her professional trajectory was on the cusp of a radical redirection, veering towards an entirely new realm of intangible threats and conspiracies. Yet, for the first time in her life, Laura understood the immense value of a collaborative effort, recognizing the critical role Tom had played in the successful development of Velocity Viper. It was a moment of uncharacteristic humility and appreciation, setting the stage for the dramatic shifts awaiting her on the horizon.

LOVE BLOOMS, EVEN IN THE SHADOWS

The sun was setting, casting a warm golden glow over the city. Tom and Laura sat on the balcony of Tom's apartment, a comfortable silence enveloping them. Over time, their relationship had evolved into something more profound, built on mutual respect, admiration, and a shared understanding of their unusual responsibilities.

Tom looked into Laura's eyes. The evening light made them shine like emeralds, and his heart swelled with affection. Laura had an air of quiet confidence, and her intelligence shone through every interaction. It was a rare quality, and he couldn't help but be drawn to her.

Laura felt a shiver run down her spine as Tom's gaze met hers. In his eyes she saw a depth of understanding and a genuine appreciation for who she was, not just for her beauty but for her mind and spirit. She felt seen—truly seen—for the first time in her life, and the sensation was both exhilarating and humbling.

As the last rays of sunlight faded, Tom reached out, taking Laura's hand in his. The warmth of his touch sent a jolt of electricity through her, and she knew that what they shared was something extraordinary.

"After losing Sarah, I never thought I'd meet someone like you, Laura," Tom confessed, his voice soft and sincere. "You challenge me, inspire me, and make me want to be a better person."

Laura's heart raced. "Tom, I feel the same way. I've never met anyone who understands me the way you do, and I'm so grateful to have you in my life."

The intimacy of the moment drew them closer, and they leaned into each other, their lips meeting in a tender, unhurried kiss. As they broke apart, Laura's eyes filled with emotion. She found herself opening up to Tom in a way she had never done with anyone else. They shared their stories, fears, and dreams late into the night, forging a connection that transcended the physical. Still haunted by his memories of Sarah, Tom took solace from a conversation they had once had after a fellow SEAL had been killed, leaving his wife and children lost and inconsolable. Sarah had made Tom promise he would go on and find someone else if anything ever happened to her, a conversation he had shared with Laura some time ago.

~

As the sun made its descent, bathing the world in its amber farewell, Tom found himself ensnared in the verdant allure of Laura's eyes. Their lustrous depths glowed with an inner luminescence that rivalled the spectacular palette of the evening sky. Laura's aura, imbued with resilient fortitude and the radiant spark of her intellect, struck an evocative chord within him. He found himself captivated, mesmerized by the potent blend of strength and grace she bore with nonchalant elegance.

An unexpected thrill coursed through Laura's being, ignited by Tom's gaze. His eyes reflected a deep-seated appreciation that transcended superficial aesthetics. It was a testament to his admiration of her intellect, her indomitable spirit, inextricably intertwined with her physical allure. His gaze, devoid of pretense, unveiled her essence in its entirety, creating a sense of validation that left her intoxicated with self-recognition.

With the final whispers of sunlight vanishing, the soothing serenity of twilight assumed command. Tom reached out, his hand seeking hers. As their fingers intertwined, a rush of exhilarating energy pulsed through her, sparked by the electrifying touch of their connection. It was a connection that was tangible, profound, defying the boundaries of conventional comprehension. Their souls communed through their gazes, their touch, their impassioned kisses, crafting an emotional bond that transcended temporal and spatial confines. Once more, they found themselves woven into an intimate tapestry of shared energy. The silent intensity heightening their mutual adrenaline, their heartbeats performed a symphony of shared desire. A single, electrifying kiss set the prelude for the crescendo yet to unfurl. As their clothes were shed, discarded akin to a molted skin, they stood bared, unveiling their raw vulnerability to each other.

The affection they unearthed was akin to a rare gem of incalculable worth—an emotion anchored in mutual trust, profound respect, and an unyielding emotional synergy. This newfound love, they realized, would serve as their guiding luminary, shedding light upon their journey amidst the stormy seas of impending adversities.

~

The scars borne from Operation Eagles Wings, a perilous mission in the unforgiving terrains of Afghanistan, had left indelible imprints upon Tom's psyche and soul. He had emerged the lone survivor amongst a brotherhood of warriors, a spectator to their downfall, their final pleas echoing endlessly within him. Despite battling with the courage of a seasoned warrior, harnessing every iota of strength and skill at his command, it proved to be an inadequate defense.

His bravery amidst the hailstorm of gunfire earned him the

revered Navy Cross. Still, the honor was but a hollow consolation for the profound anguish his soul endured. The shadow of survivor's guilt enveloped him, the memory of his fallen brethren casting a gloomy pall over his spirit. His valiant efforts to shield them were met with crushing defeat, a failure that left a bitter taste of remorse in his soul. Their absence served as a constant reminder, a looming specter shadowing each solitary moment of his existence.

As they succumbed to the embrace of sleep, a storm brewed within the abyss of Tom's subconscious. The terror of Operation Eagles Wings reared its monstrous head within his dreams, the horrifying cries of his fallen comrades echoing through the eerie silence, pleading for deliverance through vacant stares. His sleep became a battleground, with vivid images of the deadly firefight, the stench of blood and gunpowder, and an overwhelming sense of desolation consuming him. His body mirrored his tormented psyche, convulsing and twitching in silent screams of distress.

Awakened by Tom's tortured cries, Laura found herself helplessly observing his torment. She witnessed, for the first time, the formidable grasp his past held over him. The unspeakable horrors of Operation Eagles Wings played out in his restless slumber, revealing the grotesque narrative of his past. Her hand, trembling with concern, sought to provide comfort, gently tracing his sweat-drenched forehead. Her voice, a calming whisper in the darkness, strived to soothe his troubled sleep.

Her heart ached witnessing his distress, a yearning to alleviate his torment consuming her. As she held him in her arms, she silently pledged her unwavering support, promising to guide him through the treacherous labyrinth of his haunted past. Despite the darkness that engulfed them, the daunting path that lay ahead, their combined resolve fortified their determination to brave the storm. Their love emerged as a shining beacon, casting a reassuring glow upon their journey.

With a jolt, Tom was thrust back into reality from the clutches of his nightmare. His eyes, wide with residual fear, slowly adjusted to the dimly lit room, his labored breaths punctuating the silence of the night.

"Tom," Laura's soothing voice echoed in the engulfing darkness, a balm amidst the tumult of his thoughts. Her gentle hands, tenderly cradling his face, served as an anchoring force, pulling him back from the nightmarish abyss into the comforting reality of her presence. As Laura held Tom in the soothing embrace of her arms, she took a deep breath, filling her lungs with the shared air of their intimacy. The quiet hush of the night enveloped them, the only sound being their rhythmic breathing, syncing in an unplanned symphony. Her heart ached for him; for the pain he had endured, for the memories that haunted him. Her resolve strengthened; she would do whatever it took to ease his suffering. She held him tighter, her fingers tracing comforting patterns on his back, a silent promise reverberating through the room. Her journey, which had once been centered around her own aspirations, her own conquests, was evolving. The woman who had once walked a solitary path of ambition was now threading an unfamiliar territory of shared emotions, shared pain.

Her mind reflected on the changes that had slowly crept into her life. She had always been fiercely independent, her single-minded pursuit of her goals defining her. But in this room, with Tom's vulnerability etched into every line of his face, she realized that life wasn't about standing alone on the pedestal of personal achievements. It was about shared moments, shared hardships, and lending strength to each other when the world seemed too heavy to bear alone.

As the initial tide of her concern receded, she started to see the beauty of this transition. She was evolving, opening up to experiences that went beyond her personal bubble. She was learning to give, not just take. She was learning to put someone else's needs above her own. This journey was her own Operation Eagles Wings, a challenging yet fulfilling voyage that she was determined to see through.

With her heart echoing her newfound resolution, Laura kissed Tom's forehead, a promise sealed with affection. She whispered words of comfort, her voice carrying the weight of her pledge. Her arms became his fortress, her voice his lullaby, and in that moment, she realized that she was ready to fight his demons as fervently as she had been fighting for her personal ambitions.

In the darkness of the night, lit only by the soft moonlight filtering through the window, Laura's journey from selfishness to selflessness continued. It was a transformative path, strewn with challenges and discomfort, yet rewarding in ways she had never imagined. It was the birth of a new Laura, a woman who was not just a conqueror of her ambitions but also a nurturer, a giver, and a partner ready to brave storms not just for her own sake, but for the ones she loved. And as the first light of dawn made its appearance, she knew her journey had just begun.

~

The day was brimming with the brisk chill of an imminent winter, the leaves underfoot an audible testament to the season's turn. Laura, clad in her navy overcoat, walked alongside the river that traced a silver curve through the heart of the city. Her mind buzzed with questions, theories, and a slight twinge of anxiety. For weeks now, she had sensed an enigmatic sadness within Tom, an undertow of melancholy that belied his warm smile and affable demeanor. His nightmares had become more frequent, and she'd noticed the weary sighs that escaped his lips when he thought no one was watching, the subtle shadows that fleetingly danced in his eyes, the tinge of something deeper that lingered in his voice. She'd also become acutely aware of the empty bottles she'd occasionally discover. A stray bourbon bottle buried in the trash; a wine bottle subtly hidden behind his desk. Each was an echo of his solitary struggle, a silent cry for help that Laura had gradually begun to hear. On this cold day, as the river flowed steadfastly alongside, Laura had decided to unravel the mystery. Tom, her lover, her confidante, deserved more than to wage a silent war against his own demons. She needed to reach out, to extend a hand that could pull him back from the precipice. She found him hunched over the desk at his home office, his eyes heavy and his posture slouched. In his hand, he held a faded photograph, his fingers gently tracing the edges. As she moved closer, she noticed it was a picture of a woman with a vibrant smile, her belly swollen with new life, standing beside an older man who wore a striking resemblance to Tom. With an intake of breath, Laura realized who they were. The woman, radiating with maternal joy, was Tom's late wife. The man standing next to her, his eyes twinkling with paternal pride, was Tom's father. The way Tom held the picture, as if it were a fragile piece of his own heart, told Laura all she needed to know. She sat down next to him, her hand tentatively reaching out to touch his. Tom looked up, his eyes revealing a world of pain he had hidden for so long. His voice cracked as he started to speak, his words painting a picture of a cold winter's day when he'd lost the two most precious people in his life. The relentless Seasonal Affective Disorder (SAD) that had since haunted him every winter, an unwelcome guest that brought back the chill of loss and loneliness. Laura listened, her heart aching for the man before her. She realized the battle he'd been fighting, his resort to alcohol as a misguided crutch, his desperate attempts to keep his pain hidden from the world. Yet, here he was, baring his soul, his wounds raw and exposed. In the silent room, as the winter wind whispered outside, a new understanding bloomed between Laura and Tom. An understanding forged in shared pain and nurtured by empathy. Laura knew then that she would stand by Tom, help him navigate his way through the darkness that winter brought. She would be his anchor, reminding him of the spring that follows each winter, the hope that lingers beyond the shadows. And maybe, just maybe, they could find a way to turn his winter of despair into a season of healing.

~

The responsibilities that came with selflessness were heavy, but Laura found herself welcoming the weight. For the first time in her life, she didn't see these responsibilities as burdens but as a testament to the profoundness of her love for Tom. A gentle smile adorned her face as she prepared breakfast, every action, every thought now imbued with a care for another.

During the following weeks, Laura's transformation became more apparent. Her long hours at work, once a reflection of her dedication to her ambitions, now served a dual purpose. She was not only striving for professional breakthroughs but also to provide a world of peace and comfort for Tom. The very essence of her being was changing, redirecting its energy from a self-focused entity to one that embraced another's welfare.

Laura began actively participating in support groups for veterans, trying to understand the depth of the pain Tom had been hiding beneath his stoic exterior. She immersed herself in literature about post-traumatic stress disorder, aiming to provide Tom the best support possible. Her life was gradually turning into a mirror that reflected Tom's needs more than her own, and surprisingly, she found contentment in this shift.

Her conversations with Tom changed too, from discussing her own triumphs and setbacks at work to actively seeking his thoughts and fears. She held him as he opened up about his nightmares, his guilt, and his regrets, providing a safe space for him to voice his emotions. Their relationship began to transform, from being just lovers to confidantes, their bond deepening in the face of adversity.

In her journey from selfishness to selflessness, Laura learned that the essence of love was not just about sharing moments of joy but also about standing together during the trials of life. She learned that true love meant putting someone else's needs above her own, about providing comfort when required, and giving space when necessary.

Through the highs and lows, Laura's transformation was a beacon of hope, not only for Tom but also for herself. Her metamorphosis from a self-centered individual to a compassionate partner was a testament to the power of love. As Laura journeyed on this unfamiliar road, she found a new purpose, a new motivation that pushed her to strive harder and become a better version of herself. For the first time, she experienced what it meant to truly love someone else more than herself, and she wouldn't trade this experience for the world.

~

Whenever they could escape into the verdant expanse of nature, Tom and Laura felt their souls entwined. The idyllic serenity of the outdoors became the cornerstone upon which their love was built. Both possessed a passion for running, a pursuit that brought them closer than the most intricate waltzes or grandest galas ever could.

Tom was a man of quiet strength and fortitude, his character marked by an unwavering sense of duty and honor. He bore his responsibilities with grace, but his truest self was revealed only in the wilds of nature, where he could cast aside the shackles of societal expectation and embrace the freedom of the open trail. Laura was a woman of keen intellect and remarkable resilience who loved the simplicity of the outdoors. Her spirit refused to be confined by convention, and her heart soared with boundless curiosity and fierce independence.

The Marine Corps Marathon would become a cherished chapter in the story of their love. They spent the months leading up to the marathon in a whirlwind of activity, their days filled with work and their evenings with rigorous training regimens and scattered moments of respite beneath the shade of ancient trees. As their bodies grew stronger, so did their bond, each mile strengthening their connection.

The morning of the marathon dawned with an air of electric anticipation. As they stood side by side at the starting line, the thrum of excitement coursing through the crowd around them, Tom and Laura exchanged a look that spoke volumes, a silent promise of support and boundless love. Then the starting gun pierced the stillness, and the sea of runners surged forward, an undulating wave of dreams and ambition. Tom and Laura ran as one, the rhythm of their footfalls a symphony of harmonious exertion, their breaths mingling in the wind.

With every passing mile, the world seemed to fade away, until all that remained was the steady cadence of their strides and the gentle brush of their fingers against one another as they ran. The course of the Marine Corps Marathon winds through Arlington National Cemetery and passes many other iconic landmarks in Washington, DC, including the Pentagon, the National Mall, and the Arlington Memorial Bridge. But it was the Arlington National Cemetery that offered the most meaningful moments of the race for Tom and Laura. They passed many of the cemetery's most notable sites, including the Tomb of the Unknown Soldier and the John F. Kennedy Eternal Flame, and both paid their respects to their fathers as they ran.

The Marine Corps Marathon was not only a physically challenging event but an emotional and inspiring one for Laura and Tom. In the last stretch, with the finish line in sight, a surge of energy coursed through Laura, a burst of determination that propelled her forward. With the grace of a woodland creature, she overtook her competitors. The roar of the crowd was only a distant murmur as she crossed the finish line, arms raised in a triumphant salute.

Tom, moments behind her, felt his heart swell with pride and joy as he watched his beloved claim her victory. When he, too, crossed the finish line, they stood together in the center of a deafening celebration, their hearts beating in unison.

The Marine Corps Marathon would forever represent their love for Tom and Laura—a love that transcended the trappings of polite society and flourished in the great outdoors.

PROTAGONISTS AT PLAY; KEY WEST!

Far to the south, in Key West, a vivacious and spirited young woman named Georgie Roberts made her mark upon the idyllic island town. Georgie was the younger sister of the resolute Laura, a whirlwind of energy with a zest for life as infectious as it was endearing. In their youth, the Roberts sisters had formed an unbreakable bond that transcended their apparent differences. Where Laura was a paragon of stoic resolve and achievement, Georgie was a beacon of effervescence, illuminating the lives of those around her with her irrepressible spirit. Her playful name, bestowed in memory of their fallen father, perfectly encapsulated her ebullient nature.

Georgie had long idolized her elder sister, cherishing their shared confidences. Though their passions diverged in literature and academia, the sisters were united in their love for sports and their commitment to service. While Laura pursued a life of public service in the NSA, Georgie served her fellow citizens as an AmeriCorps VISTA (Volunteer in Service To America). With a heart full of compassion and a burning desire to make a difference, she embarked on a journey that eventually took her to the vibrant shores of Key West, Florida.

There she devoted her time and energy to combating the scourge of food insecurity, which plagues even the wealthiest corners of America.

In the charming streets of Key West, Georgie found her true calling, immersing herself in the vibrant local culture while striving to uplift the lives of the less fortunate. The island's carefree spirit and lively atmosphere proved the perfect backdrop for her vivacious personality, endearing her to the community and enabling her to forge lasting friendships.

The arrival of her beloved sister, Laura, and the dashing Tom Michaels sent ripples of excitement through Georgie's world. Delighting in the opportunity to play the mischievous younger sibling, Georgie would teasingly refer to Tom as "Ryan," a playful nod to his striking resemblance to the famed actor. Much to Laura's chagrin, this moniker would attract the attention of lovestruck admirers, who would follow the trio through the sun-drenched streets of Key West.

In the midst of the laughter and the teasing, the bond between the Reynolds sisters only grew stronger. As they navigated the challenges and triumphs of life, their love for one another served as a constant reminder of the strength to be found in the unbreakable bonds of sisterhood.

~

Beneath Key West's swaying palms lies a hidden history of military might and strategic importance. The tropical paradise, often associated with the melodies of Jimmy Buffett's Margaritaville, holds secrets that span generations, their echoes resonating in the manhole covers on world famous Duval Street, which still bear the inscription "Property of the US Navy."

The tale of Key West's military heritage begins before the Cold War, when the island was transformed into a formidable submarine base. The United States, determined to secure its position in the Western hemisphere, recognized the strategic significance of this sunny outpost, a mere ninety miles from the shores of Cuba, Russia's foremost power projection in the Americas.

Today the military presence in Key West endures, its footprint extending across the island. The National Security Agency operates a clandestine installation there, with myriad antennas bristling in the shadows, attuned to the intrigues of Central and South America. The Joint Interagency Task Force South (JIATFS) also maintains a stronghold on the island's southernmost tip, its mission to uphold the security of the United States in this volatile region.

A few miles from Key West, on the island of Boca Chica, lies Naval Air Station Key West, one of the nation's pre-eminent naval aviation training grounds. Here the men and women of the United States Navy hone their skills, adding to the enduring importance of this tropical haven in the grand tapestry of American military strategy.

The juxtaposition of Key West's dual identity as a haven for pleasure-seekers and a bastion of national defense is both enchanting and confounding. Visitors to this idyllic paradise, lulled by the rhythm of steel drums and the taste of salt on their lips, remain blissfully unaware of the intricate dance of power and intrigue unfolding just beyond their view. In labyrinthine corridors beneath the island, the men and women of the NSA and JIATFS work to safeguard the nation's interests, their dedication a stark contrast to the carefree revelry above. The submariners of the Cold War, their presence long faded from the island's collective memory, continue to cast shadows over the azure waters, their sacrifices an indelible part of Key West's history.

When the sun sets, the secrets of this enigmatic island slumber beneath the waves, their whispers echoing in the gentle trade winds that caress the palms. But even in this land of eternal summer, where the scents of hibiscus and rum fill the air, the shadows of the past linger, haunting reminders of the bond between the twin worlds of pleasure and power.

~

The proximity of Andrews Air Force Base in Washington, DC, makes

Key West an indispensable waypoint for the frequent comings and goings of a fleet of government jets used by the National Security Agency and the Central Intelligence Agency.

As high-ranking members of these organizations, Laura and Tom were granted the privilege of hitching a ride on these aircraft whenever empty seats were available, and they had visited Georgie several times since she was assigned to serve in Key West. One particular journey held great significance for the Roberts sisters, as it coincided with the world premiere of a film adaptation of their favorite novel.

The beloved book *Are You There God? It's Me, Margaret* by Judy Blume captured the hearts of Laura and Georgie during their youth, leading to countless treasured moments as they pored over its pages. Fifty years after the book's publication, the story had been brought to life on the silver screen. Laura and Georgie were elated to learn that the premiere would take place in a small theater in Key West, a venue that the celebrated author and her husband, George Cooper, had helped to build in the town that they both called home.

As they got ready for the premiere, Laura turned to Georgie. "Promise me you won't tease Tom tonight. It's Judy's night."

Georgie grinned at her. "I promise," she said, an unusual seriousness in her voice. "What was up with Laura" thought Georgie, "since when did she care about someone else?"

"I can't believe we're actually here," Georgie said, when they arrived at the Tropic Cinema. "Our favorite book on the big screen, right here in Judy Blume's hometown."

"And in the theater, she helped build," Laura added, her voice tinged with awe.

Despite their relatively low-key arrival, they still caused a stir as they entered the theater. The room was alive with excitement - celebrities, fans, and everyone gathered to celebrate the transformation of a beloved book into film.

As the lights went down and the movie started, Laura and Georgie found themselves transported back in time. They laughed and cried along with the story, and as the credits rolled, they knew this was a night they would never forget.

This magical weekend with her irreverent sister was exactly the break Laura needed, and she returned to Washington reinvigorated and ready to tackle whatever was to come her way.

SHADOWS UNVEILED

In the heart of Washington, D.C., Laura Roberts, and Tom Michaels found themselves unwittingly drawn into the heart of a brewing storm. As they navigated the perilous waters of international intrigue, they began to uncover the faintest threads of a conspiracy that stretched from the highest echelons of power to the darkest corners of the globe. The puzzle before them was an intricate tapestry of deceit and subterfuge that seemed to defy comprehension.

But as they delved deeper into their investigation, they began to connect the dots, slowly unraveling the true scale of the threat that loomed over the world. They suspected that the recent surge in Russia and China's interest in cryptocurrencies was no mere coincidence but rather a carefully orchestrated plan designed to undermine the global economy and challenge the supremacy of the United States.

At the epicenter of this maelstrom was Vladimir Petrov, the enigmatic figure who had spent years carefully crafting his master plan. With cold, calculating precision, he had manipulated events to his advantage, engineering crises and stoking the fires of discord. As the storm gathered, he watched from the shadows, waiting for the perfect moment to strike and bring his vision of a new world order to fruition.

As Laura and Tom raced against time to unravel the truth and expose Petrov's plan, they found themselves confronting their own demons and fears. The stakes had never been higher, and the cost of failure loomed large in their minds. As the clock ticked down and the gathering storm threatened to engulf the world, they knew that they had to find a way to stop the impending chaos.

In the face of insurmountable odds, they clung to each other, drawing strength from their shared determination and the unbreakable bond that had formed between them. As the storm raged around them, they stood united, ready to face whatever came next.

~

In the hushed whispers of the world's cyber corridors, a digital ghost listened, recording every syllable, each pause, and the fluctuating inflections of two voices engaged in a high-stakes dialogue. The conversation, flagged by sophisticated AI algorithms within the NSA's complex surveillance apparatus, was happening between Vladimir Petrov, the Russian president, and General Secretary Wei of China.

Petrov's voice, heavy with the implications of his words, echoed through the encrypted channels. "Wei, the tide is turning. The rise of cryptocurrencies is not a passing trend, but a technological revolution poised to challenge the dollar's global dominance. We're already developing a centralized cryptocurrency, the first true contender to the Western stronghold on financial power."

The skepticism in Wei's response was palpable, even though the sterile, filtered audio. "Petrov, the problems that the West claims plague our traditional currencies — the lack of transparency, volatile economies, governmental control — these will not simply disappear in a digital format. How can a digital Ruble or Yuan hope to inspire global trust?"

There was a certain fervor in Petrov's retort, "That's where Bitcoin comes into play, Wei. It's independent of any government control, hence its rapid rise in popularity. We've started accumulating it, and I suggest you do the same."

Wei, ever the pragmatist, countered with his own reservations, "Even if Bitcoin replaces the dollar, how does that benefit us? We cannot control it unless we amass over half of its total supply. A feat, as my advisors tell me, that is near impossible."

Petrov, however, wasn't deterred by the challenge, "True, control may be an uphill battle, but consider this - Bitcoin's value is skyrocketing. Increased demand, especially if it originates from the likes of us, would only propel its value higher. We stand to gain immensely."

Wei was not convinced, but he recognized the strategic implications of Petrov's argument. Even if his skepticism about Bitcoin remained, he could not afford to be left behind. "I'll have my people explore this, Vladimir. We will begin to amass Bitcoin quietly."

The conversation ended with a sense of mutual understanding, yet the air of skepticism lingered. Wei remained wary of Bitcoin, but he acknowledged the potential of a multinational digital currency that they could control. "Keep pushing forward with your centralized cryptocurrency, Vladimir. We will explore a joint initiative, a currency that is truly ours, combining the strength of our nations."

Thus, the veiled world of international politics saw a new front opening - a battleground made not of geographical boundaries but binary codes and blockchains. As the echoes of their conversation faded into the ether, the impact of their decisions set into motion ripples that would be felt across the world's financial landscapes.

~

Amidst the timeworn streets of Riga, Sergey carefully wove together the fabric of a new identity. Utilizing the infamous Silk Road marketplace as a tool, and bolstering it with his expertise in cryptocurrency, he successfully breathed life into a brand-new persona. Sergey Kuznetsov, the elusive Satoshi Nakamoto, had been laid to rest; and in his stead, Pavel Ivanov emerged, bearing the name of a beloved childhood friend as a shield.

Transplanting his life to Slovenia, Sergey – now Pavel – began establishing himself as a respected figure in Bitstorm, one of Europe's pioneering crypto exchanges. His new colleagues admired his intelligence, oblivious to the fact that their co-worker was the very architect of Bitcoin. Meanwhile, he sustained his original identity, Sergey Kuznetsov, in the realm of published cryptocurrency articles, successfully diverting the watchful eyes of the FSB. Eventually, the world ceased its hunt for Satoshi Nakamoto, leaving Sergey's original Bitcoin treasure untouched, a silent testament to his legacy.

~

The imposing edifice of the IK-6 prison stood as a grim specter against the stark skyline. Its unyielding grey walls bore silent witness to countless stories of loss, hardship, and the unrelenting human spirit. Olga Ivanov found herself on a cold winter morning within this citadel of despair.

Her purpose was a regular visit to her incarcerated mother, Yuliya, but today, the universe had other plans. As she stepped out of the black sedan, the sharp Russian chill cut through her like a knife, yet Olga remained impervious to the biting cold. She wore her uniform with an air of stoic responsibility that belied the heartache within. Every visit to her mother was a torturous reminder of her family's past and the cruel reality of her present. Still, Olga bore it with the resilience of a seasoned operative. She was, after all, a diligent servant of the state, her loyalty hardened by the circumstances of her life.

As Olga navigated the labyrinthine corridors of the prison, she was struck by a familiar voice. She turned the corner only to witness a scene that stopped her in her tracks. Nikita and Anna Kuznetsov, Sergey's parents, were being led away by stern-faced guards. The sight of her childhood companions' parents in this fortress of despair shook

Olga to her core. She called out in surprise, "Nikita, Anna! What on earth are you doing here?"

The Kuznetsovs turned in surprise. Their faces, etched with worry, lit up at the sight of Olga. But their joy was short-lived, as Olga's FSB superiors quickly closed in. "What's going on, Ivanov?" one of them demanded.

Olga turned to them, her mind racing as she grappled with the implications of this unexpected encounter. She explained her connection to the Kuznetsovs, a story of innocent childhood friendships and shared memories. But as the truth unfolded, the implications became clear to her superiors.

Olga's relationship with the Kuznetsovs was a potential asset. A light of realization sparked in their eyes. Their task was clear: they had to locate Sergey, the elusive creator of Bitcoin, and Olga was their unexpected key. They turned to Olga, their directives clear and uncompromising. "Upon your return to your post in Cuba, your primary objective is to locate Sergey Kuznetsov. The national security of Russia depends on it."

Her heart pounding in her chest, Olga nodded. She was a soldier of the state, and her duty was non-negotiable. But as she looked back at the Kuznetsovs, her heart ached. Their hopeful eyes mirrored her own desperate longing for a return to simpler times, a nostalgia for an era lost to the cruel machinations of fate. With a heaviness in her heart, she bid them a solemn farewell.

As Olga prepared for her return to Cuba, she was gripped by a swirl of emotions. Her past was catching up with her present in the most unexpected ways. The task at hand was daunting, and the consequences of failure were unimaginable. But she was determined to play her part, to navigate the treacherous waters of her mission with the courage and fortitude that defined her. For in her heart, Olga Ivanov was more than an agent of the state; she was a woman caught between her loyalty to Mother Russia, pursuit of the greater good, and the ties that bound her to the past. The path ahead was fraught with uncertainty, but she was prepared to brave the storm, armed with the memory of a friendship that had once defined her world.

~

In the distant land of Cuba, far removed from the bustling hub of the FSB, Olga Ivanov walked a path strewn with uncertainty. Despite the vibrant surroundings that camouflaged her quiet station, the very air vibrated with secrets. Olga's heart raced; her curiosity ignited like a fuse. The connection to this notorious fugitive threatened her standing in the FSB like an insidious presence, urging her to unravel the enigma. As directed, she embarked on a treacherous journey, diving headlong into the murky depths of a vast digital ocean that concealed secrets, secrets that could cost her everything. Each night, as shadows deepened, she found herself sucked into the digital vortex, the glow of her screen illuminating the darkness around her.

In the solitude of her office, Olga delved into Sergey's digital labyrinth. She discovered scholarly writings under the name Sergey Kuznetsov, indications that he was still active in cryptography. It was like following a faint trail in the dark, but at least it was something. A glimmer of hope amidst the vast sea of information.

"What are you up to, Sergey?" she muttered, her fingers flying over the keyboard.

Memories came rushing back like an unstoppable wave. Sergey had idolized her late brother Pavel during their childhood. She remembered Sergey's face when Pavel had been killed in Afghanistan, how he had screamed, "Better me than Pavel!" Sergey worshipped Pavel and always wanted to be him. Could it be that simple? Simple to Olga, but not necessarily to those who didn't know of their childhood. Could Sergey have taken Pavel's identity as a cover? He certainly knew all the details of Pavel's brief existence, and Russia did far better tracking births than deaths. Olga murmured aloud, "Are you hiding in plain sight, Sergey"?

Another digital breadcrumb fell when she cross-referenced the name Pavel Ivanov against known figures in the burgeoning world of cryptocurrencies, desperately seeking signs that would confirm her theory. She discovered an executive at Bitstorm with the same name as her late brother. A common name in Russia but not so common in Slovenia. And why was there no digital history prior to 2010 for this Pavel Ivanov? It was worth a phone call, anyway. Armed with her findings, Olga's fingers hovered over the numbers on a burner phone. Would this executive at Bitstorm be the person she was looking for or just a Slovenian man who shared a name with her late brother? The ringtone droned on, matching the rhythm of her pulsing heart. A voice answered, jolting her from her thoughts. "Pavel Ivanov, speaking."

The voice was so familiar, yet so alien. Olga swallowed the lump in her throat. "Hello, Pavel," she began. "Or should I say, Sergey? "The ensuing silence was deafening. Finally, Pavel - or Sergey - spoke. "Who is this?"

"It's me, Olga," she said softly.

~

The revelation that followed seemed to echo over the line, bridging the miles between Cuba and Slovenia. As Sergey heard Olga's voice and she outlined her role in the FSB, he was struck silent. Olga let him absorb the information, her heart heavy with a sorrowful secret yet to be shared.

The virtual cloak-and-dagger dance morphed into something much more personal during the following conversation. It was as though they were children again, sharing secrets and dreams. But amidst the nostalgia, a dreadful truth revealed itself - Sergey was unaware of his parents' fate, of their incarceration due to Petrov and the FSB.

Following the tragic news, his silence was palpable even through the static. After a while, he muttered, "I need some time, Olga." "Of course, Sergey," Olga conceded softly. "I'll be here when you're ready."

As the call ended, a silence fell over the room, punctuated only by the soft ticking of the clock. Their conversation, stretching over hours, had bridged a decade of separation, reigniting an old friendship while unraveling a labyrinth of secrets. The repercussions of their clandestine communication would take time for both of them to process.

~

Over the ensuing days, Olga grappled with the implications of her actions. By reaching out to Sergey on a burner phone, she had knowingly committed an act that could be construed as treason. The bitter taste of betrayal mingled with her resolution. She knew the consequences of her actions could be dire, but she also knew she could not abandon Sergey - the boy from her past who had emerged as the mysterious Satoshi Nakamoto.

Sergey, on the other hand, was left grappling with a different beast. The revelation of his parents' detention in the notorious IK-6 bore a hole into his soul. How could he have left them behind, allowing them to bear the brunt of his actions? Their loss, combined with the harsh reality of his existence, threatened to overwhelm him.

~

As the days melted into weeks, the two were drawn back to each other. The promise of their next conversation was the one thread pulling them through their respective turmoil. Though still reeling from the blow of his parents' imprisonment, Sergey steeled himself for the impending challenges. Despite the dangerous path she had tread, Olga was prepared to support Sergey. She had chosen to gamble her career - and possibly her freedom - for a cause she believed in.

As they reconnected, the echoes of their childhood bond reverberated through their shared resolve. Their bond, now reinforced by hardship and shared history, held stronger than ever. Their united front poised itself against the looming threats of the FSB and the cold, calculating machinations of Petrov's Russia. They could still love Mother Russia but not its current leadership.

~

When Olga and Sergey reconnected, the gravity of their shared predicament held them in its grip. Their conversation, a tapestry of truth, despair, and resolution, spanned continents, threading through the lines of secret communications. The stakes were enormous.

Sergey was a haunted man, his soul tortured by the thought of his parents suffering in the notorious IK 6 prison. His heart ached at the notion of their lost years in such a hellish place. Driven by guilt and responsibility, he reached a somber decision: he would negotiate with the FSB for their freedom. The boy who had once eluded the might of the Russian state was now ready to walk into the lion's den.

On the other hand, Olga recognized the dangers lurking within their plan. Admitting her contact with Sergey could lead to her own arrest, and negotiating with the FSB was akin to bargaining with a viper. Their promises were as mercurial as the wind, their words as trustworthy as a mirage. Yet, in the face of Sergey's determination and despair, she aligned with his dangerous proposition. Despite her doubts, she agreed to act as the linchpin in their precarious plan.

~

Their strategy was simple but treacherous. Olga would journey from the Caribbean paradise of Cuba back to the frozen heart of Russia. There, she would present herself to her superiors in the FSB, delivering the news that she had discovered Sergey's hideout. The lure would be irresistible: Satoshi Nakamoto, the genius behind Bitcoin, willing to return to Russia in exchange for his parents' freedom.

They anticipated that the FSB would demand Sergey's surrender before they considered releasing his parents. Olga pushed back, arguing for a simultaneous exchange. But the FSB's response was as icy as the Siberian winter - the agency demanded she surrender all her information first, their words laced with threats and deceit.

~

The FSB planned Sergey's surrender at the Russian embassy in Ljubljana, Slovenia's capital. They expected Olga to accompany them on their flight to Slovenia, her presence acting as insurance for Sergey's cooperation. They were clear in their instructions: if Sergey didn't appear, Olga would share the Kuznetsov's fate, a chilling warning that left her breathless.

Despite the foreboding nature of their plan, Olga and Sergey were resolved. They had a timeline - the following Monday marked the day of Sergey's surrender. The day the elusive Satoshi Nakamoto would willingly walk into the clutches of the Russian state.

~

Their conversation ended on a chilling note, their minds burdened with the magnitude of their impending gambit. They had played their cards, setting in motion a chain of events that would change their lives forever. Sergey felt a chilling wave of resignation wash over him while Olga braced herself for the storm she was about to face.

Their shared ordeal had bound them together in a web of secrets and risks. They stood on the precipice of a life-altering leap, holding on to a threadbare hope that their plan would secure the Kuznetsovs' freedom. As they braced themselves for the trials ahead, the bond between them remained a beacon of strength, an anchor in the turbulent sea of their shared adversity.

~

The following day found Sergey and Olga in an office with Petrov, a silent fortress inside the bustling FSB headquarters. The room, draped in solemnity, seemed to echo with the machinations of power and deceit. Standing tall and imposing, Petrov summoned Oleg Melnik, his aura of command filling the air.

Melnik, a veteran in the cryptology world, still harbored doubts about Sergey's claim of being Satoshi Nakamoto. His skepticism hung like a cloud in the room until Petrov laid out his demand. Sergey was to draft an email from the same email account that Satoshi had used for correspondence with Melnik in the days of Bitcoin's inception, a digital ghost that had remained dormant since 2011.

An aide materialized with a laptop, which Sergey handled deftly, his fingers flying over the keys. With a few swift keystrokes, he sent a simple email to Melnik. It read, "You are wearing a blue shirt today." The message echoed in the silence of the room, a digital signature validating Sergey's identity. The room's atmosphere shifted, a silent acknowledgment of Satoshi Nakamoto's presence. Melnik retreated, leaving Sergey and Olga with Petrov.

~

Petrov's demeanor softened, his words woven with threads of patriotism and urgency. "For the sake of the motherland, you must cooperate with us, Sergey," he implored. His gaze landed on Olga, his words continuing in a softer undertone. "Your friend here," he motioned to Olga, "has sworn an oath to her country. Your country now needs both of you more than ever."

Sergey was unyielding, his resolve as firm as a steel blade. His inquiry, voiced for the second time, echoed in the room, "Have my parents been released? I wish to speak with them." Petrov was smooth as silk, his response evasive and promising. "All in good time, all in good time," he soothed, "You will find that I take good care of my friends." His gaze rested on Sergey, his next words carrying a clear implication, "You are my friend, aren't you, Sergey?"

Petrov's attempt at a smile twisted into a snarl, a disconcerting sight that belied the seemingly cordial words. Sergey and Olga found themselves deep in the labyrinth of FSB politics, their fates entwined with that of the elusive Satoshi Nakamoto and the iron will of the Russian state.

SHIFTING ROLES

In the twisting labyrinth of power, ambition often subdues even the closest of relationships, as was tragically realized by Sergey Kuznetsov, the elusive genius known to the world as Satoshi Nakamoto. By 2011, the mysterious Satoshi had accumulated a king's ransom – over a million bitcoins – a treasure trove as elusive and mythical as the man himself. Yet, Bitcoin, his brainchild, was no longer his own. The whispers of treachery echoed through the halls of power as Vladimir Petrov set forth to claim the burgeoning realm of cryptocurrency.

In the ornate grandeur of the Kremlin, Petrov called Sergey to his office, a cloistered sanctum shrouded in veils of power and ambition. As the ornate doors closed behind Sergey, he found himself encased within the predatory silence that only power could afford.

Petrov, ensconced behind an imposing desk, leaned back, his gaze as calculating as the icy winters of Russia. "Satoshi Nakamoto needs to disappear for good," he began, his voice laden with the finality of an executioner's axe. "No more emails, no more mining, no more...inconveniences."

As the words sunk into the marrow of Sergey's reality, Petrov continued. "Now that Russia has the mining capacity, I don't want you as a competitor." His voice echoed ominously around the room, the implications chilling. He commanded Sergey to log into his Satoshi email again and step away from the computer. In the blink of an eye, the digital lifeline of Satoshi Nakamoto was severed, and the password changed to a cipher that only Petrov would know.

Sergey's protest was swift and desperate. "I need to keep up with the developments of Bitcoin for the security of our blockchain!" he pleaded, his voice reverberating with the urgency of the situation.

Petrov, however, was prepared. "A team of cryptographers," he declared, "will feed you the information you need. Your world will evolve; you just won't be able to touch Bitcoin." He paused, letting the weight of his words settle. "Sergey Kuznetsov will know everything, but Satoshi Nakamoto can never communicate again."

Despite Sergey's attempt at a rebuttal, Petrov's resolute countenance left no room for negotiation. He also demanded Sergey work with Oleg Melnik to create a digital cryptocurrency Petrov could control, and to do so quickly. His warning was as harsh as it was final, threatening dire consequences if Sergey dared to infract the agreement. An agreement was signed with the ominous shadow of the Satoshi horde hanging over it.

Petrov's strategy was as transparent as it was cunning. Sergey, the genius creator of Bitcoin, was to be contained. Yet, he was to be kept informed, a finely honed weapon that Petrov could wield when necessary. Thus, the accumulation phase of the Satoshi hoard ended, and the coins lay untouched, a testament to Petrov's tactical victory and Sergey's reluctant capitulation.

Through the desolation of solitary confinement, Sergey clung to the lifeline Petrov had thrown him. The latest developments in the crypto world were his beacon of hope, the catalyst that kept his genius mind alive amidst the cold emptiness of his surroundings.

Meanwhile, in the clandestine depths of Russia's power structures, an ambitious and covert operation was underway. Utilizing the prodigious force of nuclear energy, Petrov, through the Russian Federal

Security Service (FSB), had launched a Bitcoin mining operation of unparalleled scale. Derelict nuclear facilities were reborn in a clandestine endeavor that held the potential to reshape the global economic landscape.

And so, the tectonic plates of geopolitical power began to shift. Amid a veil of secrecy and subterfuge, Russia's growing cryptocurrency strength threatened to undermine the US dollar's supremacy. The world stood on the precipice of an impending shift; a paradigm change triggered by the silent war brewing within the heart of the blockchain.

~

The Kremlin, under the guidance of Vladimir Petrov, was accumulating cryptocurrency as a means to undermine the hegemony of the US Dollar and further its own strategic objectives. To further this ambitious plan, Petrov instructed the FSB to establish a covert Bitcoin mining operation fueled by the immense power of nuclear energy. Under the strictest veil of secrecy, the FSB embarked on the task of constructing a new, highly efficient Bitcoin mining network. They reopened Soviet-era nuclear facilities, exploiting their cutting-edge reactors to energize the resource-intensive mining process.   With an inexpensive and unlimited supply of energy, they now had a leg up on every other Bitcoin miner.

To ensure the highest level of confidentiality, the FSB assembled an elite team of scientists, engineers, and cryptographers handpicked for their loyalty and expertise. This operation remained meticulously concealed from the watchful gaze of international regulators and intelligence agencies. To hide their activities, the FSB crafted a narrative of nuclear energy as a cornerstone of sustainable development and environmental stewardship. This subterfuge enabled them to account for Russia's heightened production of nuclear power without arousing suspicions about the true objective of their endeavors. While publicly championing clean energy and the reduction of greenhouse-gas emissions, the Russian government surreptitiously channeled vast quantities of nuclear power into their illicit Bitcoin mining enterprise.

The near-boundless supply of nuclear energy at their command gave the Russians a tremendous edge over other Bitcoin miners and allowed the FSB to mine Bitcoin on an unprecedented scale. As their mining capacity swelled, so did their influence over the Bitcoin market, granting them the ability to manipulate its value and weaken the US Dollar's standing as the global reserve currency.

Yet with the burgeoning scope of the FSB's mining operation came an escalating risk of exposure. Acutely aware that any lapse in security could lay bare their entire plan, the FSB employed extreme measures to preserve the secrecy of their enterprise. They wove a thick web of misinformation and deception and even resorted, at times, to the elimination of potential threats.

So, as the international community grew increasingly skeptical of the true intentions behind Russia's nuclear energy program, the stage was set for a dramatic tableau of espionage, betrayal, and the pursuit of the truth concealed within the Satoshi Conspiracy.

~

The National Security Agency, ever watchful in its mission to protect the interests of the United States and its allies, nurtured growing suspicions regarding the enigmatic motives of Russia's new nuclear-energy program.

Whispers of an insidious connection between Russia's nuclear facilities and clandestine Bitcoin mining were echoing through the intelligence community. Determined to pierce the veil of secrecy that shrouded these nefarious machinations, the NSA had enlisted Laura Roberts and Tom Michaels to assemble an elite team and investigate. By now, their team had grown into a formidable synthesis of intellect and experience, each member handpicked for mastery in cryptography, finance, and international relations. Bound by a shared purpose, they forged ahead in their investigation into Russia's nuclear operations, excavating layers of obfuscation and disinformation in their quest for the truth.

As weeks gave way to months, the team uncovered a chilling trail of collusion and corruption. It became evident that Russia's nuclear facilities were not merely catering to the power demands of an energy-hungry nation but were fueling a covert empire of Bitcoin mining operations. This revelation sent shockwaves through the intelligence community, for the implications of such a scheme were both immense and terrifying.

~

In her office, nestled within the labyrinthine complex of the National Security Agency, Laura Roberts perched behind her desk, hands folded neatly as she regarded the man before her. Tom Michaels was a vision of discipline, his gaze sharp, carrying questions only Laura could answer.

"Tell me," Tom began, "why would Russia want to accumulate such large quantities of Bitcoin?" His tone carried curiosity more than apprehension.

Laura leaned back in her chair, observing him with an attentive eye. She always admired how Tom challenged ideas, his mind forever probing for answers beneath the surface. She crossed her legs, a soft smile tugging at her lips. "Well, Tom, consider the potential strategic advantage. With a large stake in Bitcoin, Russia has access to a store of value outside of traditional, US-dominated financial systems. By heavily investing in Bitcoin, they also influence the currency's overall value."

Tom's brow furrowed, and he shifted in his chair. "But isn't the decentralized nature of Bitcoin completely against their centralized system?" he asked, pointing out the stark contradiction.

Laura chuckled softly, nodding in agreement. "It's an excellent observation but think about it this way. By controlling a significant portion of Bitcoin, they paradoxically gain a sort of centralizing influence within a decentralized system. A clever strategy, wouldn't you agree?"

He mulled over her words, his eyes narrowing slightly. Then, as though a final piece of the puzzle slid into place, he raised his gaze to meet hers. "Are they working on some other cryptocurrency or just betting on Bitcoin? And if they succeed in making Bitcoin the new global reserve currency, what does that mean for our hegemony... for our security?"

The question hung in the air, filling the room with a potent mix of anticipation and trepidation. Laura sighed, her smile fading as she met his intense gaze. "It could fundamentally shift the global financial landscape, Tom," she answered, her tone sober. "If Bitcoin or any other digital currency becomes the global reserve currency, it erodes the power of the US dollar. We would lose our influence over global monetary policy and financial stability. It would be a new world order."

They sat in silence for a moment, allowing the weight of her words to settle. The implications were massive. Tom looked at her, his eyes reflecting a new understanding but also more questions. Laura watched him, ready to answer, ready to delve deeper. This was just the beginning. The future, as uncertain as it was, promised to be an intense, captivating journey, and they were right at the heart of it.

Laura and her team redoubled their efforts, determined to expose the full extent of Russia's entanglement in the murky world of cryptocurrency. As they unraveled the complex web of deception, the stakes soared ever higher, and the possibility of retribution loomed in their thoughts. Yet, undeterred, they forged onward, driven by the knowledge that their endeavors could potentially avert a global catastrophe.

BITCOIN'S ROLE

The audience of currency nestled snugly in Tom's leather wallet had their own tales to tell; these were stories inked in green and weaved in linen, redolent with the aroma of a hundred hands. They watched the world unfold from their humble abode; their faces etched with silent wisdom.

The $1 bill, the youngest and most nimble of the family, still bore the fresh scent of the printing press. It was always on the move, frequently trading hands, often a bit crumpled and worn around the edges, but never lacking in spirit. It reveled in its role in the everyday hustle and bustle, from the clinking of quarters in a vending machine to the gratifying snap as it was handed to a barista. Now, it was pensive, it's future uncertain, with the specter of de-dollarization looming large.

Up next was the $20 bill, older, more experienced, the backbone of many a cash drawer and ATM. It remembered the grip of countless hands, the wonder in the eyes of tourists, and the relief of the cash-strapped student. It had borne witness to acts of charity and clandestine exchanges, from the shadowy alleyways of Brooklyn to the sunny beaches of Miami. It, too, feared the inexorable march of digital currencies, aware that its grand dance might soon be a tale told to the children of the future.

Then, there were the $50 and $100 bills, the elite of the currency clan. These notes were rarefied guests, gracing only the most special of occasions. They resided in sleek money clips and plush bank vaults, relished in the reverence they were given, and savored the looks of surprise when they appeared. Yet, they too, felt the shifting winds of change. They pondered over the question - would the digits on a screen inspire the same awe, the same respect?

As the currency ensemble reflected on the world that was slowly fading away, they mourned the relationships that they would lose. They thought of their colorful comrades, from the hustling drug dealer whose livelihood they'd often greased to the charming Turkish taxi driver whose day they'd frequently brightened. Would their friends miss the tangible affirmation of their value, the cold hard cash that marked the end of a deal or a day's work? Would they yearn for the familiar crinkle, the assuring weight, the connection to an era where value was more than just numbers on a screen?

Even as the green-tinted notes contemplated the inexorable march of digital currencies, they remembered the humble, unheralded role they'd played in the lives of the world's poorest and most vulnerable. Amid the worn-out fabric of well-used wallets, in makeshift huts, within the rusting iron boxes of old, the currency brothers and sisters had been a beacon of hope.

From the labyrinthine streets of Lagos to the bustling markets of Buenos Aires, the U.S. dollars had served as a bulwark against the tide of inflation. They had witnessed the local currencies battered by economic winds, wilting under the relentless sun of hyperinflation. The people turned to them, the stable, reliable dollars, as a refuge.

Whether folded carefully and tucked into the folds of a threadbare saree by a weary Indian street vendor or stored under a fraying straw mattress by an old Venezuelan farmer, the dollars were trusted allies. They provided a measure of security and solace in a world where the value of a day's work could evaporate overnight.

As these pieces of green paper observed the financial struggles of their hosts, they wondered - could a digital currency offer the same safety net? Could a new "world's currency" arise that inspired the same trust? They knew the joy of a hidden stash of American cash, that secret lifeline that so many relied on. The comfort it provided was tangible and physical—a reassuringly real promise in a world where so much else was uncertain.

And so, they pondered while nestled in Tom's wallet. Could cold, impersonal lines of code on a screen ever replace the solace of a paper bill tucked away for a rainy day? Could the harsh light of a digital screen ever match the soft, comforting rustle of a trusted old note?

As the world raced ahead into the digital era, they saw their own obsolescence on the horizon. Yet, they took pride in the role they had played - guardians of the unbanked, protectors of the poor, symbols of hope in a turbulent world.

They had been the world's currency, an honor bestowed upon them not just by global economic tides but by the faith and trust of millions. Perhaps it was not their destiny to hold that title forever. But in the rich tapestry of human experience they had been woven into, their imprint would remain indelible and cherished long after the last note had faded from the world's wallets.

~

In the tumultuous years of Bitcoin's inception, a new world emerged that was reminiscent of the Wild West, where outlaws and pioneers sought their fortunes amid chaos and uncertainty. The untamed realm of digital currency teemed with colorful characters, each determined to leave their mark on the landscape of this expanding frontier.

Charlie Shrem was a brash, charismatic entrepreneur who rode into the Bitcoin frontier atop his digital steed. With the audacity of youth, he founded BitInstant, one of the first Bitcoin exchanges, attracting the attention of investors and regulators alike. His rags-to-riches story captured the imagination of countless others, offering a glimpse of the immense wealth that lay hidden in the digital ether.

Not far behind him, the puzzling figure of Ross Ulbricht emerged from the shadows. A gifted programmer and fervent believer in the power of Bitcoin to change the world, Ulbricht founded the Silk Road, an online marketplace infamous for its illicit trade in drugs, firearms, and other contraband. Ross, known as "Dread Pirate Roberts," skillfully navigated the dark web, earning a reputation as a cunning and ruthless operator.

Meanwhile, far across the digital frontier, Alexander Vinnik, a Russian national with an inscrutable air, established the notorious BTC-e exchange. This outpost provided a haven for money-laundering, cyber-crime, and the trade of stolen Bitcoin, drawing the ire of law-enforcement agencies around the world. Vinnik's activities in the seedy underbelly of the Bitcoin world made him a wanted man, hunted by those who sought to bring order to the wild frontier.

As both the value and the security of Bitcoin increased dramatically, it attracted not only the criminal element but a new breed of pioneers: legitimate investors, entrepreneurs, and visionaries. The wild frontier of Bitcoin soon transformed into a land of immense opportunity, where fortunes could be made and lost in the blink of an eye. This volatile landscape became a battleground between those who believed in the revolutionary potential of digital currency and those who sought to exploit it for their own nefarious purposes.

Innumerable high-stakes games, daring heists, cunning subterfuges, and thrilling showdowns played out against the backdrop of the digital frontier. The tales of Charlie Shrem, Ross Ulbricht, and Alexander Vinnik are but a few of the many recorded in Bitcoin's history. And as the story of this digital Wild West unfolded, the world watched with bated breath, eager to discover what new adventures and challenges would meet those who staked their claim in the Bitcoin frontier.

~

Laura Roberts and her intrepid team of cyber-sleuths were waging a fierce war against the criminal underbelly of the internet. Their mission: to dismantle the rogue sites that sold illicit goods, laundered money, and trafficked in stolen Bitcoin. Among their most formidable foes were the Silk Road and the BTC-e exchange, both of which had become scourges of law-enforcement agencies worldwide.

Laura and her team first targeted the Silk Road, which had become a haven for drug dealers, arms traffickers, and criminals of every stripe. Through careful analysis and dogged determination, the NSA had discovered a crucial vulnerability in the site's code, a chink in the armor that Laura would exploit to devastating effect. As she infiltrated the site's inner sanctum, she engaged its notorious mastermind, Ross Ulbricht, in a tantalizing game of cat and mouse, her flirtatious banter concealing her true intentions.

While Ulbricht scrambled to maintain his sprawling empire, Laura struck with the precision of a surgeon, draining the Silk Road's vast reserves of Bitcoin into a wallet controlled by the US government. The helpless kingpin could only watch in disbelief as hundreds of thousands of ill-gotten coins vanished before his eyes.

Soon after this triumph, in the sun-lit paradise of Greece, Laura and Tom embarked on another daring gambit. This time their quarry was Alexander Vinnik, the Russian national who had founded the BTC-e exchange. Their mission was to confirm Vinnik's identity and orchestrate his extradition, bringing him to justice for his litany of alleged crimes.

As they strolled along the picturesque Greek shoreline, Laura and Tom made a striking picture, their good looks and air of confidence drawing the eyes of other beachgoers. But even as they enjoyed the sun, sand, and surf, they were inching ever closer to their target.

As they closed in on Vinnik and confirmed his role in BTC-e, Greek security forces sprang into action, swooping down upon him with the ferocity of a raptor. Vinnik was apprehended on the pristine sands of a Greek beach, as Laura's well-coordinated plan reached its crescendo. US Marshals, accompanying the Greek security forces, whisked him away, bound for an awaiting Gulfstream G-6. This luxurious jet, its fuselage gleaming in the Mediterranean sun, had already been prepped for departure, the luggage of Laura and Tom neatly stowed within.

Vinnik, clad only in a revealing Speedo, cut a comical figure amid the well-armed and serious US Marshals. As they escorted him onto the aircraft, Laura, a consummate professional, thoughtfully handed him a towel. Though their mission was to bring him to justice, she felt a pang of empathy for the shivering man, thrust into a world he could no longer control.

Tom, on the other hand, couldn't resist injecting some levity into the tense situation. With a wry grin, he asked the US Marshals, "Has this guy been searched? Because it looks like he's smuggling grapes!" The Marshals exchanged a glance and then a smirk, sharing a rare moment of amusement in the gravity of their work.

And so Vinnik was transported back to the United States to face the consequences of his actions, his fate now in the hands of the US justice system.

Meanwhile, Laura and Tom continued their pursuit of justice. Through guile, ingenuity, and sheer audacity, Laura and her team were striking decisive blows against the digital underworld and, in the process, amassing a staggering fortune in Bitcoin on behalf of their nation. Their daring exploits would become the stuff of legend, demonstrating the tenacity of those bringing justice to the lawless corners of the internet, all while they continued to unveil the Bitcoin conspiracy.

BITCOIN; NOT THE ONLY PLAY

Even as Tom and Laura continued their investigation of the cryptocurrency conspiracy, two monumental events were about to burst forth in the world, commanding the attention of every soul and forcing every nation to marshal its forces against these unwelcome intruders.

The first was a pernicious phantom, a virulent pandemic that would emerge from the depths of the Chinese heartland, unseen but all too palpable. This insidious adversary would sweep across the globe like a merciless tempest, sowing devastation, and anguish in its path. As nations struggled to combat this unseen enemy, the once familiar tapestry of human interaction would be rent apart, leaving instead a surreal mosaic of masks, social distancing, and overwhelming uncertainty.

In the face of this maelstrom, Tom and Laura would be compelled to set aside their investigation and lend their talents to the global fight against the pandemic. With the fate of the world hanging in the balance, these two intrepid people would dive headlong into the storm.

Yet, even as they fought to contain the pandemic, another colossus would soon rear its head, demanding more of the world's attention and resources. This second cataclysm, a geopolitical maelstrom created by Russia, would threaten to engulf the foundations of international order, leaving in its wake a torrent of destruction and despair.

As the world teetered on the brink of chaos, Tom and Laura were about to find themselves enmeshed in new heights of turmoil.

~

In the lush tapestry of global geopolitics, alliances are born of necessity and tempered in the crucible of shared ambitions. One such formidable union is BRICS - Brazil, Russia, India, China, and South Africa - originally a confluence of emerging economies, a collective resounding with potential. What started as an economic endeavor swiftly transcended into a geopolitical ballet, an intriguing dance against the Western-dominated G7.

As the sun was setting on the twentieth century, the economic landscape was ready for a new dawn. The United States, having emerged as the victor in the cold theatre of the Cold War, reveled in the golden hues of economic supremacy, its dollar reigning as the global reserve currency. However, not all were content to bask in America's radiance. The burgeoning economies of the East, most notably Russia and China, harbored ambitions of their own.

BRICS was initially a vessel for these aspirations, a pathway for Russia and China to challenge America's monopoly. The idea was as ambitious as it was audacious - to establish a robust currency of their own, gradually replacing the dollar as the preferred global reserve. They perceived their collective strength, the sum of their thriving economies, as the steppingstone to realize this dream. BRICS bank, New Development Bank, and a contingency reserve arrangement were envisaged as tools to dismantle dollar hegemony, unshackling them from the influence of Western financial institutions.

Yet, the journey of BRICS was not merely an economic expedition; it was a voyage that charted the murky waters of geopolitics. As the alliance matured, the leaders of BRICS realized the potential of their shared aspirations, not just in the realm of economics but also in the theatre of global politics. The erstwhile financial venture started evolving into a geopolitical bloc, an entity with the power to shape the global order.

Their agenda began to resonate with a distinct rhythm, an alternative melody to the tunes played by the G7. While the West advocated for liberal democracy and open markets, BRICS emerged as the voice of the Rest, a champion of a multipolar world order that didn't pivot on Western values alone. This transformation was not accidental but deliberate, reflecting the shifting plates of global power dynamics.

From the icy expanses of Russia to the vibrant markets of India, from the verdant landscapes of Brazil to the industrial heartlands of China, and down to the pulsating rhythms of South Africa, BRICS countries began to explore shared diplomatic stances, voicing their concerns against Western dominance. Their aspirations had evolved, their ambitions expanded, and the collective had grown to be more than the sum of its parts. The economic alliance was now a full-blown geopolitical coalition, ready to carve its distinct narrative in the grand saga of world affairs.

The journey of BRICS was, and continues to be, a testament to the dynamism of international relations, reflecting the complexities of shared ambitions and the potential to disrupt established norms. Like a fascinating dance, this coalition continues to evolve, its members swaying to a rhythm that is both a defiance and a testament to their shared aspirations. The dance is far from over, and as the music continues, the world watches with bated breath, eager to see where the next steps might lead.

~

The charismatic lead actor, the United States Dollar, has long dominated the grand theater of global economics. Its power and prestige stem from its role as the primary global reserve currency, a position it has held with grace and resilience for over seven decades. A currency that is held in significant quantities by governments and institutions as part of their foreign exchange reserves, it represents not just economic might but the strength of a nation's political influence.

However, like all grand theaters, the stage is vast, and the wings are filled with aspiring actors eager to assume the limelight. Among them, the Russian Ruble and the Chinese Yuan have been eyeing the coveted role for some time now. These Eastern currencies, backed by strong nations, present themselves as potential challengers to the dominance of the US Dollar.

But the quest for the role of global reserve currency is not a mere walk-on part; it requires the perfect blend of stability, economic resilience, and, most importantly, international acceptance.

To understand why the Ruble and Yuan have not yet succeeded in this grand endeavor, we need to delve into the intricate choreography of global finance. For a currency to captivate a global audience, it needs to ensure stability and inspire confidence. The Dollar has done this admirably, backed by a robust economy and a stable political environment, despite periodic upheavals.

In contrast, the Russian Ruble, while rich in history and cultural significance, has struggled with instability, largely due to Russia's political volatility and reliance on commodities such as oil and gas. Such fluctuations make the Ruble an unpredictable lead, a role not many are willing to entrust their economies to.

Similarly, the Chinese Yuan, backed by the world's second-largest economy, presents a compelling case. But here, the script takes a different turn. China, with its unique blend of state-led capitalism and strict control over capital flows, does not inspire the same level of confidence in its currency. The centralization and control that mark the Chinese economy are antithetical to the very concept of a global reserve currency, which requires trust and openness.

Furthermore, to dethrone the Dollar, a currency needs wide acceptance in international trade and finance, a stage where the

Dollar has long been the principal performer. To challenge this, the Ruble and Yuan would need a network of global alliances and countries willing to use and hold their currency. This requires a level of international cooperation and acceptance that, so far, has proven elusive for both the Ruble and Yuan.

To dethrone the US Dollar as the global reserve currency is a monumental undertaking. It would require not just economic strength and stability but also a shift in global trust and acceptance. The implications are enormous, influencing everything from international trade to geopolitical power dynamics.

So, as we navigate this riveting narrative of global finance, we see that BRICS, the Ruble, and Yuan, Bitcoin, for all their aspirations, face an uphill journey. But the dance continues, and the future holds the promise of intriguing new chapters. Will a new lead actor eventually emerge, or will the US Dollar continue to dominate the stage? As our story unfolds, one thing is certain: the drama of global finance remains as captivating as ever.

~

The Chinese government maintained a careful facade of control and skepticism toward the burgeoning world of cryptocurrencies. While the nation's citizens flirted with the digital currencies, the ruling party watched from afar, contemplating their next move in the ever-evolving game of economic and technological supremacy.

In the early days, cryptocurrencies were dismissed as a fleeting curiosity, unworthy of the attention of the mighty Dragon. Yet, behind its veil of indifference, the Chinese government studied the new technology, recognizing the potential for power and influence hidden within the lines of code. As the years passed and Bitcoin gained a foothold in the global market, China began to embrace the digital currency. Its vast reserves of cheap electricity and technological prowess made China a powerhouse in the world of Bitcoin mining, securing a position of power and wealth within the digital realm.

The ruling party's relationship with cryptocurrencies, however, was fraught with tension. Fearing the destabilizing effects of these digital assets on their tightly controlled financial system, they enacted strict regulations, closing the doors to initial coin offerings and shuttering domestic exchanges. Still, the Dragon's hunger for wealth and power could not be easily denied. In the shadows, the Chinese government orchestrated a vast campaign of deceit, accumulating Bitcoin and other digital assets through state-sponsored purchases, hacking, and outright theft. The nation's vast intelligence network was turned toward the digital frontier, its agents infiltrating the wallets of unsuspecting victims and siphoning off their precious digital wealth.

All the while, the Chinese government continued its public campaign against cryptocurrencies, touting the merits of its digital Yuan and the promise of blockchain technology. The world looked on, unaware of the machinations at play beneath the surface as the Dragon's hidden hoard grew ever larger. The Chinese government's true ambitions in the world of cryptocurrencies remained shrouded in secrecy. For the time being, the Dragon continued to play its game of shadows, its eyes fixed on the ultimate prize: global economic and technological supremacy. And as the world slept, the Dragon waited for the day when the tides would turn, and the full extent of its power would be revealed for all to see. Tarasque was the ultimate prize, but in the meantime, China was accumulating over 10% of the Bitcoin supply, and the value of this continued to soar.

Alongside this delicate game of power and perception, America and Russia continued their rivalry. And it was clear that, as long as American hegemony cast its long shadow across the globe, the fires of Russian and Chinese resentment would continue to smolder.

~

In the world's vast orchestra, where each nation contributed its unique voice to the harmony of the global stage, the United States had long held the baton, wielding the power of the conductor. The American dollar, like the sweeping strokes of the conductor's hand, guided the tempo and rhythm of the world's economy. But now the music of the world was changing. The once melodious orchestra had fallen into discord, as other nations grew tired of the American maestro's command. Like a flock of birds yearning to spread their wings and soar into the skies, one country after another sought to break free from the confines of the dollar's dominion and forge their own destinies.

The reasons for this growing desire for de-dollarization were as diverse as the nations that wished for it. For some, it was a matter of pride and ambition, a longing to rise from the shadows cast by the American hegemony and take their rightful places in the sun. For others it was a quest for stability and freedom, a desire to loosen the chains that bound them to the unpredictable whims of a foreign power.

In the hearts of these nations lay the seeds of discontent watered by the memory of past crises and bitter rivalries. Whenever the American maestro faltered, sending ripples through the global economy, the seeds began to take root; eventually, they would grow into mighty trees that threatened to shatter the foundations of the old order. As their branches stretched toward the heavens, whispers of a new dawn echoed through the corridors of power. Talk of de-dollarization and an end to American hegemony filled the air as nations began to explore the possibilities of a world free from the constraints of a single, dominant currency.

One such possibility lay in cryptocurrencies, and over time more and more countries, like a flock of birds set free, discovered the boundless expanse of the digital sky. Thus the once mighty American maestro found itself facing a chorus of voices clamoring for change. As the music of the world evolved, the fading empire struggled to hold onto its baton, the echoes of its past grandeur growing ever more distant in a transforming world.

~

With the election of President Robert Harrington, the American maestro now embraced a new and powerful refrain: the siren song of "America First." As this inward-looking melody spread through the nation, it also reverberated outward, its dissonant chords clashing with the harmonies of the international stage.

The "America First" policy, with its focus on self-interest and isolation, acted as a catalyst, accelerating the process of de-dollarization. As the United States turned its gaze inward, it began to prioritize its own prosperity and security above that of the global community. Trade barriers were erected, alliances were questioned, and international commitments were reevaluated, all in the name of putting America first.

The world, accustomed to the steady hand of the American conductor, now found itself facing an unpredictable and erratic force. Trust in the United States waned as nations witnessed the once reliable maestro dance to the tune of its own self-interest, heedless of the discord it sowed. And so the seeds of de-dollarization, already taking root in the hearts of many nations, grew more rapidly, nourished by the uncertainty and instability that the "America First" policy had unleashed.

~

The proponents of the 'America First' movement are not intrinsically in the wrong and most definitely deserve representation. The interests of American citizens and taxpayers should always be paramount. The issue lies not with the movement's ideology, but with its leadership. Harrington, with his rampant corruption and demagogic tendencies, is a blight on American politics, as were many of the Senators and Congressman that spin in his orbit.

The reasonable supporters of 'America First' acknowledge this truth but find themselves clinging to an ideology they believe will chart the right course for America. For their voices to have credible impact, they must first initiate change at the top, reforming the party's leadership. Harrington's first term wreaked havoc on America's global standing, and another term could reduce America to an international laughingstock, an entity bereft of the respect it has commanded for decades.

The 'America First' proponents must understand that while the nation's interests are crucial, a narrow, self-serving approach can erode America's global credibility. A balance between national interests and global cooperation is key to maintaining America's status as a global leader. Otherwise, the country risks becoming an isolated entity, scorned, and mistrusted by the rest of the world.

Countries have tried to insulate themselves from the whims of a single, dominant power, to diversify their reserves, and to seek alternate means of conducting trade and financial transactions.

Cryptocurrencies, with their decentralized nature and freedom from the influence of any one nation, became an increasingly attractive option. As the American maestro's grip on the global stage weakened, nations flocked to these digital assets. Thus, in a tragic irony, the "America First" policy, intended to strengthen and protect the nation's interests, ultimately hastened its decline. The once mighty maestro found its baton slipping from its grasp as the world embraced a new and decentralized refrain, accelerating the crescendo of de-dollarization.

~

The discordant strains of "America First" reverberated throughout the symphony hall of global politics, the cacophony echoing in the ears of nations worldwide. Yet this disquieting melody was but one instrument in the ongoing orchestra of events.

High US inflation, once a tamed beast, now stirred to life again, darkening the concert hall. As the greenback's purchasing power dwindled and the cost of goods and services swelled, the world's confidence in the stalwart dollar faltered. The American currency's role as the global reserve was called into question, its notes tarnished by the stain of inflation.

Next came the weaponization of the dollar, its once harmonious chords twisted and contorted into a fearsome coercive tool. Sanctions and economic warfare became the new leitmotif as the United States sought to bend other nations to its will, leveraging the dominance of its currency to force compliance. This, in turn, pushed countries to seek new melodies, yearning for the dulcet tones of financial autonomy, free from the grip of the dollar's newfound ferocity.

The rise of "BRICS, added yet another layer to the symphony: Brazil, Russia, India, China, and South Africa, once mere accompanists in the global orchestra, now took center stage, their collective crescendo demanding attention and respect. These nations, disillusioned with the dollar's dominance, began to seek out their own harmonies, exploring other instruments that would allow them to compose their own financial destinies.

And so, a maelstrom was born, a flurry of discordant notes that accelerated de-dollarization. The self-serving strains of "America First," the ominous drumbeat of inflation, the weaponized chords of the dollar, and the rising crescendo of BRICS all converged, each adding to the pandemonium that threatened to consume the maestro. In the face of this uproar, nations worldwide began to pursue the promise of cryptocurrencies. And as the concert raged on, the de-dollarization movement swelled, a chorus of voices united in their desire for a more balanced and harmonious world order.

~

In the hushed confines of Laura's office at the NSA, a chess game of geopolitical strategy was being played out. The players – Tom Michaels and Laura Roberts, intelligence veterans, their battlegrounds a high-tech landscape dominated by cryptocurrency. The prize, none other than the balance of global economic power, teetered perilously on the edge of upheaval.

Against the tableau of global finance, the Titans of the East - Russia and China - had quietly amassed an impressive fortune in

Bitcoin. Rumors of the infamous Satoshi's Horde under Russian control added fuel to the fire of uncertainty. Their intentions, however, lay shrouded behind a veil of political maneuvering, leaving the rest of the world in a state of tense speculation.

As the discussion unfolded, the flickering glow of the computer screen cast an eerie glow upon their faces, a stark reminder of the digital reality they now inhabited. Their gaze, more often than not, fell upon a single line graph: Bitcoin's soaring trajectory, a stark reminder of the shifting sands of the global economy.

"The US dollar," Tom began, his voice mirroring the gravity of their situation, "is under siege. Our erstwhile supremacy is being challenged, undermined." His gaze flicked to the growing figures of Bitcoin's market capitalization. "And yet," he paused, a thoughtful frown crinkling his forehead, "our potential usurpers are playing an opaque game. The scale of their Bitcoin accumulation is undeniably alarming, but what if it's just the first move? The opening gambit in a grander scheme?"

Laura's intelligent eyes mirrored the same uncertainty. "The foundation of our concerns lies with Bitcoin's ascendance. It has surpassed being a mere curiosity or a fad. Its rise in value, its acceptance as a legitimate asset class... it's beginning to wield real power. The question remains, though: does it hold the potential to disrupt the existing global economic order?"

"And what would that mean for American hegemony?" Tom added, voicing the fear that lay unspoken between them. "We've had the upper hand for decades. This could tip the scales."

"It wouldn't take much more to tip them", Laura added. "What else can go wrong"?

IN THE SHADOW OF A GLOBAL PANDEMIC

Zhang Wei, a man of unmatched cunning and ambition, stood in his office, gazing out over the vast expanse of Beijing. The city, with its intricate landscape of commerce and industry, was the throbbing heart of China, pumping the lifeblood of a nation on the precipice of greatness. Wei was no stranger to the perilous game of global power, having spent a lifetime navigating its treacherous waters. Yet, as he contemplated the world beyond his window, he began to envision an even grander scheme.

At the epicenter of Wei's grand design lay the Wuhan Institute of Virology, a state-of-the-art research facility in the heart of China's Hubei province. A citadel of scientific inquiry, the Institute was dedicated to the study and containment of infectious diseases, a bulwark against the unending march of pathogens that threatened humanity. Its laboratories, staffed by some of the world's most brilliant minds, were a testament to China's commitment to scientific progress and the safeguarding of global health. Renowned the world over for its cutting-edge research and pioneering innovations, the Wuhan Institute of Virology stood at the vanguard of the battle against infectious diseases.

But the Institute's stellar reputation belied the dark secrets that lurked within its walls, the machinations of a man with a singular vision of global dominance. As Wei surveyed the sprawling cityscape, his thoughts drifted to the Institute, a symbol of his nation's prowess and a harbinger of the change he sought to bring about. Little did the world know that this bastion of scientific excellence would soon be the birthplace of a cataclysm, a weapon of unimaginable power that would be unleashed upon an unsuspecting planet. In the shadows of Wuhan, a storm was brewing, and as its winds gathered force, the fate of nations hung in the balance.

~

Wei's plan was as audacious as it was insidious, born of a merciless intellect that saw an opportunity in chaos. The United States, a titan of the world stage, had long been the dominant player in the global economy, their mighty dollar a beacon of stability and prosperity. But Wei saw something more: a vulnerability, a chink in the armor of the West that could be exploited to devastating effect.

In the shadows of a tumultuous world, an unseen enemy, a creation of human ambition and hubris, awaited its moment to strike. The world, battered by the waves of the global financial crisis and The Great Recession, had become fertile ground for the rise of Bitcoin, the digital marvel that promised to disrupt the established order. Meanwhile, impatience over Petrov's repeated delays in releasing Tarasque, and the insatiable desire for dominance and control had driven Zhang Wei to devise a sinister plan.

In Wuhan, China, lay his silent, invisible instrument of chaos, a virus of unimaginable virulence and potency. Wei, fueled by a desire to see the global hegemony of the United States crumble, sought to undermine the fragile state of the world by releasing this malevolent specter upon an unsuspecting populace. He reasoned that the resulting devastation would necessitate an unprecedented level of deficit spending on the part of the United States, exacerbating the nation's economic woes and hastening its decline.

In the Wuhan laboratory, a dedicated team of scientists refined and perfected the virus to ensure its devastating potential. Little did they know that their work would soon spiral out of control, thrusting the world into a nightmare from which there would be no easy escape.

~

The lab in Wuhan, a fortress of cutting-edge technology and impenetrable security, was intended, in Wei's scheme, to be the cradle from which a deadly serpent would be unleashed—but only after China had perfected a vaccine to protect its people. Fate, however, had other plans. Before the completion of their work, a series of unforeseen events led to a catastrophic failure in the lab's containment protocols. The virus, no longer bound by the shackles of human control, slipped through the cracks and out into Wuhan.

Like a wildfire the virus spread from city to city, country to country, leaving a trail of death and destruction in its wake. It cared not for borders or allegiances, cutting a swath through both the West and the East with equal ferocity. As the world reeled from its devastation, China found its own economy ravaged by the weapon it had sought to wield against others.

The flaw in Wei's plan revealed itself in the most cruel and ironic of ways. The virus, intended as a tool to bring about the downfall of the West, turned on its master, consuming friend, and foe alike. While the world began the arduous process of rebuilding, Zhang Wei was left to ponder the cost of his ambition and the terrible price he had paid for power.

In the wake of the devastation wrought by the WUHAN FLU pandemic, the full extent of Wei's machinations remained shrouded in mystery. But one thing was certain: the landscape of global power had been forever altered, and the shadowy puppeteers who sought to shape the course of history would continue to ply their trade from the darkness, ever watchful and ever scheming.

~

When the scale of the WUHAN FLU pandemic first became clear, President Harrington was still serving his first term in office. His response to the global pandemic was muted, as he saw in the virus no threat to American dominance. But the virus spread with alarming speed, soon reaching every corner of the globe. Panic and fear gripped the world, as governments struggled to contain the disease and stem the tide of mounting casualties.

It was in this chaos that Wei's plan began to unfold. With the global economy in freefall and the pandemic showing no signs of abating, the United States found itself facing an existential crisis. President Harrington, already grappling with the fallout from his disastrous "America First" policy, was ill-equipped to deal with the catastrophe. As the nation's coffers drained and the dollar began its downward spiral, it seemed that Wei's plan was on the verge of succeeding.

The world, already reeling from the financial crisis, teetered on the brink of chaos. The emergence of Bitcoin had not only shaken the foundations of the global financial system but had laid bare the inherent vulnerabilities of traditional currencies. And as the digital juggernaut continued to gather momentum, the virus, a microscopic harbinger of doom, also spread silently, poised to plunge humanity into the abyss of despair and darkness.

~

Zhang Wei envisioned a future in which the United States, a nation with a history of rising to challenges and lending aid to a beleaguered world, would once again try to lead world events. His plan hinged on the nation's propensity to follow the patterns of the past. He recalled the aftermath of World War II and the birth of the Marshall Plan. In this unprecedented initiative the United States had poured vast resources into the reconstruction of Europe, a testament to its capacity for benevolence and resolve.

Now, in a world ravaged by disease and disarray, Wei believed that the United States would once again felt compelled to act, stepping forward as the would-be savior of a crumbling order. As so many times before, the nation would print vast quantities of the one thing everyone desired: US dollars. And this deluge of currency, Wei surmised, would destabilize the mighty dollar, dethroning it from its exalted position and clearing the path for China's meteoric rise.

~

Tom and Laura had been making significant progress in their investigation of the cryptocurrency conspiracy, but the world beyond their clandestine realm had other plans. Now Tom and Laura were desperately needed to aid in the Herculean efforts to combat the dreaded WUHAN FLU virus. Their unique talents were in high demand as the United States and its allies sought to protect their citizens and preserve their way of life. Though they were loath to abandon their work on the cryptocurrency case, they could not turn a blind eye to the suffering around them.

Meanwhile, as the world reeled from the pandemic, Russia's military aspirations surged to the forefront. The Russian bear flexed its muscles, asserting its influence and challenging the delicate balance of power that had existed for decades. This shift in the geopolitical landscape could not be ignored, and Tom and Laura were once again called upon to lend their expertise to the cause. Their focus torn between these two seemingly insurmountable challenges; the pair struggled to complete their original mission amid the pressing demands of a world in chaos.

As they fought to stem the tide of these twin disasters, they could not shake the nagging feeling that the Bitcoin conspiracy was but a single thread in a much larger, darker tapestry. They wondered what other secrets lay hidden beneath the turbulent surface of a world unraveling. And their suspicions were correct: as the deadly virus spread, Wei prepared to launch the next stage of his plan: the revelation of China's immense Bitcoin accumulation. The ensuing chaos, he believed, would fatally undermine the United States' position, hastening its decline and propelling China to the forefront of the global stage.

~

President Harrington stood at the helm of a nation in turmoil. Faced with the most significant global crisis of his tenure, he faltered, unable to perceive the true scope of the threat before him. To Harrington, the virus was nothing more than an inconvenience, a blip on the radar that could be easily dismissed in the pursuit of his own ambitions.

But as the death toll mounted and the world crumbled under the weight of the pandemic, the American people began to see through Harrington's self-serving facade. His callous disregard for the suffering of millions, both at home and abroad, galvanized a nation to action, and as the election approached, it became clear that change was in the air.

In the waning days of President Harrington's tenure, the nation had found itself on the brink of collapse. The self-centered agenda that had once seemed so alluring now lay exposed: its hollow promises and short-sighted policies had brought the United States to the edge of a precipice.

~

The pandemic had laid waste to the global economy, and the United States, crippled by Harrington's stubborn refusal to acknowledge the gravity of the situation, had been hit particularly hard. As businesses shuttered their doors and unemployment soared, the American people looked to their leader for guidance, hope, and a plan to steer them through the storm.

But Harrington offered them nothing. Instead, ensconced in the gilded confines of his White House, he stayed deaf to the cries of his constituents, blind to the suffering that had enveloped the land. His focus was squarely on his own interests, his own legacy, and the preservation of his own power. He had long ago abandoned any pretense of concern for the people he had sworn to serve.

In the midst of the chaos, a new figure emerged on the political scene, a herald of hope and unity for a nation battered by adversity. Bob Myers, a charismatic and compassionate leader, captivated the hearts and minds of the American people. Myers embodied the virtues of empathy, kindness, and a genuine concern for the well-being of others.

With a message of resilience and a renewed commitment to global cooperation, Myers offered a stark contrast to the isolationist policies of his predecessor. His gentle demeanor and dedication to unity struck a chord with a populace weary of conflict and division, who yearned for the warm embrace of solidarity and shared purpose.

As the election approached, the cracks in Harrington's once impenetrable armor began to widen. A stream of revelations about his administration's misdeeds, from corruption to human-rights abuses, fueled a growing disillusionment among the American public. They had been betrayed by a man who had promised them the world, only to deliver them to the brink of destruction. But it was not the scandals, the corruption, or even the incompetence that ultimately spelled Harrington's demise. It was the dawning realization among the people that their leader was not a savior but a false prophet, a man who had sold them a dream buried beneath his own selfish desires.

Turning their backs on the man who had once captivated their hearts and minds, the American people found solace in the arms of Bob Myers. In him, they saw a leader who would guide them through the darkness into the light of a new day. With each passing day, the tide of public opinion shifted in Myers' favor. And as the election neared its conclusion, the inevitable became reality: Harrington, the man who had once seemed invincible, fell under the crushing weight of his own hubris.

His defeat marked the end of an era, a dark chapter in American history that would not be forgotten but would rather serve as a cautionary tale, a reminder of the perils of unchecked power and the corrosive influence of self-interest on the soul of a nation. But could it recover?

In the days that followed his historic victory, President Myers set about the monumental task of mending the fissures that had rent the fabric of the nation. Armed with an unyielding faith in the American people and an unwavering belief in the power of empathy and compassion, he embarked on a journey to restore the values that had once defined the land of the free and the home of the brave.

~

Under President Myers, the United States became the vanguard in the battle against the WUHAN FLU pandemic. With a renewed commitment to international collaboration, the nation marshaled its considerable resources, leading the charge in the development and distribution of vaccines, providing aid and support to struggling nations, and spearheading a global effort to rebuild the shattered world economy.

The results were nothing short of miraculous. As nations came together, united in their fight against the pandemic and the economic devastation it had wrought, the global community began to heal. And in the midst of this resurgence, the dollar, once thought to be moribund, grew stronger than ever, buoyed by the strength of a revitalized and united world.

~

Zhang Wei watched in frustration as his carefully orchestrated plan unraveled before his eyes. The American response to the pandemic, led by the indomitable President Myers, had not only averted the crisis but had strengthened the very institutions he had sought to undermine. The dollar, once poised to fall, had risen like a phoenix from the ashes, demonstrating the resilience of the human spirit and the power of unity.

As the world moved forward, emerging from the darkness of the pandemic into a new era of hope and cooperation, Zhang Wei was left to contemplate the consequences of his actions. The machinations he had set in motion had failed, and in their wake, a brighter future was taking shape, a future where the power of unity and compassion could stand against even the most insidious of plots.

SHADOWS AT HOME

Bob Myers' meteoric rise to prominence had been not a product of chance but rather the culmination of a life spent in service to others. Born to a family of recent immigrants, he had seen firsthand the challenges faced by those who sought a better life in the land of opportunity. His early experiences had instilled in him a deep compassion and empathy, qualities that would come to define his political career.

Throughout his time in public service, Myers championed the rights of the marginalized and the dispossessed, earning him the respect and admiration of those he served. And as the WUHAN FLU pandemic ravaged the world, his dedication to the betterment of humanity became the foundation of his campaign for the Presidency.

In the midst of an unprecedented global catastrophe, Bob Myers' message of hope, unity, and perseverance resonated with a nation reeling from the consequences of Harrington's divisive and self-serving policies. As his campaign gained momentum, it became clear that he represented a new dawn for the United States, a beacon of light in the dark age of Harrington. And it was not just his message that captivated the American people; it was the man himself. Bob Myers was a living embodiment of the principles he espoused: a man of integrity, boundless compassion, and a fierce determination to fight for the common good. His humility, warmth, and genuine concern for the well-being of others stood in stark contrast to the callous, selfish nature of his predecessor.

Bob Myers' election heralded the beginning of a new era for the United States, a time of healing, renewal, and a rekindled commitment to the ideals that had once defined the nation. With Myers at the helm, the United States rose to meet the challenges of the WUHAN FLU pandemic and emerged even stronger than before, a testament to the spirit of the American people and the power of hope to triumph over despair.

At Bob Myers' inauguration as President, a sense of hope permeated the air. The nation, beleaguered by the ravages of the pandemic and the chaos sown by Harrington's regime, looked to their new leader with a mixture of relief and cautious optimism. In Myers they saw a man of integrity, a leader who placed the interests of his people above his own.

In his first days in office, President Myers wasted no time in addressing the most pressing issue of the time. He convened a task force of the brightest minds in science and medicine, directing them to work around the clock toward a solution that would stem the tide of illness and death now washing over the globe. Under Myers' guidance, the United States reasserted its role as a world leader, working hand in hand with other nations to combat the scourge of the virus. The international community, skeptical of American intentions after years of Harrington's isolationist policies, welcomed its renewed spirit of cooperation with open arms.

As the United States marshaled its resources to fight the pandemic, it also set about repairing the internal damage wrought by Harrington's divisive reign. Myers moved swiftly to root out corruption, holding those who had abused their positions of power accountable for their actions. He also took steps to address the nation's deep-seated social and economic inequalities, launching ambitious programs to uplift the most vulnerable members of society.

In the face of these sweeping changes, the nation began to heal. Businesses reopened, jobs returned, and the economy gradually regained its footing. More importantly, the American people rediscovered their sense of unity and purpose, embracing the notion that on the path forward they must walk hand in hand.

Zhang Wei, the architect of this part of the plan to undermine American hegemony, watched these developments with consternation. The plan he had crafted had backfired. As he stared at the reports detailing the resurgence of the American economy, the strengthening of the dollar, and the resurgence of international goodwill, Wei felt a deep pang of frustration. His plans had been thwarted by a nation that refused to be broken and a leader who had rekindled the flames of hope.

~

While the world still languished beneath the oppressive yoke of the WUHAN FLU pandemic, the boisterous engines of commerce and industry slowed to a grinding halt. The very fabric of society began to unravel, its threads frayed by the unrelenting grip of disease, fear, and uncertainty. Desperate measures were needed to stem the tide of despair and restore hope to the hearts of millions.

In this dark hour, the United States turned to an unconventional solution that had once been perceived as the province of economic heresy: qualitative easing. As the pandemic continued to spread, the United States government embarked on a bold experiment, venturing into the uncharted waters of fiscal policy to avert the looming specter of economic collapse.

Qualitative easing, the cornerstone of this daring gambit, was a policy born of necessity. With the global economy teetering on the brink of ruin, the United States injected much-needed liquidity into the financial system by purchasing vast quantities of government bonds and other financial assets. In so doing, they hoped to spur lending and spending, catalyzing a resurgence of economic activity that would lift the world from the depths of despair.

This policy of qualitative easing, accompanied by the attendant relaxation of monetary constraints, came to be known as "loose money" policies. The approach was predicated upon a simple yet powerful truth: in times of crisis, the United States, with its unparalleled ability to borrow money, its economic might, and its vast influence, possessed a unique ability to spend with abandon, unleashing a torrent of capital and investment that reverberated through the world.

By flooding the financial system with a deluge of capital, the United States aimed to lower interest rates and stimulate borrowing, thereby reigniting the dormant fires of economic growth. This grand design hinged on the belief that, by restoring confidence and stability to the markets, the United States could foster a resurgence of prosperity that would ripple across the globe, banishing the shadows of despair that had settled upon the world.

The echoes of an earlier triumph lent credence to this scheme. Following the devastation wrought by the Second World War, Europe lay in ruins, its cities reduced to smoldering husks, its people weary and bereft of hope. In the aftermath of this cataclysm, the United States embarked on an audacious endeavor to breathe new life into the once proud civilization: the Marshall Plan. Through the Marshall Plan, the United States provided aid and assistance to the beleaguered nations of Europe, helping to heal the wounds inflicted by the war and fostering a spirit of unity and cooperation that would endure for generations.

Decades later, in the desperate struggle to conquer the insidious WUHAN FLU virus, the United States once again donned the mantle of leadership, channeling the spirit of the Marshall Plan as it sought to stem the tide of economic devastation and chart a course to recovery. The age of qualitative easing had dawned and with it, the promise of a brighter future, where disease and despair would be vanquished by human determination and ingenuity.

The implementation of qualitative easing, like the Marshall Plan before it, faced a chorus of naysayers and skeptics. But in both instances the United States persevered. As the wheels of industry creaked back to life and the embers of commerce flickered once more, the world experienced the transformative power of the strategy. From the smoldering ruins of a global economy laid low, a phoenix began to rise, its wings fanned by the winds of change, its ascent propelled by human resilience.

Throughout history, humanity has faced innumerable trials and tribulations, each seemingly insurmountable. Yet, time and time again, we have risen above the ashes, our spirit unbroken, our resolve undiminished. In the annals of history, the age of qualitative easing would come to be remembered as a time when the world was pulled back from the abyss by the unyielding resolve of a nation and the unwavering belief in the power of hope.

~

As the United States continued its ascent under President Myers' leadership, the world marveled at the nation's remarkable transformation. Gone were the dark days of the pandemic and the strife that had festered under Harrington's rule. In their place a new era had dawned, in which the United States stood tall as a beacon of hope and progress.

Emboldened by their success in combating the virus, Myers and his administration turned to other pressing global issues. They spearheaded efforts to address climate change, forging alliances with nations around the world to develop sustainable solutions to protect the planet for future generations. At home, they tackled economic inequality, creating opportunities for those who had long been left behind. Education, healthcare, and social services were revamped and expanded, ensuring that every American had access to the resources they needed to thrive.

But the road to recovery was not without challenges. Many

clung to the old ways and resisted the changes that Myers sought to implement. Still, he remained steadfast, refusing to back down in the face of adversity. His determination inspired a new generation of leaders, both within the United States and beyond its borders. These individuals, galvanized by Myers' vision of a better world, soon rose to prominence, championing justice, equality, and progress.

Meanwhile, Zhang Wei seethed as he watched the world rally behind the resurgent United States. His dreams of toppling American hegemony had been dashed, and he grappled with the fact that his efforts had only served to strengthen his adversary. For all his bitterness and frustration, Wei could not deny the truth: the world was changing, and the old ways of thinking no longer held sway. As nations came together in pursuit of a brighter future, it was clear that the age of division and strife was giving way to one of unity and cooperation.

As the United States embarked on the road to recovery, the world stood with them, hand in hand. Together they faced the challenges ahead, knowing that a world of peace, prosperity, and justice could be built only through the collective efforts of all who called this planet home.

~

Inside the familiar comfort of Tom's home office, Tom and Laura found themselves engaged in a charged discussion on monetary policies, their views clashing in an animated interplay of differing economic ideologies.

Tom, the pages of the latest economic report spread across his desk, was the first to voice his concern, his words carrying the weight of the economic turmoil he saw threatening the globe. "Laura," he began, his voice filled with concern, "we stand at the edge of a global depression if no action is taken. We need to stimulate the economy."

Laura, ever the champion of sound money policy, countered. "Tom, I understand the crisis at hand, but loosening the monetary reins isn't always the solution. It may bring about a short-term relief but also potential long-term instability."

Tom, ready to defend his position, responded, "Qualitative easing allows more money to flow into the market. Yes, it risks inflation in the long run, but right now, we need to boost spending, stimulate growth."

But Laura, recalling the principles she held dear, retaliated, "And what about the tale of Icarus, Tom? Do we want to fly too close to the sun only to fall? We mustn't forget the lessons from the past. Overreliance on such policies can lead to unwanted inflation and asset bubbles."

Their eyes then shifted to the digital ticker that showcased Bitcoin's soaring value. Laura, seeing an opportunity, pointed to it, "Look at Bitcoin, Tom. It's a symbol of fiscal discipline, a finite supply, no qualitative easing there. Its success is a validation that enduring prosperity comes from restraint, not unrestrained spending."

Tom considered her words, the subtle shadows in his eyes reflecting the intricate dance of their differing ideologies. "Yes, Bitcoin has seen remarkable growth," he conceded, "But it's not a one-size-fits-all solution. It thrives in its own unique environment. The global economy is more complex, and sometimes it requires us to adapt and respond."

Their spirited dialogue, far from reaching a conclusive end, ebbed into thoughtful silence. Here, within this small room, they echoed the grand global debate, a testament to the eternal economic dance between restraint and abundance, the pursuit of prosperity and its potential perils. As they turned back to their work, the conversation lingered in the air, an unresolved symphony of ideas, as they both sought a path to navigate the complex terrain of global finance.

~

As the winds of qualitative Easing swept across the globe, there were also those who sought to reap the whirlwind. Within the tumultuous storm, avarice and ambition found fertile ground, sowing seeds of discord in a world eager to emerge from despair.

In the heart of this maelstrom, former President Harrington, once the standard-bearer of the America First Party, surveyed the landscape with a covetous eye. In the perils of qualitative easing he perceived an opportunity to fan the flames of resentment and breathe new life into his political aspirations. With cunning and guile, he seized upon the specter of deficit spending, decrying its use for the benefit of others while conveniently overlooking the fact that it had been a hallmark of his own administration. In the twisted mirror of his ambition, deficit spending was only palatable if it served the interests of Harrington and his acolytes.

So, with the zeal of a man possessed, Harrington set to work, stoking the fires of division and enmity within the United States. Unperturbed by the success of the new administration's policies that had revitalized the global economy, he pursued his own myopic agenda, ever inward-looking. With every fiery tirade and impassioned speech, Harrington sought to cleave the nation in twain, his rhetoric a clarion call to the disaffected and the disillusioned, who yearned for a return to a past that had never truly existed.

As the world looked on with a mixture of concern and bemusement, the divisions sown by Harrington threatened to rip apart the fabric of American society. In his relentless quest for power, he seemed oblivious to the fact that his actions played directly into the hands of those who wished to see America falter and fail.

~

Meanwhile, the sinister machinations of Petrov, Zhang Wei, and their collaborators slowly expanded, their nefarious plans inching ever closer to fruition. With each passing day, the threads of the sinister web they wove drew tighter, threatening to ensnare the world in a dark and perilous embrace.

Unbeknownst to the world's leaders, Russia and China's conspirators had infiltrated far and wide, their malevolent influence spreading like cancer through the veins of the global body politic. But as the storm gathered strength, whispers of subterfuge and betrayal began to circulate among the vigilant. The world's intelligence agencies sensed that a dark force was at work, a puppet master who was pulling the strings behind the curtain of international diplomacy.

Amid the gathering storm clouds, Laura Roberts and her team forged ahead on their journey into the heart of the tempest, determined to unravel the conspiracy that threatened to engulf the globe in the cold embrace of tyranny and fear. With each step they took, the storm drew closer, the winds of change howling with fury. And as the final pieces of the conspirators' intricate puzzle began to fall into place, the world hung unknowingly over a chasm.

BITCOIN PLAYS UNVEILED

The Russian Oligarch, a specimen of the modern gentry, evokes an image of an individual embodying power, influence, and opulence. Rising to prominence from the ashes of the Soviet Union, these corporate tsars emerged as commanding actors in the anarchic play that was Russia's transition to capitalism.

Most dwell in the illustrious neighborhoods of Moscow. Rublyovka, the Beverly Hills of Russia, is particularly teeming with them. This plush enclave is a fortress of luxury, sequestered from the chaos of city life by towering fir trees and stringent security measures. There behind iron-wrought gates are nestled the grand mansions - edifices of Western and Slavic architectural fusion, a testament to the blend of influences that underpin these new elites.

These homes, though brimming with extravagance, serve not only as mere residences but symbols of their owner's social standing. They are fortresses of solitude, stocked with art collections rivaling the Hermitage, fleets of European luxury cars, and private chefs catering cuisines from every corner of the world. Yet, the grandeur of Rublyovka's mansions, while an obvious display of wealth, also betrays an undercurrent of paranoia; high-tech security systems, thick perimeter walls, and private security details are as much fixtures of these residences as marble floors and silk drapes.

These are the dwellings of the oligarchs – the new aristocrats who owe their ascension not to lineage but to guile, cunning, and unrelenting ambition. But how did they rise to such heights in the relatively brief interlude following the fall of the Soviet Union?

When the Iron Curtain collapsed in the early 1990s, Russia was a land of economic disarray. The transition from a centrally planned economy to market capitalism was as swift as it was chaotic. Amidst this turbulence, those with the audacity to seize the moment found themselves at the helm of the economic ship.

The government, grappling with a tumultuous economy, embarked on a grand scheme of privatization, with state-owned enterprises being sold off to the highest bidder, often for a pittance. There were many of those – former party functionaries, clever entrepreneurs, astute intellectuals – who recognized the tidal wave of opportunity this chaos presented.

Armed with their networks and astute understanding of the economic landscape, they snapped up state assets. Mines, oil fields, and vast tracts of real estate changed hands, often overnight. This was the age of the 'wild east,' a period marked by lawlessness that only the most ruthless could navigate.

Some ascended through the tangled bureaucracy, leveraging their Soviet-era connections and inside knowledge. Others seized the moment through sheer entrepreneurial audacity, recognizing that in the wild dance of capitalism, fortune favors the bold. Yet others built their fortunes upon the age-old pillars of speculation and graft, exploiting the weaknesses of a fledgling system of law and order.

In a few short years, these men – and they were mostly men – transformed from humble apparatchiks and businessmen into the oligarchs, the new tsars of Russia's burgeoning capitalist empire. Their rise, swift as a Siberian winter storm, was not without controversy. They were simultaneously admired and reviled, seen as both symbols of Russia's newfound prosperity and the very embodiment of its deep-seated corruption.

They reign over Russia's economic landscape like modern tsars, their power intertwined with the political fabric of the nation. They are the oligarchs of Russia, born of chaos and cunning, heirs to a fortune written in oil, steel, and the whirlwind of economic change.

~

In stark contrast to the tumultuous post-Soviet world that birthed the Russian oligarchs, China's most influential business figures emerged from a different backdrop: the transition from a closed, centrally planned economy to a market-driven one while still under the firm grip of the Chinese Communist Party (CCP).

Among China's business elite, Ya Chang stands out as one of the most successful and influential figures. His rise to power started with close ties to the CCP and a keen understanding of the changing economic landscape in China. Using his political connections, Chang obtained favorable policies and financial backing, allowing him to create an e-commerce company that eventually outstripped giants like Amazon in scale and profitability.

His company, leveraging China's burgeoning manufacturing industry and its rapidly growing consumer market, became a central hub for online trade not just in China but also globally. It capitalized on China's massive population, whose increasing disposable income and internet access fueled a boom in e-commerce. Additionally, by offering an extensive array of products and services, it became an integral part of people's daily lives, enhancing its market position. This meteoric rise led Ya Chang to amass a staggering fortune, ultimately making him the wealthiest man in the world.

Even as Ya Chang built a global e-commerce empire, he remained beholden to his Chinese Masters in the CCP and served as a convenient shield for Chinese Bitcoin aspirations. Given his extensive resources and commercial reach, Ya Chang could accumulate Bitcoin on a massive scale. His Bitcoin wallets, reputed to contain over 1,000,000 Bitcoins, represented a fortune in digital currency, surpassed only by Satoshi Nakamoto who had disappeared years before, his vast fortune untouched for well over a decade.

This digital wealth served multiple purposes. Beyond Zhang Wei's grand scheme, it was used to integrate Bitcoin payments into his e-commerce platform, driving further adoption of the digital currency.

~

Frustrated by the lack of a digital Ruble or something similar, Russia and China had set their sights on the digital currency that had begun to redefine the global economy—Bitcoin. Yet the public nature of the blockchain, a digital ledger that recorded every transaction for all to see, posed a significant challenge to their clandestine endeavors. To navigate these waters, they needed to draw upon centuries of intrigue, weaving a tapestry of deception that would shield their true intentions from the prying eyes of their rivals.

In Moscow, Petrov devised a cunning plan to cloak Russia's Bitcoin acquisitions in secrecy. He established a Bitcoin Holding Company funded by Russian Oligarchs, a seemingly innocuous front that obfuscated the extent of Russia's digital wealth. Behind the veil of this unassuming corporate entity, Vladimir Petrov held the keys to Russia's digital empire.

In the Far East, a parallel effort unfolded: China, too, sought to amass a trove of Bitcoin, a digital war chest that would bolster its standing on the world stage. So, Ya Chang had been directed to form a Bitcoin Holding Company, mirroring the Russian strategy, and serving as a cover for China's own purchases of the coveted digital currency. But China's Bitcoin accumulation was not limited to mere purchases. They also employed a more insidious strategy, enlisting the expertise of North Korean hackers to infiltrate and plunder the digital coffers of their adversaries. Through a complex web of cyber-espionage, these skilled operatives managed to siphon off hundreds of thousands of Bitcoins, funneling the stolen wealth into China's burgeoning crypto reserves.

North Korea, a pariah state with little to lose and much to gain, soon found itself in a unique position. The regime, desperate for hard currency to fund its weapons programs and purchase Western technology, willingly sold its stolen Bitcoin to the Chinese holding company in return for American currency. Thus, ironically, the US dollars that had once symbolized the dominance of the West now fueled the ambitions of China and North Korea.

As the nations of the world danced on the edge of a knife, the hidden fortress of Russia and China grew ever stronger, a specter that loomed ominously over the uncertain future.

~

Petrov had been harboring suspicions for some time now. He was not one to be blinded by the grandeur of his plans nor the excitement of the new technology he wielded. He saw patterns and shadows that danced just out of sight, always hinting at a larger game afoot.

The WUHAN Flu pandemic had brought the world to its knees, and Russia, despite its might, had not been spared. The virus had swept through the nation like an unseen enemy, its invisible tentacles reaching into every corner of the country, its effects all too visible.

As Petrov sat in his office, the gravity of the situation bore down on him. Was it mere coincidence that China had remained relatively unscathed in the wake of the virus, or was there more to it? The question gnawed at him, and he found it increasingly difficult to ignore the insidious thoughts creeping into his mind. Had he been double-crossed? Had the pandemic been a calculated move by China, a pawn sacrificed in a much larger game of geopolitical chess?

His thoughts were interrupted by the quiet knock on his office door. Sergey entered; his usual air of calm confidence replaced by concern.

"Sir," Sergey began tentatively, "You wanted to see me?"

Petrov stared at him momentarily, studying Sergey's face before speaking. "Yes, Sergey. We need to discuss Tarasque, the project Melnik and his team are developing."

Sergey looked puzzled but nodded. "What about it, sir?"

Petrov steepled his fingers, his gaze fixed on Sergey. "It still doesn't work, and I want you to take over the project. I also want you to modify the code. Tarasque was designed to provide centralized control over the Bitcoin network, with equal powers to Russia and China. I want you to change that. I want Russia to have sole control." Petrov knew that he could trust no one but himself.

Petrov, the embodiment of power and control, towered over the mahogany table separating him from Sergey. His voice, imbued with a grit born of countless political battles, echoed in the room. "And another thing, Sergey, it's time we wielded the power you've created. The future of the global power balance is tied to the Bitcoin currency you've fathered. It's time to turn the tables in our favor. But we need to control it."

Sergey's pulse throbbed at the base of his throat, an icy undercurrent of fear coursing through him. "Mr. President, Bitcoin's strength is in its freedom, its immunity from any controlling entity. It's a counterforce to the monopoly of the US dollar."

Petrov's gaze, icy and unwavering, held Sergey in place. "Then we must modify it. I need to wield that control."

Sergey shook his head, conviction fueling his rebuttal. "I understand your position, sir, but altering Bitcoin would defeat its purpose. Its freedom from any central control is its charm. It's a fresh respite from the dollar's dominance."

Petrov's furrowed brows betrayed his contemplation. "Then propose another way."

An idea ignited in Sergey's eyes. "We could enable Tarasque by constructing a centralized cryptocurrency using Bitcoin's protocol by holding sway over a substantial portion of the Bitcoin network. It's a marriage of blockchain technology and the control you seek."

Petrov's retreating figure suggested a pensive mood. "But it's a waiting game. And time is a luxury we can't afford."

"True, sir," Sergey replied, seizing the momentum. "However, this approach is more realistic, ensuring the control you yearn for. In parallel, Russia could continue to invest in Bitcoin. Our centralized currency would be exchangeable with Bitcoin, enabling our presence on both fronts."

A heavy silence hung in the air as Petrov's scrutinizing gaze bore into Sergey's. At last, he nodded. "Begin immediately. This endeavor isn't just economic. It's about our nation's survival."

~

Thus, Sergey Kuznetsov found himself ensnared in a complex web of deception and power play. His genius was being weaponized for a cause that risked undermining the very principles he held dear. Holed up in his small office, the shadows of an imminent tempest only faintly registered in his consciousness. The toll for his brilliance was yet to be exacted.

~

Sergey felt the weight of his predicament grow heavier with every passing day. His brilliant mind was being exploited to weave a dangerous gambit that went against the very principles of Bitcoin. But what choice did he have? Petrov held the cards; he held Sergey's parents.

It was time to make a stand. "Mr. President," Sergey began, his voice measured yet resolute. "I will do as you ask, but only if you release my parents."

Petrov looked at him, his steely gaze piercing Sergey. "Your parents are in good hands, Sergey," he replied nonchalantly. "You know that."

"But I need them free," Sergey persisted. "They deserve freedom. And I deserve to have them by my side. Especially now."

Petrov considered him for a moment. "All in due time, Sergey.

All in due time."

Sergey knew he was walking a tightrope. His parents' freedom was at stake, and he had little leverage. But he also understood that Petrov needed him, needed his brilliance to make Tarasque a reality. It was a delicate balance of power, but for the moment, he had a slight edge.

Sergey took a deep breath and raised the stakes. "Mr. President, I want to be clear. I will develop Tarasque. But I need a guarantee that my parents will be released. This isn't just a request; it's a condition."

The silence in the room was deafening as Petrov took in Sergey's demand. He leaned back in his chair, steepling his fingers together, scrutinizing Sergey with a steely gaze. The air between them crackled with tension, the balance of power tilting on the edge of a knife.

Finally, Petrov broke the silence, "You tread on dangerous turf, Kuznetsov." His gaze never leaving Sergey, he picked up the phone and dialed a number. After a brief exchange, he replaced the receiver. "Your parents will be moved to a more comfortable location within the prison. And you'll be allowed to visit them."

Sergey held his breath, biting back the urge to demand immediate release. But he knew better than to push Petrov too far. His parents' lives were at stake. He had to play this game carefully. "Thank you, sir," he finally responded, hoping he was making the right choice.

So Sergey Kuznetsov, the genius cryptographer, the elusive Satoshi Nakamoto, became a pawn in a game far more complex than he had ever envisioned. Under the watchful eyes of the FSB, he would work on the very project that threatened to undermine the essence of his creation, all the while desperately hoping that he had bought his parents' safety at the cost of his ideals. The fate of Tarasque, and indeed his own fate, hung in the balance, a dark uncertainty looming over the brilliance of his genius.

In keeping with the lessons ingrained by his parents, Bitcoin was designed to be a force for the greater good. Instead, Kuznetsov would soon find himself at the center of a struggle that would be a force for evil.

~

The dim light from a computer monitor cast eerie shadows on the face of Sergey Kuznetsov, who was still unknown to the world as the enigmatic Satoshi Nakamoto. In the privacy of his office, the hum of his computer was the only sound to break the oppressive silence that had settled Before him lay the monumental task of altering the foundation of the world's first cryptocurrency, Bitcoin, to give birth to an entirely new entity — Tarasque.

Despite the inherent contradictions of creating a centralized cryptocurrency, Kuznetsov found himself lost in the mechanics of it. For all his initial resistance to the idea, the intellectual challenge had taken root in his mind. Could it really be possible to build a centralized entity within the decentralized framework that Bitcoin offered? Could a lion-headed, bear-clawed, dragon-tailed creature of myth and power come to life within the digital realm?

The Bitcoin protocol was a complex, self-regulating ecosystem designed to prevent any one entity from gaining absolute control. Satoshi's groundbreaking work had made it so, forming a trustless, decentralized network where transparency and collective consensus were key. It was, in essence, the antithesis of centralization.

In his exploration, however, Kuznetsov discerned a delicate and fascinating balance. Yes, Bitcoin was inherently resistant to centralized control. Yet, it was not completely immune. There was a potential vulnerability, a subtle chink in the armor, rooted in the Proof-of-Work consensus mechanism.

~

In the Bitcoin protocol, the mechanism relied on the majority of computational power (hash rate) to validate and add new transactions to the blockchain. This ensured that no single participant could manipulate the transaction data. But what if a single entity controlled more than half of the network's hash rate? This entity would hold disproportionate influence over the network, potentially overriding the rules of transaction validation and even rewriting transaction history. The so-called '51% attack.'

Though the feasibility of such an attack was negligible due to the astronomical computational power and electricity required, it was this loophole that Kuznetsov now pondered. Could he exploit it, altering the Bitcoin protocol to shift control to a centralized entity?

And so, he delved deeper into the cryptographic abyss, threading together strings of code, each one meticulously designed to circumvent Bitcoin's intrinsic safeguards. His task was navigating a labyrinth, each twist and turn presenting new challenges and obstacles to overcome. He felt a mixture of excitement and dread, a sense of trespassing into forbidden territory. Yet, he pressed on, driven by the same insatiable curiosity and intellectual ambition that had propelled him this far.

In the wee hours of the morning, the last string of code fell into place. Kuznetsov leaned back in his chair, staring at the lines of code that formed Tarasque. It was done. The lion's head, bear claws, and dragon tail had taken the form of a digital entity — a centralized cryptocurrency built on the foundations of Bitcoin's protocol.

Tarasque was designed to be different. Unlike Bitcoin, the majority of mining power would be controlled by Russia This would allow them to control the creation of new blocks and, thus, the transaction history. Moreover, Russia would have the power to censor transactions, something that was fundamentally against Bitcoin's principle of financial freedom.

~

Tom's office at the CIA was an intimate space filled with artifacts and mementos that told tales of a career steeped in clandestine dealings and nuanced diplomacy. Laura Roberts and Tom Michaels huddled over an antiquated globe that dominated the room, their figures illuminated by the dim light of the desk lamp.

"This," Laura began, her finger tracing the contours of the Crimean Peninsula, "was just the start, wasn't it? Russia's occupation in 2014... We responded with economic sanctions, but they proved to be little more than a minor inconvenience."

Tom's hands clasped behind his back; his gaze focused on the geographic chessboard spread before him. "The process of de-dollarization had already been in motion," he mused, "Has it now reached a stage where Russia can disregard our sanctions, our economic might, with such impunity? Have we lost that leverage?"

Laura pursed her lips, considering the question. "It's certainly a possibility," she conceded. "Sanctions, traditionally our primary tool of deterrence, lose their sting in the face of a robust cryptocurrency economy. With Bitcoin, transactions become anonymous, bypassing the traditional financial systems entirely."

She paused, her eyes narrowing in contemplation. "But if this de-dollarization continues at its current pace, and Russia were to make a move against a non-NATO country...how would we respond then? Economic sanctions would lose their deterrent power."

"Indeed," Tom nodded, "We are bound by Article 5 to protect our NATO allies. But what about countries that fall outside of that alliance? With Bitcoin potentially undermining our sanctions, what would our response look like?"

Silence filled the room as both veteran agents grappled with the reality of this newfound uncertainty. Russia's previous actions in Crimea had set a worrying precedent, a demonstration of their capacity for opportunistic aggression. With the power dynamics of the global economy shifting, the prospect of further such acts seemed increasingly plausible.

"The world has been preoccupied with the WUHAN Flu pandemic," Tom noted, his voice carrying an edge of grim anticipation, "But as it winds down, it feels like the chess pieces are slowly being moved back into position. If this is indeed part of a larger plot, it won't be long before we see the next move."

Their shared dread hung heavily in the air as they pondered the intricate web of possibilities stretching out before them. The once-clear paths of diplomacy and international relations were growing increasingly murky, obscured by the rise of Bitcoin and the disruption it brought with it. As they watched the shadows lengthen in the dim light of Tom's office, they both knew that they were in the midst of a world teetering on the precipice of profound change. And in that suspense-laden silence, they could only watch, wait, and prepare for whatever came next.

UKRAINE, PART II

The decision to invade Ukraine was not made lightly. Petrov and Wei had been waiting for too long, biding their time and watching as America continued to hold the spotlight. But they were both growing tired of waiting in the shadows and now they decided it was time to act. Petrov convinced Wei that Russia should be the first to strike. He argued that military action on the European continent would have greater destabilizing effects on the West. Moreover, Wei believed Petrov had already amassed control over 15% of the Bitcoin supply, and controlled Tarasque, giving the Russian Bear a stronger hand in the negotiations.

Wei, not known for his patience, was eager to get started. But Petrov assured him that his "special military operation" would last only a few weeks; he doubted he would even need China's military assistance. So, with Petrov's assurances, Wei agreed to support the invasion.

Petrov had selected Ukraine as the target because it was a non-NATO country with which Russia had a significant history. Indeed, Russia already occupied a large portion of Ukraine in the south.

Petrov and Wei were not interested in drawing others into the fight. They simply wanted to weaken America's influence, which had remained stubbornly high even after the disastrous America First administration of President Harrington.

The invasion of Ukraine began quickly and with great force. Russian troops poured into the country, seizing control of critical infrastructure and military installations. The Ukrainian military was no match for the might of the Russian military machine. Beyond Ukraine's borders, the invasion caught the world by surprise. Many countries condemned Russia's actions and called for an immediate end to the conflict. The United States, however, was slow to respond. The Myers administration was deeply divided on how to handle the situation. Some advisers called for military action, while others urged caution, fearing that American military intervention could trigger a wider conflict. Laura Roberts and Tom Michaels worked day and night to gather intelligence on Russia's plans and capabilities.

As the conflict dragged on, it became clear that Petrov's "special military operation" was not going according to plan. The Ukrainian military, with Western support, was putting up a more substantial fight than Petrov had anticipated. Russian casualties were mounting, and the international community was increasingly outraged. Soon the invasion of Ukraine had become a major global crisis, and the world watched to see how it would be resolved. Petrov had taken a huge risk by launching the invasion, and now he was struggling to control it.

~

Vladimir Vladimirovich Petrov had always viewed human life as a commodity to be used and discarded at will. To him, the lives of ordinary citizens were simply pawns in a larger geopolitical game, to be sacrificed without a thought if it meant advancing his own interests and ambitions. His contempt for human life was on full display during the actions in Ukraine. As Russian soldiers flooded into Ukrainian territory, Petrov saw nothing wrong with using them as cannon fodder, sending them into battle without regard for their safety. To him, their lives were expendable, a small price to pay for expanding Russia's influence.

And it wasn't just Russian soldiers whom Petrov viewed with total disregard. Ukrainian civilians were also deemed to be of no value and were treated with brutal violence and cruelty. As Russian-backed separatist forces seized control of key areas in eastern Ukraine, countless innocent civilians were caught in the crossfire. Petrov's lack of concern for human life extended well beyond the battlefield. Russian journalists and political opponents who dared to speak out against him were silenced with ruthless efficiency, often disappearing without a trace. To Petrov, these people were only obstacles to his quest for power, and their lives were of little consequence.

As the conflict in Ukraine raged on, Petrov remained steadfast in his belief that the ends justified the means. He saw no problem with using violence and intimidation to achieve his goals and viewed the lives of ordinary people as mere collateral damage in the pursuit of his ambitions. For Petrov, the value of human life was determined solely by its usefulness to him. Anyone or anything that stood in his way was expendable, and he would stop at nothing to achieve his goals. His attitude was a chilling reminder of the dangers of unchecked power, and a warning to those who dared to oppose him.

~

Picture the US dollar as a mighty sword, wielded by a powerful warrior. In today's global economy, this warrior is the United States, and the sword represents the dollar's dominant role in international trade and finance. When trouble brews, the warrior can use his sword to protect his allies and deter his enemies, showcasing his strength and influence.

The United States, watching the battle in Ukraine, finally decided to intervene. The Americans unsheathed their mighty sword, the US dollar, and struck at the heart of Russia's economy. Here's how such a warrior wields his sword:

First, he freezes the enemy's treasure: The US and its allies locked away Russia's assets, blocking them from the global market that relied on the US dollar. Second, he cuts off the enemy's lifelines: The Americans limited Russian banks' access to the US dollar, making it difficult for them to trade with other nations and obtain necessary resources. Third, he excludes them from the world's trading posts: The US and its allies banned certain Russian banks from using the global messaging system, making it harder for them to conduct business. Fourth, he restricts trade and supplies: The Americans imposed restrictions on trade with Russia, limiting that country's access to critical goods and technologies and reducing its revenue from exports.

All of these actions took a deep toll on Russia's economy, causing its currency to lose value, inflation to soar, and economic growth to slow. The US dollar's weaponization demonstrated the immense power and influence that can be exerted through control over the global financial system.

As the conflict in Ukraine continued, the people of Russia grew weary and started to question Petrov's leadership. They longed for peace and saw the invasion as a disaster that would lead to isolation and strained relations with the rest of the world. Petrov's impatience had resulted in a costly and ultimately futile military adventure, with the mighty sword of the US dollar playing a significant role in their failure.

~

Nine months into the Russian invasion, a glimmer of hope for Ukraine emerged amid the desolation and chaos. The once seemingly unstoppable Russian forces had been pushed back, their advances stymied by the fierce determination and resourcefulness of the Ukrainian military. In a stunning reversal of fortune, Ukrainian forces had managed to reclaim over a thousand square miles of territory, including the critical northeastern region of Kharkiv. This astonishing victory infuriated Petrov and showed the world that Ukraine could not be easily subdued.

In the early days of the invasion, Russian forces had appeared invincible, sweeping across the border with seemingly inexorable momentum. However, as the conflict wore on, the cracks in the Russian military machine began to show. The incompetence and corruption within its ranks became increasingly apparent, with multiple examples of ineptitude highlighting the dire state of the Russian forces.

One such instance occurred during the Battle of Luhansk, in which Russian forces had been ordered to take the city at all costs. Despite superior numbers and equipment, the Russians found themselves ensnared in a deadly game of urban warfare. Ukrainian forces, using their intimate knowledge of the city's layout, were able to isolate and ambush Russian units, inflicting heavy casualties. The Russian commanders, struggling to adapt, ordered a reckless frontal assault on the city center, resulting in the needless deaths of hundreds of their own soldiers.

A series of logistical failures also plagued the Russian military. In one notable example, a Russian armored column was forced to halt its advance after running out of fuel, leaving it stranded and vulnerable to attack. It was later discovered that corrupt officers had been siphoning off fuel supplies to sell on the black market, leaving their own troops dangerously under-supplied.

But it was the atrocities committed by Russian forces that truly shocked the world. As the invasion continued, reports of war crimes and human-rights abuses committed by Russian soldiers began to surface. The intentional targeting of civilian infrastructure, including hospitals, schools, and residential areas, was documented and shared with the international community. In one heinous incident, Russian soldiers were reported to have executed an entire village of civilians, including women and children, in retaliation for a successful Ukrainian ambush.

As the ninth month of the invasion drew to a close, the scale of the devastation became clear. Tens of thousands of lives had been lost on both sides, and countless more had been irrevocably altered. The Ukrainian landscape was scarred with the remnants of battle, and the future of the nation looked grim. Yet, through all the darkness and despair, a sense of hope had emerged. The Ukrainian people, having endured unimaginable suffering and loss, continued to fight for their freedom, pushing back against the might of the Russian military. And as the world witnessed their resilience and defiance, the tide of the conflict began to turn, setting the stage for a new chapter in the struggle for Ukraine's independence.

~

As the brutal conflict raged on, the significance of superior Western technology became apparent. The United States and its European allies, deeply concerned by Russia's aggressive actions, began to provide Ukraine with advanced weaponry, military equipment, and intelligence. This assistance proved invaluable, allowing Ukrainian forces to match the might of the Russian military and, in some cases, even outmaneuver them.

The battle for Bakhmut served as a harrowing testament to the importance of this technological edge. A strategically vital city, Bakhmut was the center of a fierce and bloody struggle that ultimately turned into a deadly stalemate. For weeks, Ukrainian and Russian forces traded blows, each side attempting to gain the upper hand in a savage contest of attrition.

Then Ukrainian forces, newly armed with cutting-edge Western technology, inflicted heavy casualties on their Russian adversaries. Advanced anti-tank weapons proved remarkably effective, allowing Ukrainian troops to neutralize Russian armored vehicles and disrupt enemy formations. Meanwhile, precision-guided artillery and advanced surveillance systems allowed them to target and destroy key Russian assets, turning the tide of the battle in their favor.

Despite these advances, the battle for Bakhmut remained a

grueling and exhausting affair. With both sides entrenched and unwilling to yield, the city was transformed into a hellish landscape of shattered buildings and lifeless streets. And as the death toll mounted, the hopes of a swift resolution to the conflict began to fade.

Recognizing the importance of breaking the deadlock, Ukrainian commanders, in coordination with their Western allies, planned a bold spring counteroffensive. Their objective: to drive the Russian forces from Ukrainian soil once and for all. In preparation for this ambitious operation, a stream of Western weapons and equipment flowed into Ukraine. Advanced drones, which could provide real-time intelligence and surveillance, were delivered alongside state-of-the-art communication systems to ensure seamless coordination between units. New shipments of anti-aircraft and anti-tank weaponry bolstered the Ukrainian forces, giving them the tools they needed to combat Russia's formidable arsenal.

At the same time, Western intelligence detected a dramatic decrease in China's support of Russian efforts, while the United States, under President Myers' selfless leadership, committed vast quantities of money and supplies to the conflict, rehabilitating America's reputation as an ally that could be trusted and undoing a lot of the damage that Harrington had inflicted. These actions had the further effect of strengthening the dollar and slowing Bitcoin's rise.

As spring approached, the Ukrainian forces, now equipped with the most advanced technology the West had to offer, stood ready to launch their counteroffensive. With the hopes of a nation resting on their shoulders, they prepared to push back against the Russian invaders and reclaim their homeland. The stage was set for a dramatic showdown, one that would determine the future of Ukraine and the balance of power in the region.

~

Spring brought with it newfound hope and determination for the people of Ukraine. Empowered by the advanced weaponry provided by their Western allies and buoyed by a series of tactical successes, Ukrainian forces launched their sweeping counteroffensive, aiming to wrest control of their homeland from the clutches of the Russian invaders.

The primary objective of this daring operation was to sever the strategic land bridge connecting mainland Russia to Crimea, thereby isolating the disputed peninsula, and dealing a significant blow to Russian military capabilities in the region. The secondary objective was to liberate key cities and territories occupied by Russian forces, expelling the invaders and restoring Ukrainian sovereignty.

As the operation commenced, the Ukrainian military, now a formidable fighting force, sprang into action with a level of coordination and precision that had been unthinkable mere months prior. The new anti-tank and anti-aircraft weaponry proved to be devastatingly effective, cutting through Russian armored columns and neutralizing their air superiority. The battles for key cities such as Kherson, Mariupol, and Melitopol were fierce, with Ukrainian forces employing a mixture of guerilla tactics and conventional warfare to dislodge their adversaries. In each engagement, the superior technology and unwavering resolve of the Ukrainian military proved to be deciding factors. As the Russians fled from these urban centers, their losses mounted at an alarming rate, in terms of both lives and materiel.

The breaking point came as the Ukrainian forces reached the land bridge itself. With defeat looming large, the morale of the Russian troops began to crumble. Exhausted and facing a relentless onslaught, large numbers of Russian soldiers chose to surrender rather than continue fighting. These captured troops were treated with respect and dignity, as per the rules of the Geneva Convention, and were transported to prisoner-of-war camps in western Ukraine.

As the dust settled and the smoke cleared, the enormity of the Ukrainian counteroffensive became apparent. The strategic land bridge had been severed, and Russian forces had been expelled from all occupied territories save for Crimea itself. The people of Ukraine rejoiced at the sight of their flag flying over liberated cities, while the international community hailed the operation as a resounding success.

The thunder of retribution had sounded across the land, showcasing the spirit of the Ukrainian people and the power of unity and resolve in the face of adversity. Yet, as the world watched, it was clear that the struggle for the region was far from over.

~

As the tide of Ukrainian retribution swept back across their beleaguered nation, the gaze of its resolute people turned toward the jewel of the Black Sea: Sevastopol. Nestled in the rocky embrace of Crimea's southern coast, this storied city had long been a bastion of Russian power in the region, a symbol of domination and defiance. Now, in the final phase of the counteroffensive, the Ukrainian military prepared to bring the fight to the invaders' stronghold.

The battle for Sevastopol proved to be the most daunting and grueling challenge faced by the Ukrainian forces, as they confronted the full might of the Russian military machine, entrenched within a fortress-like enclave. The city's defenses had been bolstered steadily over the years, its harbor containing a veritable armada of warships, submarines, and coastal batteries.

When Ukrainian forces encircled the city, they were met with a formidable array of Russian firepower. In the face of such overwhelming odds, many armies would have hesitated, but the Ukrainian soldiers, unyielding and steadfast, pressed forward, employing a cunning combination of land, sea, and air assaults to breach the enemy's defenses.

In the waters of the Black Sea, a flotilla of Ukrainian naval vessels, augmented by American support, engaged the Russian fleet in a pitched battle. Aerial dogfights between fighter jets filled the skies, while the percussion of artillery duels echoed throughout the contested city. The fighting on land was equally intense. Ukrainian infantry, supported by armored columns, descended from the north, clashing with Russian defenders in a brutal street-by-street struggle for control. Every building, every alleyway, became a crucible of courage and sacrifice. The superior training and advanced weaponry of the Ukrainian forces proved invaluable as they slowly, inexorably pushed the Russian defenders back.

As the days of the siege turned into weeks, the once imposing Russian bastion began to fall apart. Supplies dwindled, and the beleaguered defenders found themselves cut off from any hope of reinforcement. The end, when it came, was swift and decisive. Ukrainian forces, sensing the enemy's desperation, launched a final assault that broke the back of the Russian resistance.

As the Ukrainian flag was raised over the liberated city, a great cry of triumph and relief resounded through the streets of Sevastopol. The final vestiges of Russian occupation had been expunged, and the people of Crimea welcomed their liberators with open arms.

Yet the scars of war remained, a somber reminder of the price paid by those who had fought for freedom. For Ukraine, the battle for Sevastopol would be forever etched into their history, a testament to the indomitable spirit of a nation reborn. Though they faced an uncertain future, they did so with the knowledge that they had confronted the forces of tyranny and emerged victorious.

RUSSIAN PLAY

Laura Roberts and Tom Michaels had been working for years to protect America's national security. As two of the top intelligence officers in the country, they had seen it all, from cyberattacks to terrorism to espionage. But in recent years, they had become increasingly concerned about the ties between Russia, China, and the global Bitcoin market. Meeting with their team in a conference room at the NSA one day, Laura and Tom began outlining where things currently stood.

Laura began "it all started with those seemingly harmless clues. Reports of Russian and Chinese hackers targeting Bitcoin exchanges and mining operations, making off with millions of dollars in digital currency".

Tom continued, "Yeah, and then we heard whispers about Russian and Chinese investors pouring billions into Bitcoin, driving up its value. That's when things started to click for us".

Laura summarized, "But what really set off the alarm bells were the events of the past few years. The Russian invasions of Ukraine, both in 2014 and 2021. It's become clear that Russia and China are using Bitcoin to assert their economic dominance and wage economic warfare against Western democracies".

Tom added, "Exactly. By accumulating massive amounts of Bitcoin, they could disrupt global markets, destabilize economies, and create chaos and confusion"

Laura continued "And let's not forget the global pandemic. We discovered a connection there too. China initially tried to cover up the outbreak, downplaying the severity of the crisis while heavily investing in Bitcoin. It was a calculated move to further their economic goals"

Tom added "The pandemic was being used to create chaos and disruption in Western democracies, creating the perfect conditions for a massive transfer of wealth from West to East."

Laura concluded "All these clues lead to a dark and sinister truth. Russia and China are using Bitcoin as a weapon on the world stage, waging economic warfare. The stakes couldn't be higher."

Tom reminded the team "We know we can't act on our suspicions without concrete evidence. So we've been investigating tirelessly, gathering intelligence from every possible source, government agencies, private companies, and individual hackers. But our hard work has paid off. Laura was able to connect with the architect of the scheme."

~

Laura's first encounter with Sergey Kuznetsov came during her investigation into Russia's clandestine Bitcoin mining operation. When she intercepted encrypted communications between Sergey and his superiors in the FSB, Laura was intrigued by his brilliant cryptographic work and soon realized that he, (rather than Melnik) might hold the key to unraveling Petrov's grand scheme.

Reaching out to Sergey was a risky move, but Laura was determined to find the truth behind Russia's secret operation. She skillfully encrypted a covert message, using Sergey's own cryptographic techniques to pique his interest. Upon receiving the message, Sergey was both impressed and intrigued by Laura's ingenuity. He cautiously replied, curious to know more about the person who had managed to crack his code. As the two began to communicate in secret, Laura discovered that Sergey was not only a brilliant cryptographer but a disillusioned and resentful genius who felt unappreciated by his government and overshadowed by Petrov's inner circle. She appealed to Sergey's ego and resentment, suggesting that they work together to expose the truth and bring Petrov's plot to light. Finally, someone was giving Sergey the recognition he craved, and they might even be able to protect his creation from Petrov's dangerous hands.

Over time, Laura and Sergey forged a bond built from their shared desire to reveal the truth and their appreciation for each other's intellectual prowess. Laura provided Sergey with evidence of the depravity of Russia's actions in Ukraine, as well as the damage caused by the secret Bitcoin mining operation, both to the global financial system and to the people of Russia. Slowly but surely, Sergey's loyalty to his country began to waver as he saw the extent of the corruption and deception perpetrated by Petrov and his inner circle.

The turning point came when Sergey discovered that his beautiful Russian accomplice, the FSB agent Olga Ivanov, who had long been his sole confidante and source of support, had been tasked with monitoring his activities and ensuring his loyalty to Petrov. The FSB purposely disclosing this "truth "to drive a wedge between Olga and Sergey. Feeling betrayed and furious, Sergey decided to join forces with Laura, turning against his government in a bid to expose the truth and bring the architects of the Satoshi Conspiracy to justice.

~

Emerging from the tapestry of cloak and dagger that bound the FSB's shadowy dominion, the figure of Olga Ivanov towered with an alluring mix of danger and beauty. A woman of formidable intellect and athletic prowess, she had become an essential cog in the Russian intelligence machinery. Her latest task: to ensure that Sergey Kuznetsov, a mathematics prodigy, and the state's secret weapon, stayed faithful to the Motherland's cause.

However, behind the cloak of the obedient agent was a woman haunted by her past and driven by a mission to protect her family. Her mother, Yuliya Ivanov, had become a political prisoner, her voice of dissent against the Russian leadership silenced behind the stone walls of a maximum- security facility. The loss of Yuliya's son, Pavel, in the brutal Afghan war and the disintegration of the Soviet Union had only amplified her protests, leading her to a fate shared with the famous dissident Alexei Nostrov.

As an FSB agent, Olga managed to secure marginally better conditions for her mother within the bleak and formidable prison. The proposition to monitor Sergey, her childhood friend, was initially met with resistance. Yet, when her loyalty to the state was questioned, Olga had no choice but to acquiesce. She had deep feelings for Sergey, and a fond nostalgia for a simpler, happier time when they, along with Pavel, were just children. Every moment with Sergey was a reminder of a past that was no more, but every move she made was a bid to secure a future for her mother. Now suffering through Moscow's freezing winters, Olga had faced her fair share of challenges. The loss of her brother and the imprisonment of her mother shaped her character, toughening her spirit in a world that offers little mercy. However, beneath her cold exterior lay a soul yearning for tranquility, warmth, and the enlightenment of the heart—a yearning that found solace during her five-year assignment in the sun-drenched paradise of Cuba. As the primary representative of Russian power in the Americas, Cuba hosted a significant presence of the FSB. Throughout her time stationed there, Olga discovered an inexplicable attraction to the island's vibrant beauty, where lush landscapes and boundless skies filled her with awe and a sense of belonging that she had never experienced amidst the icy expanses of her homeland.

Despite the natural magnetism of her beauty, Olga was a seasoned actress in the theatre of deception. Although she was Sergey's closest confidante, Olga disclosed very little of her conversations with Sergey.

Her charade satisfying her superiors' interest so long as she assured them Sergey was working 24/7 on Petrov's behalf.

The suggestion of a vacation to Cuba from Sergey sparked a glimmer of interest in Olga. An opportunity to return to her cherished island and reconnect with her past associates was tempting. She assented to the proposition, and as they prepared for their journey to Cuba's sun-kissed shores, they unwittingly set the stage for a plot thick with intrigue, desire, and deception,

~

In a world consumed by ambition and deceit, the tendrils of love and longing sought to find purchase amid the rocky soil of intrigue. It was in this uncertain landscape that Laura discovered Sergey's unrequited passion for the enigmatic Olga Ivanov. Sergey was feeling increasingly disillusioned with his life in Russia. Treated with disdain, forced to work for evil, and his parents unfairly imprisoned, he yearned for a chance to escape the suffocating confines of his existence.

Laura sought to exploit Sergey's simmering discontent to secure the precious private keys to Petrov's digital vaults. As the two moved through their delicate dance of manipulation and desire, she discovered the one thing that captured Sergey's imagination: the prospect of a life with Olga beyond the cold shores of Russia. He viewed Cuba as a ripe fruit just out of reach, but Laura proposed a second destination, which would offer the promise of freedom and a new beginning: Key West. This suggestion struck a chord in Sergey's heart, for Olga herself had once confessed a fondness for this tropical paradise second only to her devotion to her beloved Cuba.

Emboldened by the prospect of finally winning Olga's heart and escaping the shadow of Russia's oppressive regime, Sergey agreed to a clandestine rendezvous in Key West with Laura. In exchange for the Satoshi Hoard private keys, he would receive the deed to a home in Key West, political asylum, and a lifetime stipend to ensure his continued comfort and security.

As Laura and Tom worked feverishly to navigate the labyrinthine bureaucracy of the State Department and secure the necessary arrangements for Sergey's escape, they maintained a careful veneer of secrecy. Worried that Olga might still be loyal to the Kremlin, they urged Sergey to keep the plans hidden from her until the moment they set foot upon the sands of Key West.

~

In the swirling vortex of power and politics, Sergey and Laura found themselves drawn into a web of passion and deceit. Sergey, trapped in a life of unfulfilled dreams and seething resentment, saw in Laura a way out. And Laura, determined to secure the keys to Petrov's virtual vault, exploited Sergey's affection for Olga.

With the promise of a new life in Key West, away from Russia's oppressive clutches, Sergey found himself ensnared in Laura's plot. In return for protecting his creation and a chance at love, he had to betray Petrov and grant Laura the keys to the vast wealth of Satoshi's hoard.

Laura's palms were damp as she dialed the number. The secure, encrypted line was the only link she had with Sergey. She could hear the anticipation in Sergey's voice as he picked up the call.

"Laura," he greeted. His voice was calm, but Laura sensed an undercurrent of tension.

"Sergey, we need to act fast," she warned, her voice dropping into a lower register." We don't have much time. Olga needs to convince Petrov to allow you to travel to Cuba, even if it means relinquishing complete control of the Satoshi Hoard."

"Petrov wants that more than anything, so that will undoubtedly be the condition," Sergey admitted, a hard-edge creeping into his tone. "But it's a risk we have to take. I'll give him access, but he won't be able to touch the Bitcoin without attracting global attention, and I will ensure that I can regain access to the Satoshi Hoard."

"Good," Laura acknowledged, the relief audible in her voice.

"Now we need to focus on getting you out of Russia."

She heard Sergey draw in a deep breath on the other end of the line. "What's the plan?"

"You already suggested the trip to her, now Olga needs to get you both to Cuba," she explained.

Sergey's voice was thoughtful when he replied. "Olga is still loyal to the FSB, Laura. I can't tell her about the escape plan yet."

"I understand," Laura assured him, her heart pounding. "Just keep up appearances for now. Once you're in Cuba, we'll arrange a boat to take you to Key West."

Laura could hear Sergey's breathing slow down on the other end. "Key West, huh?" he mused, a hint of excitement coloring his voice.

"Yes," Laura confirmed, a smile playing on her lips. "You'll be safe there. We're working with our contacts at the State Department to ensure you'll be granted political asylum."

"And Olga?" Sergey asked, concern creeping into his voice.

"We'll do our best to ensure she's safe, too," Laura promised. "But we need to move quickly, Sergey. Are you ready?"

There was a pause, then a single, determined word echoed back at her. "Yes."

With that confirmation, Laura was set into motion, her mind racing with plans and contingencies. She knew this was the most dangerous part of their plan, but it was also their only chance to bring down Petrov's plot. They were about to ignite a chain reaction that would ripple through the world, and for the first time, Laura felt hopeful that they could really pull it off.

Laura quickly hung up the phone, her hands shaking. Each call and each word they shared was a risk, but they were all necessary gambles.

"Tom, we're moving ahead," she informed her partner, who had been waiting impatiently on the edge of the conversation.

Tom gave a short nod, pulling out his phone. "I'll arrange the boat. We'll use one of our smuggler contacts in Cuba. The FSB can't know we're involved."

As Tom busied himself with the arrangements, Laura turned her attention back to Sergey. He was their key to unlocking the Satoshi Hoard and exposing Petrov's conspiracy. They needed to keep him safe, not just for their mission, but because he was one of the few who could decipher the tangled web of cryptocurrency that Petrov had entwined around Russia's economy. If anything happened to him...

No, Laura wouldn't let that happen. They had a plan. Sergey would get out of Russia, meet her in Key West, and they'd start the process of tearing Petrov's operation apart, bit by bit.

On the other end, Sergey ended the call and stared at the blank screen. It was official. He was going to betray his country to protect his creation and to expose the truth. Olga... he couldn't bear to think of her reaction. But it was the only way. And if he could secure a better life for her, it would be worth it.

~

Olga's high heels clicked across the polished floors of Petrov's grand office as she approached the formidable man. His stony face softened slightly as he looked up from his files and saw her standing in front of his desk.

"Olga, to what do I owe this pleasure?" He asked, his tone smooth as he studied her.

"Mr., President, we need to talk about Sergey." Olga began, keeping her voice steady.

"Ah, our prodigious mathematician. What about him?" He queried, his eyes not leaving her face.

"He's stressed, Mr., President. Overworked. He hasn't been sleeping, and I fear he might be on the brink of a breakdown." Olga spoke, her words punctuated with concern.

Petrov leaned back in his chair, considering her words. "Is he faltering in his tasks? Is he a liability?"

"No, not at all." Olga was quick to reassure him. "His loyalty to Russia has been reaffirmed. He's fully cooperating with our goals. It's just that the development of Tarasque has taken a toll on him.

A vacation could do wonders. He needs some time to rejuvenate."

"A vacation?" Petrov scoffed, "Now is not the time for a vacation. The plan is nearing fruition."

"But that's exactly why he needs it, Mr., President." Olga persisted. "You need him at his 100%. A brief reprieve could ensure that. Two weeks in Cuba. It's all he needs."

Petrov stared at her for a moment, his gaze probing. Finally, he sighed, "Very well. But there is a condition. Before he will be allowed to leave Russia, I must have sole access to the Satoshi Hoard."

Olga felt her heart clench at the demand, but she gave a curt nod. "Very well, Mr., President. To ensure his loyalty to Russia, I will convince Sergey to hand over the keys."

And with that, the deal was sealed. The countdown to a dangerous game had begun.

The next few days passed in a blur for Sergey. He played the part of the loyal servant, bowing to Petrov's demands and granting him control of the Satoshi Hoard. Inside, however, his mind was already on the move, preparing for the daring escape.

~

Up to now, Sergey maintained control over the Satoshi Hoard. Petrov had initially demanded a copy of the private key from Sergey, but he remained confident that, since Satoshi Nakamoto's disappearance in 2011, Sergey would be unable to transfer any of the Bitcoins stored within the hoard, especially with the entire world closely watching. Technically, until now, they had shared access to the Satoshi Hoard, but Petrov now insisted on having exclusive access.

The air was thick with tension when Sergey walked into Petrov's office. The weight of the world seemed to press down upon them, the stakes so high that even a small mistake could spell catastrophe.

Petrov's icy gaze met Sergey's as he began, "Sergey, I've been giving some thought to our next move. It's time to unleash the Russia-only controlled version of Tarasque."

Sergey stiffened, "But sir, we discussed this. It could destabilize the Bitcoin network, turning the entire Bitcoin community against us."

Petrov waved a dismissive hand, "The risks are worth the rewards. We can control the network."

But Sergey was adamant, "We already have enough control, sir. The Satoshi Hoard is ours. With the other Bitcoins Russia controls, that's over 2 million Bitcoins. We don't need to force centralization. We can exercise influence without arising suspicions."

Petrov paused, considering Sergey's words. He had always valued Sergey's counsel. "And what of China?" he asked, his voice tight.

"We continue with the plan, sir," Sergey suggested, "As far as they know, Tarasque is ready to be deployed any day now. They have no reason to suspect anything different."

Petrov nodded, "What about the additional Bitcoins China has been accumulating? Can we seize them?"

Sergey paused, weighing his words carefully before speaking words that would further cement his value to Petrov, "Yes, sir. I believe I can develop an approach to gain access to their Bitcoin holdings. It will not be easy, but I am confident it's achievable."

Petrov's eyes gleamed with satisfaction, "Then get to work on it, Sergey. I know you need the vacation but if you don't want your trip to Cuba cancelled, you will report good news to me before you will be allowed to leave."

As Petrov dismissed him, Sergey hesitated, "Sir, there's something else you should know. I'm working on a new algorithm, one that allows us to change the private key of a Bitcoin wallet without disturbing the public key. I call it 'ReKey'."

Petrov raised an eyebrow, "Meaning?"

Sergey held his gaze, "Meaning, if someone steals our wallets and has our private keys, we can change the key without anyone's knowledge.

Petrov leaned back in his chair, a slow grin spreading across his face, "Sergey, you never cease to amaze me. I knew I could count on your loyalty."

As Sergey left the office, he knew he had won a battle, but the war was far from over.

~

Petrov sat in his lavish office within the Kremlin, his mind consumed by concerns surrounding Sergey's potential ability to outwit them and retain control over the cryptocurrency wallets. Seeking reassurance, he summoned his head of cyber security, Oleg Melnik, to discuss the matter at hand.

Melnik, known for his arrogance and unwavering self-assurance, entered the room with a confident stride. He firmly believed that he was far superior in intellect to Sergey and felt compelled to put Petrov's worries to rest. With a self-assured grin, Melnik began addressing Petrov's concerns.

"Rest assured, sir," Melnik declared, a hint of superiority in his voice. "Once Sergey surrenders exclusive control of the wallets and we have them in our Vault, there will be no way for him to access the Bitcoins. The good news you sought to allow his trip to Cuba came with Sergey's delivery to me of the final Taresque code, which I can release at any time. We hold the upper hand."

Petrov leaned forward; his eyes fixed on Melnik. "But Sergey once mentioned something called the private seed," Petrov interjected, his voice tinged with concern. "He claimed it could recreate all the wallets if we lost access to the hard drives. Is that true?"

Melnik chuckled dismissively. "I've anticipated that scenario, sir," he replied confidently. "As you directed, I compelled Sergey to relinquish the private key to the wallet containing the Satoshi Hoard and the crucial part is that I am the sole possessor of the written copy of that 64-character code. Without that, accessing the Satoshi Hoard is impossible."

A glimmer of relief flickered in Petrov's eyes, but he couldn't help but harbor lingering doubts. "What if Sergey memorized those characters or developed a way to change the Private Key?" he asked cautiously.

Melnik's confident expression didn't waver. "Absolutely impossible, sir," he countered swiftly. "No human mind is capable of such a feat. Besides, I have all the knowledge required to manage your Bitcoin holdings at this point. Perhaps it's time we eliminated Sergey and put your mind at ease."

Petrov's face remained impassive; his thoughts conflicted. The notion of permanently silencing Sergey sent shivers down his spine, but the idea of securing their control over the wealth was even more enticing. After a brief moment of contemplation, Petrov made up his mind.

"Yes," Petrov concurred, his voice cold and resolute. "Sergey will have his final vacation. I granted him permission to go to Cuba because I had arranged that he would never return alive."

~

The quiet reverberation of their sinister scheme hung in the air, an unspoken weight that throbbed with dark anticipation. Petrov's gaze returned to the panoramic view of the Moscow skyline outside his office window, his mind already wandering to the next steps of their plan. Melnik, left in the shadows of Petrov's imposing figure, let a triumphant grin seep into his stern expression. Control over the Satoshi Hoard, and by extension, a significant part of the Bitcoin network, would soon be theirs.

Petrov, however, was not lost in a vision of grandeur. Instead, his thoughts turned back to Sergey and his unexpected accomplice, Olga. The brazen programmer and the fiercely intelligent woman had become dangerous thorns in his side. Their brilliance was an undeniable threat to his plans, and he pondered over how best to leverage their skills without giving them a chance to topple his carefully laid schemes.

His thoughts turned to the infamous IK- 6 prison. Both Olga's mother and Sergey's parents were held there, their freedom forfeited as collateral for the young tech-savants' cooperation. As further insurance, Petrov would arrange for Olga's father to join them in the same dreaded prison, also inhabited by Alexei Nostrov, a staunch critic of Petrov's rule. Sergey and Olga's options were surely limited with their families imprisoned some 200 kilometers away from Moscow. Petrov could almost taste the sweetness of his forthcoming triumph.

Yet, Petrov knew that, with intellects such as Sergey's and Olga's, certainty was a fleeting luxury. He turned his icy gaze back towards Melnik, his tone steady and relentless. "See that every possibility is accounted for, Melnik. We have too much to lose."

Melnik gave a curt nod, continuing ominously. "Sir. I assure you we have sufficient insurance for their loyalties. They will be helpless."

With that, Petrov dismissed Melnik, a wolfish smile creeping onto his face as the door to his office closed. The chessboard was set, the pawns in their place, and the time had come for Petrov to make his play. The Bitcoin revolution would soon be within his grasp, the fate of Russia hanging in the balance.

The room fell silent, heavy with the weight of their conspiratorial intentions. Petrov's decision had been made, and the wheels of a dark plot were set into motion.

~

The corridors of the Kremlin were filled with unease, the once lively and bustling halls now eerily quiet. Whispers of betrayal and treachery slithered through the air as paranoia tightened its icy grip on the Russian government. President Vladimir Petrov, once a figure of strength and control, found himself isolated and haunted by failure. The debacle in Ukraine shattered his reputation on the world stage and ignited a fire of dissent among his own people.

As mistrust festered within him, Petrov saw enemies in every shadow, and every whispered conversation became a plot against him. He employed a personal food taster, much like the medieval Popes of old, fearing that even his most loyal servants might be tempted to slip poison into his meals. With each day, he retreated further into his private quarters, the walls closing in around him as his once untouchable empire began to crumble.

Amid the darkness of his downfall, there remained only a single ray of hope—Bitcoin. The cryptocurrency, secretly nurtured and harvested by the Russian government under Petrov's watchful eye, had experienced a dramatic surge in value. China's unexpected change of heart and their subsequent mass purchasing of the digital currency had driven its price to astronomical heights, and with Russia using nuclear power to mine Bitcoin, their stockpile had grown to an immense fortune.

The only ones aware of this incredible wealth were Petrov, Zhang Wei, Sergey Kuznetsov, Oleg Melnik, Tom Michaels, and Laura Roberts. Now, with the Russian propaganda machine baying for his blood, Petrov was desperate to reveal his ace in the hole. If he could demonstrate the vast economic power that the Bitcoin reserves bestowed upon Russia, he would silence his critics and reaffirm his position as an indomitable leader.

Summoning Kuznetsov to his office, Petrov demanded a plan to showcase Russian control over all of their Bitcoins without risking the loss of the precious cryptocurrency. Kuznetsov proposed the use of a digital signature authenticated by Petrov's private keys. By signing the transactions with his unique code, Petrov could prove his dominion over the immense fortune without relinquishing any of the assets themselves.

With no alternative in sight, Petrov agreed to Kuznetsov's plan. He knew he should never trust another soul with his private keys, but his survival depended on the success of this endeavor. As Kuznetsov turned to leave the dimly lit chamber, Petrov's steely gaze bored into him. Both of their fates rested on the success of the plan.

~

Petrov strode down a long dark hallway toward a secret vault. The guards stationed at the entrance stepped aside to allow him through, and the heavy steel door slid open with a deafening rumble. Inside the vault, Petrov approached a large safe that had been concealed behind a false wall. He entered a series of codes into the keypad and turned the combination lock, causing the door to swing open with a metallic groan.

Before him lay a sight that would have made any Bitcoin enthusiast gasp in awe. There, stacked high in neat rows, were countless drives containing the digital currency that had taken the world by storm. For years, Russia had been quietly accumulating Bitcoin, both through mining operations and through more nefarious means. Now Petrov had decided to make a bold move. Sergey had electronically coded the word "Petrov" over all of Russia's Bitcoin stash, as well as the elusive Satoshi Hoard, proving to the world that Vladimir Vladimirovich Petrov controlled over 15% of the total Bitcoin in circulation.

Petrov entered a digital code Sergey had provided him, and the Bitcoin blockchain was forever altered.

~

Satoshi had returned! And apparently, he was working with Russia. The Genesis Block and millions of Bitcoins had been signed "Petrov" At once, the eyes of the world were fixed upon the Bitcoin Blockchain. The Chinese and their North Korean hackers were especially quick to react, launching a major cyber-attack in an attempt to gain control of the wallets with their priceless cargo. The attack was relentless, with sophisticated algorithms and brute-force tactics aimed at breaching the security protocols that protected the stash.

But Petrov was one step ahead. Sergey had anticipated the attack and put in place a series of countermeasures to protect the hoard of Bitcoins from any would-be intruders. As the hackers tried in vain to gain access to the wallet, they were met by a barrage of firewalls, encryption codes, and other security measures that proved impossible to crack.

The attack was ultimately unsuccessful, but it did expose to the world Russia's control of not only the Satoshi Hoard but another huge cache (soon nicknamed the Petrov Hoard) that had been accumulated over the past decade, mostly through mining but also through theft and direct purchasing. For the first time, the world confronted the reality of a major world power holding a huge portion of the world's most valuable currency. Questions were raised about the ethics of such an accumulation, and fears were stoked about the potential for such a concentration of power.

Petrov remained defiant. He saw the Bitcoin hoards as a valuable asset for Russia, one that could be used to cement his place on the world stage and provide a bulwark against economic instability. As he closed the vault door behind him, he knew he had taken a bold step toward securing his future.

~

The revelation of Petrov's proof of control of over two million Bitcoins sent shockwaves through the world. It was a day when the balance of power began to lurch, subtly yet inexorably. And amid this shift, Laura and Tom grappled with a new set of challenges. Their efforts to secure asylum for Sergey Kuznetsov had taken on a new urgency, as the forces that sought to control the enigmatic genius closed in around them.

Laura's assertion that Sergey was, in fact, Satoshi Nakamoto now appeared more credible than ever. This revelation had stirred the State Department into action, as they recognized the invaluable asset that Sergey represented. Petrov's arrogant assumption of control over the Satoshi Hoard strengthened the resolve of those who sought to protect Sergey and his secrets.

Blinded by his own hubris, Petrov believed that he had secured the keys to the kingdom—or, more accurately, the keys to the Satoshi Hoard. Little did he know that Sergey, a master of misdirection and subterfuge, had engineered a means to regain control of the vast fortune, regardless of his physical proximity to the Kremlin vault.

Once Sergey and Olga were enroute to Cuba, Petrov sent out new orders: their lives were forfeit once they had outlived their usefulness The icy grip of the FSB closed around the unsuspecting pair. But all was not lost: Laura and Tom had concocted a daring plan to spirit Sergey and Olga from Cuba away to the safety of Key West. They had established contact with a network of covert American agents who had been operating in Cuba for years, their identities closely guarded and their loyalties certain.

As the wheels of this audacious plot began to turn, the stage was set for a confrontation that would determine the fate of not only Sergey and Olga but also the future of the world as they knew it.

RETURN TO KEY WEST

Laura's heart leapt with joy upon hearing of Sergey's departure from Russia. The stars seemed to have aligned, and destiny appeared to be guiding them toward a fateful encounter. With haste, Laura planned a journey with Tom to the shores of the idyllic island of Key West. Excitement coursed through her veins as she reserved seats on a US Government Gulfstream, knowing that the culmination of their mission was at hand.

Laura's excitement was contagious. As she picked up the phone to share the news with her sister, her voice was brimming with elation. "Georgie, Tom, and I are heading down to Key West again to meet up with his old friends, Olga and Sergey. They're visiting from Russia, and it's going to be quite the reunion!"

Georgie, always eager for a new adventure, was swept up in the tide of her enthusiasm. "That's amazing, Laura! I can't believe you're visiting again so soon!"

As the sisters chatted, Laura could barely contain her excitement. The knowledge that she would soon secure the keys to the Satoshi Hoard while also being able to provide Sergey with a new life as John

Kinsley, an American citizen, filled her with a sense of purpose and anticipation.

In the days leading up to their departure, Laura and Tom made careful preparations for their rendezvous in Key West. They reviewed their plans in detail, ensuring that every aspect of the operation was flawless. Their mission was of the utmost importance, and they knew that even the smallest misstep could have dire consequences. The tension in the air was palpable. But for Laura, the prospect of success outweighed any fear or uncertainty. As she looked forward to her upcoming journey, her heart swelled with the hope that they would soon bring about a brighter future for all.

~

The sultry Caribbean air embraced Sergey and Olga as they set foot on Cuban soil, a world away from their icy homeland. As they ventured deeper into the sun-kissed landscape, memories of days long past stirred in Olga's heart.

A warm reception awaited them, as Olga's former FSB comrades welcomed their erstwhile compatriot with open arms. The years had done little to weaken the bonds forged during their time together on this tropical isle. Sergey was travelling under his Pavel Ivanov passport, just in case anyone still remembered the name Sergey Kuznetsov. Laughter rang out through the night, as Olga and her friends reminisced about their daring escapades to the fabled shores of Key West. Undeterred by the strictures of their homeland, they had defied convention and risked all in pursuit of the freedom and revelry that lay just ninety miles to the north.

The mention of Key West ignited a fire in Olga's soul: she longed for the warmth and excitement that the island paradise offered. And it was not long before she learned, to her delight, that her friends still made clandestine excursions to the place dear to her heart.

With the prospect of a journey to Key West now tantalizingly within reach, Olga shared her desire to visit Key West with Sergey.

Sergey agreed, delighted by this alignment with his own secret arrangements and buoyed by Laura's promise of safety—telling Olga he had already arranged the trip before they had left Russia.

Soon, with the help of Laura and her web of contacts, Sergey came into possession of a mysterious package containing the key to their escape: a thousand American dollars and a Visa card bearing the name John Kinsley. And so, the groundwork was laid for their daring escape.

~

The warm Caribbean night unfurled like a velvet tapestry, studded with distant stars. Sergey and Olga readied themselves for a journey across the sea. As they boarded the clandestine go-fast boat, a sense of anticipation and danger electrified the air.

As the boat cut through the sultry Caribbean darkness, unknown to them, a figure stood at the secluded dock, gazing at the departing boat with suspicion. The FSB agent who had been tasked to keep a close eye on Olga didn't recognize the boat - it was not one of the vessels they typically used for their surreptitious trips to Key West. His instincts tingled ominously.

In a matter of moments, the man and his FSB team were roaring into the night, the powerful engine of their own go-fast boat a deafening challenge to the quiet stillness. As they gained on their quarry, the dim silhouette of the escaping boat grew larger in their sight.

Meanwhile, on board their vessel, Olga and Sergey were suddenly jolted by the sound of gunfire. The tranquility of their escape shattered by the shrill sound of bullets piercing the night. A quick glance over her shoulder confirmed Olga's worst fears - they were being pursued.

Sweat trickled down the drivers brow as he fought to maintain control of the boat amidst the flying bullets. Their smuggler crew, who had signed up for a simple transportation job, were now considering cutting their engines, fearing for their lives.

Just when the situation seemed to spiral into chaos, the roar of a helicopter overhead pierced the night, its spotlight illuminating the churning waters around them. Sergey craned his neck to see the insignia of the US Coast Guard emblazoned on the underbelly of the helicopter.

The chopper had been dispatched from the US CGC Thetis, a 270 ft Famous class cutter, out of Key West that had been quietly lying in wait near the international border line. As the helicopter swooped closer to the water, a loudspeaker blared out a warning, demanding the chasing vessel to halt its pursuit.

When the warning was ignored, a deafening roar echoed through the night. The Coast Guard helicopter had deployed its 50-caliber machine gun, aiming for the outboard engines of the chasing boat. Within seconds, the high-powered slugs had shredded the engines, leaving the FSB agents stranded, their vessel dead in the water.

As the dust settled, Olga and Sergey, unharmed but shaken, breathed a sigh of relief. Their future was uncertain, but for the moment, they were safe, speeding away from the chaos behind them and into the welcoming arms of a Key West sunrise.

~

Laura, nervously flipping through a dossier containing a new identity for Sergey Kuznetsov, now John Kinsley, felt the weight of her plan all over again. With each document—a passport awaiting a photograph, the deed to a charming conch house on Elizabeth Street—the operation became more real. Laura had also secured a lifetime stipend for Sergey of $3,000 per month, the first installment of which lay in crisp notes inside a secured briefcase. Everything was set, waiting at a secure location in Key West that was guarded by unseen NSA operatives.

Tom and Laura had arrived on the island earlier in the day and were escorted to secure quarters, an innocuous-looking building that belied the high-level operation it housed. Down the hall another room was ready for Sergey, soon to be John. The air was heavy with anticipation as their intricate plan was set in motion.

The next day Sergey and Olga were to arrive by boat, docking at a private slip reserved next to Fort Zachary Taylor. The strategic location, owned by the US government, offered an easy escape route, and was conveniently situated near downtown Key West, a stone's throw from Sergey's soon-to-be home.

The plan was not without its complications. Sergey had not yet revealed to Olga that their departure from Cuba was a permanent one. He feared her reaction and the possibility of her refusing to leave Russia behind. This secret placed an extra layer of complexity on the already intricate operation, compounded by the fact that Laura and Tom were intent on addressing Sergey as John from the moment of his arrival, to avoid unnecessary danger.

Georgie, Laura's sister, was unaware of the tensions simmering beneath the surface of the planned reunion. All she knew was that she was meeting a couple named Sergey and Olga for drinks on Duval Street. When she received a message that they would now be meeting "John" and Olga, she didn't ask any questions. She knew that her sister and Tom were involved in matters far beyond her understanding, and she trusted their judgment.

As the sun set, Laura looked out over the idyllic landscape, her mind buzzing with anticipation, apprehension, and hope. The next day would bring with it a new dawn, not just for Key West but for Sergey and for them all. The new identity, the stipend, the house—it was all a carefully crafted illusion but one set to become reality. As they moved forward, she was acutely aware of the risks involved but also of the immense potential for a new beginning.

~

As the remnants of their dramatic escape were swallowed by the dark expanse of the Florida Straits, the reality of their situation began to descend upon Sergey and Olga. Underneath the blanket of the night sky, only occasionally pierced by the coast guard chopper's searchlight,

Sergey guided Olga away from the curious gazes of their Cuban crew.

Breaking the quiet tension that had blanketed them, Sergey's voice cut through the roaring sound of the boat's engines. "Listen carefully, Olga. I'm no longer Sergey, from this point forward, you should know me as John Kinsley."

His words crashed into Olga like the sea spray whipping against the hull. This wasn't a mere alias for a covert operation. This was a fundamental shift, an absolute severance from their past lives. As the boat forged ahead, Sergey filled in the blanks of their impending existence in Key West, Florida. He spoke of the bargains struck with the American authorities, their sanctuary assured, and his conviction that this was their only path to wield their knowledge for a righteous cause.

Olga was trying to wrap her mind around the concept of this new world, a world of sun-drenched beaches and swaying palms, so radically different from the wintry boulevards of Moscow. It was a world that promised the allure of freedom and countless opportunities. Yet, it also filled her with unease. Among the swirling questions in her mind, one worry was paramount. "What about our parents, John?"

He looked at her, his gaze steady, offering a silent promise of protection. Sergey outlined his plan to orchestrate their parents' release from the noose of the Russian regime. He explained that the Americans held considerable influence, enough to negotiate their parents' freedom. In exchange, he would become an invaluable asset to the United States, providing critical information. He committed to leveraging all his resources to guarantee the safety of their parents.

Their hushed conversation was abruptly cut short by the ringing of Olga's phone. The screen displayed an encrypted message that made her heart freeze. "All agents return to your post immediately, massive explosion in China; all agents recalled to Moscow within 48 hours." The world seemed to be spiraling towards an unprecedented crisis, and they were caught right in the middle.

But there was no turning back now. Their past was a receding shadow on the horizon, and their future, albeit uncertain, lay ahead.

As the Floridian coastline loomed closer, the magnitude of their decisions washed over them. They were venturing into unknown waters, both literally and metaphorically, where the stakes had never been higher.

~

The boat slipped through the sapphire waters and arrived at a private pier on the southernmost tip of Key West. Sergey and Olga were greeted by a tall handsome man and a striking woman. The Cuban smugglers, despite their numerous visits to Key West, had never ventured to this secluded location. Their only desire now was to deliver their human cargo and make a swift departure.

As the boat bumped against the pier, the tall man reached out to steady Sergey. "You must be John," he murmured, his voice as warm as the tropical air. Sergey nodded, passing him their bags. Olga followed, stepping onto the solid ground of their new life.

The quartet moved toward an awaiting car flanked by two stern men. They journeyed a short distance to a nondescript building where a uniformed woman greeted them. She asked about weapons, and after she had apologetically conducted a brief search, the four were led to a comfortable room, completed with a spread of sandwiches and Russian pastries.

Another woman, this one in plain clothes, introduced herself as Linda and offered them drinks. She met Sergey's request for something stronger than coffee with a smile and a gesture toward a bottle of Stolichnaya vodka. They raised a toast— "To new friends and a better world"—and the clink of glasses followed by the burn of vodka served to ease the tension in the room.

As Linda slipped away, Laura took the lead. Her warm reassurances and promise of support eased the concerns of the newcomers. She invited Olga to voice her questions and concerns, a sentiment met with relief and a request for another glass of vodka.

Over the next three hours, the room echoed with stories and

quiet laughter. Olga relayed the message she had received on the boat, unsurprised to learn the Americans were already aware of the explosion in China. But her curiosity about their future was palpable. As the evening unfurled, a new reality began to take shape—far removed from their former lives, full of uncertainty, but also brimming with the promise of freedom and adventure.

~

After hours of debriefing the next day, everyone looked forward to dinner with Georgie in downtown Key West. They headed out after receiving a stern warning from the local intelligence services to be on the lookout for any familiar faces from Cuba.

The sun dipped below the horizon, casting long shadows on the bustling streets of Key West. With the languid sway of palm trees and the heady scent of sea air, the tropical island seemed an unlikely stage for spy games. Yet, as the group navigated the throngs of sunburned tourists, Olga recognized two men in the crowd who seemed to be following them. Danger lurked just beyond the warm embrace of the setting sun.

Sanctuary materialized in the form of Sloppy Joe's, a boisterous bar that promised respite and anonymity. With its worn wooden floors and cheerful din of laughter and talk, the establishment seemed a perfect hideaway. Yet, as they slipped into the welcoming shadows, Tom warned Laura and Georgie about the man Olga had seen: an FSB agent was dogging their steps.

A game of subterfuge and misdirection unfolded within the crowded bar as the agent, eyes narrowed and senses alert, moved ever closer to his quarry. But fate had other plans, and in a moment of inspiration, Georgie called out a name that would change the course of their evening: "Ryan!"

At the utterance of this single word, the bar erupted into a frenzy of excitement as a wave of eager tourists surged forward, believing the handsome actor Ryan Reynolds to be in their midst. The FSB agent, caught off guard by the sudden commotion, was swept away in the tide of jostling bodies and flashing cameras.

The noise, the crowd, and the confusion were all gifts. Grabbing John and Olga by the arms, Laura guided them toward the side door of Sloppy Joe's. A glance over her shoulder confirmed that their pursuer was still entangled in the mob, his attention diverted. They slipped out into the warm night, the clamor of the bar receding behind them. The labyrinthine streets of Key West greeted them, along with the thrum of nightlife in the air. The teeming masses of tourists providing the perfect camouflage.

They moved swiftly, weaving through the crowd, their pace brisk but measured. It was crucial not to attract attention, to seem like just another trio of tourists intoxicated by the tropical allure of Key West. A glance shared between Laura, John, and Olga spoke volumes—alert, aware, but calm. This was not their first dance with danger.

Laura's fingers sped over her phone, firing off a quick message to Tom and Georgie. They were safe for now, heading back to the NSA facility. As the message zipped through the airwaves, Laura slipped the phone into her pocket, her gaze returning to the path ahead.

Despite the adrenaline that coursed through their veins, they couldn't help but notice the beauty of Key West at night. The palm-fringed streets were bathed in the warm glow of streetlamps, while the distant roar of the ocean provided a soothing soundtrack. It was a surreal contrast to their reality—a paradise with danger lurking in its shadows.

When they arrived at the NSA facility, the secure structure seemed a stark contrast to the carefree vibrancy of Key West. The door closed behind them with a soft click, and they felt a familiar rush of relief. They were safe, at least for now, and ready to face whatever lay ahead. After all, danger was a part of their lives, and they had learned to treat it lightly.

When Tom and Georgie finally returned, Georgie's presence breached too many protocols to count, but the five of them ignored these violations, drinking and laughing the night away. It wasn't the night they had chosen, but they made the best of what they were given. Tomorrow would most certainly bring more challenges, but for now they could wait.

~

As the night wore on, casting elongated shadows from the amber glow of the Key West streetlamps, Stanislav Petrov and Akim Zakharov reluctantly abandoned their pursuit. Orders from Moscow echoed in their ears, and they knew their time on this island paradise was drawing to an end. With heavy hearts and a shared sense of duty, they embarked on their final task in America: procuring a mountain of cigarettes.

Driven by the urgency of their mission, they scoured the local shops, their arms soon laden with cartons of American tobacco. Once their quarry was gathered, they made their way to the slip at the Key West City Marina. A sleek vessel awaited there, poised to whisk them back to Cuba.

Upon their arrival in Cuba, they joined the ranks of their fellow FSB agents. The island's contingent was preparing for their imminent departure. As the early morning light touched the horizon, an Aeroflot jet stood ready. Its engines hummed softly, preparing to ferry the agents back to the heart of their homeland.

As the jet soared through the skies, the agents exchanged weary glances, their thoughts consumed by the rapidly deteriorating world. Tension filled the cabin, the knowledge that the once-mighty Russian intelligence services now faced an uncertain future weighing heavily on their collective conscience.

Upon their arrival in Moscow, they were summoned to Lubyanka Square, the iconic headquarters of their storied organization. They gathered with their fellow agents in the heart of the city, a sea of stern faces and grim determination. They stood shoulder to shoulder, prepared to face the consequences of a world on the brink of catastrophe.

Then, in a single, earth-shattering moment, a thunderous explosion rocked the building. The force of the impact tore through the city's heart, obliterating everything in its path. In an instant, 95% of the FSB agents in the world were wiped from the face of the earth. Their fates sealed by the brutal hand of fate.

Back in Key West, John and Olga remained blissfully unaware of the cataclysmic event that had transpired across the globe. They reveled in their newfound sanctuary, with the tropical breeze carrying the distant echoes of a world on the precipice of change.

As the sun dipped below the horizon once more, the island held its breath. It stood poised between the promise of tranquility and the specter of danger. Yet, for Sergey and Olga, the future seemed a little less uncertain. Their enemies had been vanquished in a single, devastating stroke of luck. In the heart of paradise, they stood ready to embrace whatever lay ahead as the world continued to teeter on the edge of the unknown.

~

The frangipani trees were in their prime, as if touched by Midas himself. They burst into a riot of colors that painted the Meadows neighborhood of Key West with pink, red, white, yellow, and every shade in between. These blossoms, much like summer's fireworks, adorned the stems in clusters, each bloom reminiscent of an orchid, radiating a subtle yet intoxicating perfume that lingered in the air, a mélange of jasmine, citrus, and gardenia.

It was under the shadow of these trees, their fragrance a constant companion, that Tom and Laura took their daily walks, punctuated by the soft rustle of fallen blossoms underfoot, treasures that Tom would lovingly tuck behind Laura's ear. Their favorite frangipani, a riotous spectacle of pink and white, grew near their NSA-owned property in the front garden of a charming single-family home.

Their admiration for the tree did not go unnoticed. One day they caught the eye of the house's owner, Lucy Buffett. Known to all as LuLu, she was a vibrant character, a Key West staple and the sister of the town's famous son, Jimmy Buffett. The owner of a chain of successful restaurants, LuLu exuded a genteel southern charm that made you feel right at home.

An instant connection was made, and she extended an impromptu lunch invitation to the couple. Eagerly they agreed: LuLu's world-famous gumbo was not to be missed. In the days that followed, their walks took on a new routine, a friendly chat with LuLu becoming as essential as the frangipani blossoms tucked behind Laura's ear.

One day Laura noticed a change. Tom, usually attired casually for their walks, was instead resplendent in his white dress uniform, its brightness rivaling the summer sun. His chest was adorned with campaign medals, testaments to his service in Iraq and Afghanistan, alongside the Trident pin of a Navy SEAL and the Navy Cross, symbols of his extraordinary valor.

Their daily path led them, as always, to LuLu's frangipani tree, but this day held a twist. Under the shade of their beloved tree, Tom knelt, a frangipani blossom in hand. With a deftness that took Laura by surprise, he drew out a small box from his pocket, revealing a diamond ring that glittered as if it held a piece of the sun itself. Laura was taken aback; her heart pounded as Tom voiced the words she had yearned to hear: "Laura Roberts, will you marry me?"

The world seemed to blur around her, the fragrant scent of the frangipani blossoms filling her senses as his words echoed in her ears.

LuLu, catching sight of the momentous event, rushed out with a bottle of champagne and an armful of glasses. Tom popped the cork, pouring out the bubbling liquid.

It was only after a sip of the celebratory drink that Laura found her voice. Her heart full to bursting, she shouted her joy to the world: "Yes, yes, yes!" she cried, under the shadow of the resplendent frangipani tree.

~

Over the next couple of days, Key West became a vortex of revelations and reconfigurations, a microcosm of the shifting global stage. Far removed from the island, the world's intelligence machinery hummed with urgency, its collective gaze fixated on Moscow. The sudden recall of all FSB agents globally, including those cloaked in the heat of Cuba, followed by the cataclysmic explosion, documented the imminent storm brewing.

With the Russian intelligence web pulled away, the threat to Sergey—or rather, John—and Olga diminished, creating an unanticipated sanctuary within Key West. Tom and Laura began to outline their return to Washington, but they were keen to extract every possible insight from John and Olga before their departure.

The jewel in the trove of information was Sergey's recreation of the wallet housing the Satoshi Hoard, a task made possible by his remarkable subterfuge which enabled him to recreate the private key. For now, the US government, holding the reins to this digital fortune, chose to keep the Bitcoins untouched.

Amid the high-stakes game of global intrigue, the personal lives of our protagonists found surprising turns. Olga discovered a newfound affection for Sergey—now John—an undercurrent of emotion that ran deeper than she had previously acknowledged. She reveled in the notion of sharing a home with him, a man who could understand and share her nostalgia for a homeland crushed under Petrov's iron fist. They were stepping into the promise of a tranquil existence in their Elizabeth Street abode, with John's brilliance in mathematics ensuring a comfortable life.

Meanwhile, Tom and Laura, captivated by the charms of Key West, had embarked on a journey of their own. They revealed their wedding plans to Georgie, who was overjoyed at the prospect of her sister's marriage in her beloved tropical paradise.

They had even discovered the ideal setting for their nuptials: the Basilica of St. Mary Star of the Sea, its aged stones whispering stories of countless lovers who had pledged their vows within its walls. Father John Baker, the gentle Rector, agreed to officiate at the ceremony in the fall following the Presidential elections—though, even after hours of conversation, he was no closer to unraveling the enigma of the couple's professions.

Georgie, meanwhile, delighted in showing John and Olga the myriad joys of Key West. Oblivious to their true identities, she happily accepted the story of John as a remote-working math professor.

As their flight carried them back towards the heart of Washington, the plane's interior hummed with the low murmur of their ongoing dialogue, the topic at hand resonating with the gravity of the wealth they'd uncovered - the Satoshi Hoard.

"Tom, I can't stop thinking about the Satoshi Bitcoins," Laura voiced her thoughts, her eyes on the changing landscapes below.

"I know, Laura," Tom responded, his gaze locked with hers, "the enormity of it is... daunting."

His hand moved to tap on the armrest, a sign of his mind at work. "We should transfer them," he proposed, the words carrying a resolute ring. "Into a new wallet, publicly. It could symbolize our intention to use this wealth for the reconstruction of Russia, Ukraine, and China. The American taxpayer should not have to bear this expense."

Laura, however, wore a veil of uncertainty. She chewed her lower lip, her eyes revealing the depth of her contemplation. "But have we considered the implications of such a move, Tom? Those Bitcoins are skyrocketing in value due to their limited number. What if we leave them untouched?"

Her concerns went deeper, worries about the threat this digital currency could pose to their nation, the world order. "And what about American hegemony, Tom? This digital currency could destabilize things, even tip the scales of world order."

Their conversation hung suspended in the air, thick with uncertainty and pregnant with the weight of decisions yet to be made. As they moved closer to their destination, their minds grappled with the profound implications of the treasure they now held in their hands.

~

In the nerve center of the National Security Agency's Key West installation, Sergey Kuznetsov, known now by his American name, John Kinsley, sat poised in front of an array of high-tech computer screens. A symphony of electronic hums and whirrs from the servers provided a rhythmic backdrop to the momentous task he was about to undertake. He was on the cusp of recreating the illustrious Satoshi Hoard using the digital code he had Petrov enter when he signed the Bitcoins "Petrov". This action allowed Sergey to enable the private recovery seed—a sequence of 24 seemingly random, yet strategically significant words, committed to his formidable memory while operating within the highest echelons of the Kremlin.

This string of words performed an intricate dance in his mind, a choreography of perfect order and precision. They held immense power, for upon their correct entry, the private key—a digital skeleton key to the veritable Fort Knox of Bitcoin—would be recovered. It was this key that stood as the final barrier between the world and a wealth that was beyond most people's wildest dreams.

Methodically, Sergey began to type. Each keystroke drew him closer to the precipice of his monumental goal. Time seemed to hang in balance as the final characters were entered, and then, with one last tap of the enter key, the screens flooded with a wave of confirmation messages. The digital incarnation of the Satoshi Hoard sprang to life, its existence blinking back at him from the screen. He had done it.

In the wake of this extraordinary achievement, Sergey handed over the reins of this immense wealth to the US government. His chosen intermediary was none other than Laura Roberts, a woman whose integrity he had come to respect and who served as a bulwark against potential misuse of the funds. Through her, he fulfilled his agreement with the State Department, delivering access to the Bitcoin treasure trove in exchange for his new identity and safety.

But the handover was not without its concerns. Laura, though relieved at Sergey's successful completion of his part of the deal, was dogged by a haunting uncertainty. The ability of Sergey to reproduce the wallet once raised the possibility of him doing it again, thereby accessing the government's new wealth stash. Could she fully trust John Kinsley to act in the best interests of his new homeland?

Sergey, an individual gifted with perceptiveness and intuition, picked up on Laura's apprehensions. He understood her fears—the trust they were attempting to establish was precarious, especially given the high stakes and their chosen line of work. In an effort to assuage her anxieties, he proposed a solution: a modification to the old wallet to a new type called "multi-sig", requiring both his and Laura's signatures for any Bitcoin transaction. It was an offering of trust, a peace offering designed to bridge the gap between them.

This adjustment offered an additional layer of security, preventing unilateral action on the part of John. It gave Laura some semblance of peace, a small sign that John Kinsley was indeed committed to his new life and newfound allegiances. Despite the enormity of the responsibility, it was never about the money for Sergey. His dream had always been for Bitcoin to serve as an instrument for the betterment of the world, and he was now placing his faith in Laura Roberts and the US government to ensure this vision came to fruition.

~

In a world where digital currencies like Bitcoin were increasingly dominating global financial transactions, the importance of securing one's wealth could not be overstated. The unique nature of Bitcoin and its underlying technology, blockchain, presented a complicated set of challenges and opportunities. Among these, the concept of a multi-signature (or multi-sig) Bitcoin wallet stood as a beacon of security in the uncharted waters of digital finance.

To understand the concept of a multi-sig Bitcoin wallet, one must first grasp the role of private keys in Bitcoin transactions. A private key can be thought of as a secret password that grants its holder full control over a specific Bitcoin wallet. However, unlike a physical key that can be duplicated or a password that can be written down, a lost or stolen private key could lead to the permanent loss of one's

Bitcoin, like losing the combination to a safe and having no means of retrieving it. The safe, though secure, then becomes a prison for the treasures within.

Herein lies the beauty of a multi-sig Bitcoin wallet. Instead of a single key, a multi-sig wallet requires multiple private keys to authorize a Bitcoin transaction. Picture a safety deposit box that requires two different keys to be turned simultaneously in order to open. This is the essence of a multi-sig wallet. It distributes the risk and increases the security of one's Bitcoin by ensuring that no single point of failure can lead to the loss of one's digital wealth.

A multi-sig wallet can even be configured to require three private keys, with the condition that any two of them are sufficient to authorize a transaction. This is referred to as a "two-of-three" multi-sig wallet. The holder of such a wallet might keep one key on their person, put another in a secure location, and entrust the third to a trusted friend or family member. Even if one key is lost or stolen, the Bitcoin within the wallet will remain secure.

In this way, multi-sig wallets address many of the fears and uncertainties that surround the safekeeping of Bitcoin. The risk of hacking is significantly reduced because a potential thief would need to obtain multiple keys, probably stored in different locations, to access the wallet. Similarly, the accidental loss of one key would not result in the loss of Bitcoin, as the remaining keys would still provide access.

The multi-sig wallet was an elegant solution to a complex problem, a testament to the innovative spirit that had birthed Bitcoin itself. It was a digital fortress, secure yet accessible, offering peace of mind in a world where the lines between physical and digital wealth were increasingly blurred.

~

In the labyrinths of a world intertwined with the ethereal web of the blockchain, the newly developed multi-signature or 'multi-sig' wallets stood as vaulted fortresses, the epitome of digital security. However, at the dawn of Bitcoin's genesis, such fortifications were yet a glimmer on the horizon. The Satoshi wallet, a mythical trove architected by Sergey and laden with a treasure of over a million Bitcoins, was of this early lineage. Only the genius developer himself was capable of modifying this early vintage wallet without notice.   Since Sergey's coerced disappearance in 2011, it lay dormant, a digital Sleeping Beauty untouched by the world's restless ebb and flow.

Yet, parallel to this hushed crypt, another tale of intrigue unfolded. Russia's additional Bitcoin wallets, pulsating with the heartbeat of relentless transactions, echoed a narrative that resonated far beyond the borders of the Russian Federation. These wallets, unlike their dormant brethren, ebbed and surged with Bitcoin's lifeblood as it flowed into their digital coffers, swelling their numbers. The orchestration of this grand ballet of bits and bytes fell to Oleg Melnik, Petrov's trusted head of cybersecurity.

Sergey, even in the confines of his isolation, had witnessed these wallets' movements prior to affixing the signature "Petrov" on each Bitcoin in them. While the Satoshi wallet slept in silence, these behemoths of the blockchain, known colloquially as 'Petrov's Hoard,' roared into life with the ceaseless movement of Bitcoins. Yet a nagging uncertainty gnawed at Sergey. Had Melnik kept a backup of the recovery seed? Could he recreate these wallets, mirroring the vast repositories of Bitcoin they held? If so, Melnik could access the Petrov Hoard even without Petrov or the digital hardware wallets themselves.

The answer lay buried deep within the cold recesses of a vault, where Petrov kept the keys to his digital kingdom. The vault held not only the hardware wallet containing the Satoshi horde but also the hardware wallets and private keys granting access to Petrov's Hoard. Sergey, under Petrov's relentless gaze, had witnessed these keys, their intricate alphanumeric sequences a testament to the digital wealth they guarded. Despite his best efforts, the rush to sign Petrov's name had robbed Sergey of the time to etch those keys into his memory. The daunting prospect of memorizing a 24-digit alphanumeric code under such pressure had proven too great a challenge.

Yet the world of the blockchain bore witness to the existence of these digital fortresses. The two grand repositories, together holding a king's ransom of approximately one million additional Bitcoins, had carved their place in the annals of the Bitcoin ledger. Now bearing the moniker 'Petrov,' they loomed large on the blockchain, drawing awed whispers and fevered speculation from across the globe. Although 'Petrov's Hoard' and the 'Satoshi Horde' stood as distinct entities, the shadow of Vladimir Petrov enveloped both. Like an inscrutable puppeteer, he pulled the strings, the destiny of these digital troves dancing to his tune.

RUSSIAN FURY

The ever-shifting sands of power and loyalty were as ancient and treacherous as the game of politics itself. Zhang Wei had long understood that no alliance is eternal. As resentment and dissatisfaction took root in his heart, the Chinese mastermind found himself contemplating the unthinkable: the betrayal of his Russian ally, Vladimir Petrov. Russia's failure in Ukraine and the growing disparity between the two nations' Bitcoin hoards gnawed at Wei's pride. He had expected their partnership to bolster China's position in the world, yet Russia's humiliating defeat had left them weakened and vulnerable. The Satoshi Hoard, a treasure trove that could tip the balance of power irrevocably, beckoned to Wei like a siren's call.

As the sun cast long shadows across the bustling streets of Beijing, Wei made his decision. The time had come to sever the alliance and seize Russia's Bitcoin Hoard for China. With this audacious act, he could both secure his nation's dominance and undermine Russia's position in the world. So, in a clandestine Chinese cyberwarfare facility, a team of elite hackers was assembled, their orders straightforward: infiltrate Russia's digital wallets and transfer the coveted Bitcoins to a Chinese-controlled account. These skilled operatives, handpicked by Wei for their expertise and loyalty, knew the magnitude of their task and the consequences of failure.

The hackers hunched over their glowing screens, orchestrating a symphony of code and subterfuge. They breached layer upon layer of security, navigating the labyrinthine digital defenses surrounding Petrov's wallets with the finesse of master thieves.

But Wei's treacherous gambit had not gone unnoticed. The realm of geopolitics was a stage on which all players were under constant scrutiny, and the delicate balance of power left little room for error or secrecy. News of China's audacious cyberattack soon reached Petrov's ears, and the Russian leader was not one to suffer betrayal lightly.

~

The frigid winds of the Russian winter swept through the Kremlin, carrying with them the bitter sting of betrayal. Vladimir Petrov paced the length of his opulent office, his anger a fire that threatened to engulf all in its path. The alliance between Russia and China, once a bastion of shared ambition and mutual gain, now lay in tatters, rent asunder by the treacherous Zhang Wei.

The Chinese had failed Petrov in his darkest hour, providing only limited support for his invasion of Ukraine. The bitter taste of defeat still lingered in his mouth, a constant reminder of the humiliation that he and his nation had suffered at the hands of their supposed ally. Now, to add insult to injury, the Chinese were daring to attempt the theft of Russia's Bitcoins.

The audacity of their betrayal was almost beyond comprehension. Petrov had long known that the game of power was one of deception and cunning, but Wei's treachery surpassed even his most pessimistic expectations. The Russian leader seethed with righteous fury, his every thought bent on retribution and revenge.

He summoned his most trusted advisors. The time had come to strike back, to make the Chinese pay for their duplicity in a currency of blood and fire. Russia would not suffer such indignities without reprisal, and the Chinese would learn the folly of crossing the Bear. The Kremlin's war room buzzed with tense energy as plans were laid and contingencies considered. A new chapter in global conflict was about to be written, one that would pit the might of Russia against the cunning of China. The world held its breath, watching as the clouds of war gathered on the horizon.

As the first salvos were fired and the wheels of retribution set in motion, the full cost of betrayal began to reveal itself. Friends turned to enemies, alliances shattered like glass, and the foundations of the world order trembled. In this new era of mistrust and enmity, only one thing was certain: none could predict the outcome of the tempest that now loomed over the world.

~

Under skies as gray as the somber mood of the Kremlin, President Vladimir Petrov prepared to act. The defeat in Ukraine still gnawed at him, a festering wound to his pride that refused to heal. He saw his reflection in the frost on his window—a betrayed, weakened, belittled man. But Petrov was not one to accept defeat lying down. His eyes, cold as the Siberian tundra, showed an icy resolve. A purge was necessary, a culling of the treacherous and the incompetent—a bloody reclamation of control.

Among the first to feel the sting of Petrov's wrath was Defense Minister Ivan Vavich. A bullish man with a bristling mustache, Vavich had been a staunch advocate for the invasion of Ukraine. But when the campaign faltered, his bluster had proven as empty as the promises he'd made. Petrov had him arrested on charges of dereliction of duty and treason, an example for all others who dared to fail their leader.

Next was Valery Popov, Chief of the General Staff. Popov, a man of strategic brilliance, had initially opposed the Ukrainian invasion, cautioning against the risks. However, his objections had been swept aside in the fervor of war. As the tide of battle turned against them,

Petrov saw Popov's earlier caution as sabotage. Popov was removed from his position, his once stellar military career extinguished in the blink of an eye.

Foreign Minister Ivan Lavrov, once a trusted advisor, also found himself in Petrov's crosshairs. It was Lavrov who had peddled the idea of the invasion, his silver-tongued assurances of a swift victory luring Petrov into the quagmire. For his role in the debacle, Lavrov was relieved of his duties, his political influence reduced to rubble.

The purge was swift and brutal, a chilling testament to Petrov's ruthlessness. Yet, amid the chaos, one man remained untouched. Ramzan Umarov, the autocratic leader of Chechnya, was rumored to be on his deathbed. Petrov reasoned that Umarov's imminent demise was punishment enough, and besides, Umarov's forceful grip on the volatile Chechen region and his sizable following among Russia's Muslim population made him a risky target.

It was a grim time. The halls of the Kremlin echoed with the ghostly whispers of the condemned. But Petrov's purge, while brutal, was a calculated move. He believed that by cutting off the rotten branches, he could save the tree. Still, in his quest for redemption, he failed to see the growing rot at the roots, a decay that threatened to bring the whole tree crashing down.

Meanwhile, the Russian winter raged on, its chill seeping into the heart of the Kremlin. Amid the snow and ice, the seeds of dissent were sown, waiting for the spring thaw to bloom into a reckoning. As Petrov looked out over the frozen landscape, he saw only the cold desolation of his reign, unaware of the upheaval brewing beneath the surface. The purge was only the beginning of his troubles, the first flakes in a future blizzard of rebellion and revolution.

~

Ilya Vavilov was a man of immense power and influence, whose name was spoken in hushed tones in the grand corridors of the Kremlin. He was a businessman, a billionaire, and, to many, a puppet-master, his strings stretching up to the highest echelons of the Russian government. Known as "Petrov's Driver" for his ride-sharing empire, Vavilov also controlled the Wagner Group, a private military company whose soldiers had fought and died on the Ukrainian front lines.

In the aftermath of the Ukrainian debacle, Vavilov found himself a target of Petrov's fury. Petrov labeled him a traitor, a moniker that carried a death sentence in the harsh world of Russian politics. It wasn't merely Vavilov's failure in Ukraine that ignited Petrov's wrath; it was the insidious rumors of his duplicity—whispers that Vavilov had been secretly negotiating with the Americans. Whether these rumors were true or not mattered little. In Petrov's world, even the shadow of disloyalty was enough to warrant execution.

The death of Ilya Vavilov was swift and brutal, carried out in the same ruthless manner as the rest of Petrov's purge. On a bitterly cold Moscow night, a group of masked operatives broke into his opulent mansion. His security team was neutralized with ruthless efficiency, the alarm system sabotaged to remain silent. The operatives found Vavilov cowering in his private study, surrounded by antique books and expensive art, a glass of vintage brandy clutched in his hand. He was given no opportunity to plead for his life or protest his innocence. Two gunshots echoed through the room, and the puppet master's strings were severed.

Petrov ensured that the news of Vavilov's assassination was swiftly disseminated, a warning to any who dared to cross him, a chilling reminder that betrayal would be met with swift and fatal retribution. The message was clear: Petrov's reign was absolute, his justice uncompromising. And, as he had intended, the assassination sent shockwaves through the Kremlin. Those who had once felt secure within the walls of power now found themselves looking over their shoulders, their confidence replaced with paranoia. The death of the powerful oligarch was a grim reminder that no one was safe from Petrov's wrath.

The execution of Vavilov marked a turning point in Petrov's rule. His reign was no longer marked by strength and stability but by fear and uncertainty. The purge had claimed its highest-profile victim, and the remaining members of Petrov's inner circle could only wonder who might be next. As the Russian winter tightened its grip, the chill of fear and mistrust seeped deeper into the Kremlin. The stage was set for a seismic shift in the Russian government, and all of its officials waited to see what the next act would bring.

~

The grandeur of the Kremlin's war room offered a dramatic contrast to the grim deliberations taking place within its walls. Vladimir Petrov stood at the head of the long, mahogany table, his steely gaze sweeping over the room, pinning each of his advisors with a stare that promised retribution for the faintest hint of dissent.

He began to speak, his voice echoing off the vaulted ceilings, filling the room with palpable tension. "Comrades," he began, "I believe you understand the gravity of the situation we face. Zhang Wei has betrayed our trust and threatens the very existence of our great nation."

There was a murmur of agreement around the table, a chorus of assent from advisors wary of their volatile leader's wrath.

"Our constitution," Petrov stressed, "permits a nuclear response in the face of an existential threat. I argue that this is precisely the situation we face today."

A new chill descended upon the room. Nuclear aggression was not a topic to be broached lightly, even in the high-stakes world of international politics. Yet Petrov's conviction was irresistible.

"The Chinese," he spat, "have not only failed to support us in our righteous struggle in Ukraine, but they have also attempted to steal our Bitcoin—our treasure."

The room was deathly silent as Petrov paced, his fingers tracing the edge of the map spread across the table.

"This is not a mere act of treachery; it is a declaration of war. They seek to cripple us, to leave us weak and vulnerable. We cannot, we will not stand for such blatant aggression."

There were nods of agreement, murmurs of support. Yet beneath the veneer of compliance ran an undercurrent of unease. Many suspected that Petrov's fiery rhetoric was a smokescreen, an attempt to divert attention from the failures of his Ukrainian campaign. Nevertheless, no one dared voice these suspicions for fear of inviting their leader's vengeance.

Finally, General Antonov, a bear of a man with decades of military experience, spoke up: "Sir, if we may consider... Are there no other options available? Diplomatic actions, perhaps?"

Petrov turned his gaze to Antonov. "Diplomacy," he scoffed, "is for those who lack the courage to take what is rightfully theirs. We have been wronged, and we will respond in kind."

With those words, the fate of Russia—and perhaps the world— was sealed. The game of power and retaliation had begun, with the stakes higher than they'd ever been. As the advisors left the room, their decision heavy on their shoulders, the Russian winter seemed to seep into the very bones of the Kremlin as if in anticipation of the horrific war that loomed on the horizon.

~

Vladimir Petrov, a master of deception and manipulation, soon spotted the perfect opportunity to maintain the facade of his alliance with China while enacting his plan for revenge. The upcoming Operation Red Storm, the largest military exercise in China's history, would be the ideal stage for his scheme.

Petrov knew that the Chinese would jump at the chance to study the advanced Western weaponry that had been captured during Russia's disastrous campaign in Ukraine. He was well aware that China had become adept at copying Western technology, particularly the advanced electronic optics and targeting systems found in vehicles like the Abrams tanks and Stryker armored vehicles. The prospect of acquiring this knowledge would undoubtedly entice the Chinese and help maintain the illusion of the Russo-Chinese alliance.

By sending the captured arms to China after his own engineers had studied them in detail, Petrov sought to kill two birds with one stone. First, it would help maintain the appearance of cooperation between the two nations, even as Petrov plotted his retaliation. Second, he felt confident that the Chinese would focus their attention on the vehicles' cutting-edge technology, thus remaining oblivious to the deadly surprises he had concealed within.

This ploy was a cunning move on Petrov's part, demonstrating his ruthlessness and strategic acumen. He took advantage of both China's eagerness to acquire Western technology and its belief in the strength of its alliance with Russia. By exploiting these factors, he concealed his true intentions. He set in motion a plan that would have devastating consequences for China, reshaping the global balance of power in the process.

Petrov's plan to exact vengeance on his former ally had reached its final stages. Concealed within the fuel tank of each of the captured vehicles, Petrov had hidden his own devastating payload—a five-megaton nuclear warhead. The Abrams tank, a symbol of American military might, was known for its large fuel capacity, a necessity given its powerful turbine engine. This cavernous compartment, the largest in the vehicle, provided the perfect hiding place for the deadly payload that Petrov had chosen to deliver. An American Stryker armored personnel carrier concealed a second five-megaton nuclear warhead in the hopes that it would be separated from the tank and thus help to destroy more than the entire Chinese base. Although not as large as the Abrams, the Stryker's fuel tank was more than large enough to secure the miniaturized device.

Transported by train from Russia to China, the armored vehicles arrived at their destination with their deadly secret still hidden. The fuel gauges read "full," posing no cause for suspicion, as the vehicles were not expected to be operational during their journey.

When the Chinese scientists eagerly examined the captured Western technology, they paid little heed to the fuel tanks. There was little to be gained from reverse-engineering such a mundane component. And so the stage was set for a cataclysmic betrayal, one that would plunge humanity into a new era of annihilation.

CHINA PAYS A TERRIBLE PRICE

The Zhurihe military base, built in the desolate expanse of the Inner Mongolia Autonomous Region, stood as a testament to China's military prowess. Here the might of the People's Liberation Army Ground Force (PLAGF) was honed to a razor's edge, ready to be wielded by their master, Zhang Wei. Operation Red Storm was to be the crowning achievement of the PLAGF, a grand display of strength that would eclipse the humiliations of the past and herald a new era of Chinese supremacy.

Tens of thousands of soldiers stood at attention, their faces a sea of stoic determination, as five elite divisions of the Chinese military prepared to take the stage. These warriors, specialists in armored warfare, were the tip of the spear, the vanguard of China's inexorable march toward global dominance. As their vehicles' engines roared to life, the earth itself seemed to tremble beneath their power.

Yet a serpent lay coiled in their midst, a deadly retribution sent by Vladimir Petrov. The machines of war he had bestowed on them, gleaming with the promise of technological secrets, were a tantalizing prize for Wei and his ambitious designs, but within them lay a pair of deadly devices, two five-megaton tactical nuclear warheads primed to unleash devastation on an unimaginable scale. Petrov's fury had found its mark, and the seeds of chaos were about to be sown in the ranks of China's most elite fighting force.

As the Chinese soldiers marveled at the Western technology now at their fingertips, their minds filled with visions of conquest and glory, the countdown to destruction began. With each tick of the clock, the specter of retribution grew ever closer, and the fate of Operation Red Storm hung precariously in the balance.

~

The sun had barely risen on the first day of Operation Red Storm, and the vast expanse of the Zhurihe military base teemed with activity. Over 150,000 soldiers of the People's Liberation Army Ground Force had assembled, their hearts swelling with pride and anticipation as they prepared to showcase the might of the Chinese military. The rumble of engines and the thunder of marching boots echoed across the sprawling facility.

Then, in a moment that would be seared into the memories of those who survived, a blinding flash of light consumed the base. The detonation of two five-megaton nuclear devices, hidden within the fuel tanks of captured American armored vehicles, unleashed a fury, unlike anything the world had ever seen. A combined-ten-megaton explosion is much more powerful than the bomb dropped on Hiroshima. In fact, it is about 666 times more powerful, with an explosive yield of ten million tons of TNT. The effects were catastrophic, with a blast radius of twenty-three miles and extreme heat and lethal radiation extending even farther.

The explosion tore through the base, leveling buildings and incinerating soldiers and support personnel alike. In an instant, the lives of over 150,000 soldiers were snuffed out, their bodies reduced to ash in the all-consuming firestorm. Tens of thousands more perished in the surrounding towns, their lives cruelly snatched away by a force they could neither see nor comprehend.

Zhurihe, the pride of the Chinese military, was reduced to a smoldering wasteland. Over two thousand of China's most advanced tanks lay twisted and mangled amid the devastation, their once imposing forms now little more than radioactive scrap. Thousands of artillery pieces, the might of China's ground-based firepower, had been obliterated in the blink of an eye.

The destruction did not end there. A staggering 3,000 transport and supply vehicles, vital to the support of the Chinese military machine, were melted into radioactive waste. Millions of artillery shells and countless other munitions were consumed by the inferno, their deadly potential snuffed out in an instant.

But the loss of equipment paled in comparison to the irreplaceable knowledge and expertise that had been wiped away. Advanced communications equipment, night-vision goggles, and the supplies needed to equip one-quarter of China's land-based forces had also vanished in a heartbeat, along with the men and women who had dedicated their lives to mastering their use.

The repercussions of this catastrophic event would reverberate across the globe, shaking the foundations of the world order and leaving a power vacuum that would take years to fill. China's capacity to wage war had been dealt a crushing blow, one from which it would struggle to recover. In a single, devastating instant, the scales of global power had been irrevocably tipped, plunging humanity into a new era of uncertainty and fear.

~

Dressed in his immaculate military uniform, the insignia of his high rank prominently displayed, Zhang Wei stood on an elevated platform overlooking the sprawling base, an emperor surveying his kingdom. His eyes gleamed with an intoxicating blend of ambition, excitement, and determination. He carried a sense of invincibility, the audacious confidence of a man standing on the precipice of altering the course of history.

As the vehicles made their way past the saluting stand, Wei's pride swelled, oblivious to the reality that the very machines symbolizing China's military might were, in fact, harbingers of their imminent doom.

With the eerie silence of death itself, the nuclear devices activated. Wei's triumphant smile froze as a blinding flash of light engulfed the base, consuming the armored vehicles, the soldiers, and everything else in its path. He barely had a moment to register the shocking turn of events before the deafening blast wave hit, catapulting him into oblivion.

Heat equivalent to that of the sun's core incinerated everything within its reach. Zhang Wei, the architect of Operation Red Storm, was caught in the epicenter of this monstrous nuclear inferno. The man who sought to ascend to unprecedented heights of power was instantly reduced to nothing but atoms, his existence extinguished as swiftly as a candle snuffed out by a gust of wind.

Wei's death marked the brutal end of an era and served as a harsh reminder of the dangers of unchecked ambition and power. His grand vision for Chinese supremacy had been reduced to radioactive dust, a grim symbol of the cataclysmic power of nuclear weapons and the unforeseen consequences they carried.

Thus, Zhang Wei, who began the day as the harbinger of China's destined rise, met his end in the most tragic and shocking way possible, consumed by the very power he sought to control. The echoes of his fall reverberated through the annals of military history, a stark reminder of the destructive capability of mankind and the fleeting nature of power.

~

As the embers of Operation Red Storm cooled and the dust settled on the devastated landscape, the enormity of the nation's loss became apparent. Yet, even as the Chinese government reeled from this catastrophic blow, the wheels of Wei's plan continued to turn, inexorably driving the nation toward the invasion of Taiwan.

Wei had been instrumental in the planning and execution of Operation Red Storm. He had intended this vast military exercise as both a display of China's power and a smokescreen for his true purpose: the invasion of Taiwan. A man of cunning and foresight, Wei understood the importance of his presence at the Zhurihe military base on the first day of the operation, lending his authority and expertise to the proceedings. His presence was to serve as a beacon to the troops, a symbol of the determination of the Chinese state to assert its dominance in the region.

Despite the chaos that ensued following the nuclear strike and Wei's untimely demise, the invasion plan he had so meticulously crafted proceeded. The intricate web of preparations, deception, and strategy had been woven so tightly that the momentum of the plan carried it forward, even in the face of calamity.

In the wake of Wei's death, the highest echelons of the Chinese government were thrown into turmoil. Factions vied for power, seeking to fill the void left by the fallen mastermind. But even as the political landscape shifted and churned like storm-tossed seas, the invasion of Taiwan remained a constant objective, a lodestar guiding the nation through the darkness.

The invasion plan was of such magnitude that it transcended individual ambition, having become an essential component of China's broader goals. For the Chinese government, the invasion represented not only the fulfillment of Wei's vision but also a chance to reassert China's strength and resilience in the face of tragedy.

As the days passed, the Chinese Navy and Marines continued their preparations, undeterred by the upheaval that gripped their nation. They trained and drilled, refining their tactics and strategies in anticipation of the coming assault. The element of surprise, painstakingly cultivated, remained intact, ensuring that Taiwan would be caught unawares.

In the end, it was the dedication of the Chinese military, coupled with the sheer force of Wei's vision, that carried the plan forward. The invasion of Taiwan would proceed, emerging from the chaos of Operation Red Storm, demonstrating the will of a nation and the legacy of a man who had dared to strive for world domination.

~

Before the explosion, as the fateful day of Operation Red Storm approached, the air within the inner sanctum of the Chinese government had been thick with anticipation. From the beginning, Zhang Wei, aware of the monumental risks involved in his audacious plan to invade Taiwan, had known that his own life would be in the balance. In the high-stakes game he was playing, the slightest misstep could spell disaster not just for himself but for the entire nation. So, Wei made a calculated decision to entrust the Chinese nuclear launch codes to his most loyal ally: Mao Chang, the President of China.

Chang's earlier ascent to the rank of full general had been a testament to his unwavering loyalty to Wei, and now he found himself in a position of unparalleled responsibility. The office of the President was largely ceremonial in nature, yet this transfer of power held unprecedented weight. With a single stroke, Wei had placed the fate of millions in the hands of his trusted confidant. Chang was granted full launch authority, a move that shocked the upper echelons of the Chinese government.

The order was communicated to the military and the Central Committee in no uncertain terms. Wei's power was such that no one dared to question his decision, despite the gravity of the situation. In the halls of power, whispers of unease echoed among the bureaucrats and military leaders, but their voices were hushed by Wei's iron grip on the nation.

Chang, for his part, felt the weight of the world pressing down upon him. The nuclear codes, now in his possession, represented a force beyond comprehension, the power to unleash destruction on a scale never before seen in human history. As he gazed upon the small, unassuming briefcase that contained the keys to the apocalypse, he shuddered at the thought of what might come to pass.

Only days later, the Russian bombs exploded, Wei was killed, and Chang found himself leading the vast nation of China.

~

In the harrowing aftermath of the nuclear detonation at Zhurihe military base, China reeled from the shock and confusion of the unexpected tragedy. Amid the swirling fear and grief, the nation desperately sought answers to the terrible questions that haunted the hearts and minds of its people: Who was responsible for this unimaginable act of destruction? And what could have motivated them to unleash such a weapon upon the innocent?

As the Chinese National Nuclear Safety Administration swung into action, the race to unravel the mystery of the attack began in earnest. Deploying sophisticated drones and remote sensing equipment, the investigators scoured the blast site for clues that might lead them to the source of the deadly explosion. Each day brought new revelations, painting a chilling picture.

In the smoke and fire of the devastated base, a terrible truth began to emerge. The molecular analysis conducted by the drones, coupled with satellite imagery tracing the origin of the blast to the Western military equipment recently transported from Russia to China, pointed to an inescapable conclusion: Russia, once a staunch ally of the Chinese regime, had turned its formidable nuclear arsenal against them.

The revelation sent shockwaves throughout the Chinese government. Zhang Wei had warned the Central Committee of Petrov's fury following the calamitous events in Ukraine, but few imagined that the Russian leader would be mad enough to resort to a nuclear strike. Yet the evidence was irrefutable, etched in the radioactive signatures that lingered like a deathly pall over the scorched earth of Zhurihe.

As the weight of the terrible news settled upon the nation, Mao Chang, now the de facto leader of China, summoned the Central Committee for an emergency meeting. In the Great Hall of the People, the most powerful men and women in the country gathered, their faces etched with grim determination as they grappled with the enormity of the crisis before them.

In the Great Hall of the People, Mao Chang stared out at the assembled members of the Central Committee, their faces filled with grim determination and simmering rage.

"There is no easy way to say this," he began, his voice echoing through the cavernous hall. "We believe the nuclear attack on the Zhurihe military base was perpetrated by Russia."

Outraged murmurs rippled through the room. Chang held up a hand, signaling for silence. "The evidence is irrefutable. The fallout signatures, the satellite imagery, the blast origin… all point to Russia."

"What do we do now?" demanded a committee member. The room erupted into a heated debate, some demanding immediate retaliation, others counseling restraint, and diplomatic engagement. One thing was clear - the invasion of Taiwan would proceed as planned. Years of intricate planning would not be wasted over this treachery.

Chang's gaze swept over the room. The decision to retaliate was his, and he carried the weight of it heavily. As he prepared to address the room once more, he knew that the choice he made would forever alter the fate of his nation and the world.

With the world watching, Mao Chang steeled himself to make his stand, knowing that a man's true character was revealed in such moments of crisis.

IT CAN'T GET ANY WORSE, CAN IT?

For the United States, the shock of the explosion at the Chinese military base thrust the nation into a vortex of uncertainty. There could be no hiding from the catastrophe, and the US government found itself under immense pressure to respond to the rampant speculation that had engulfed the world.

The leaders of the US intelligence community were hastily summoned to the White House, tasked with addressing the President's urgent queries. The atmosphere within was fraught with tension as the finest minds in American espionage scrambled to make sense of the incomprehensible. Even the usually unflappable Bob Myers appeared shaken, giving way to an outburst of uncharacteristic anger, as he demanded, "What the hell happened?" Those present could not recall ever the President displaying such raw emotion.

Reports continued to pour in, painting a harrowing picture of a nuclear device detonating in the heart of the Mongolian plains. Yet, despite the mounting evidence, a fundamental question remained unanswered: How could such an event have occurred without any prior indication of a launch detected across the globe? Tom's best analysts were forced to confront the unsettling possibility that the explosion might have been the result of a catastrophic mishap involving tactical nuclear weapons. Though the notion seemed scarcely believable, it remained the only plausible theory that could be constructed on such short notice.

With the Chinese authorities remaining conspicuously silent, the United States launched a series of intelligence-gathering drones to ascertain the full extent of the disaster. However, this bold move was not without its perils, as the violation of Chinese sovereignty and airspace threatened to ignite a powder keg of international tensions.

As the world held its breath, satellite imagery revealed the horrifying aftermath of the explosion but provided no insight into the cause of the catastrophe. Desperate for answers, Tom reached out to his extensive network of intelligence assets, only to discover that Wei had perished in the blast and that the Chinese Central Committee was now convening around the clock.

In a rare glimmer of hope, however, it appeared that Tom's old friend Li Chen was emerging as the leading potential successor to Wei, his rise offering a promise of stability amid the chaos. The sudden vacuum left by the demise of the enigmatic leader, notwithstanding Mao Chang's assumption of the country's leadership, had sent ripples throughout the international community, with all acutely aware of the precarious balance of power.

In addition to these moves on the chessboard of world command, the ominous build-up of Chinese naval and ground forces in the Guangdong province off the coast of Taiwan exacerbated the world's growing sense of unease as its leaders struggled to decipher the intentions behind these troubling developments.

~

The grand chamber of the Chinese Central Committee echoed with voices—voices tinged with anger, resentment, and a hunger for retribution. Each voice represented a strand in the web of China's political and military power. And amid the clamor, two voices stood out.

Li Chen, a figure known for his caution and moderation, surprised all with his aggressive stance. He argued vehemently for a direct, fatal strike on Moscow. His reasoning was simple yet brutal: "If you strike the king, you must kill him," he declared. "Russia's power resides in Moscow. Petrov, ensconced in the Kremlin, is the head of the serpent. We must sever it."

Mao Chang, now the de facto head of the nation, echoed Chen's sentiments. "Petrov's defenses are turned towards the Americans. He's blind to our threat," he stated with grim satisfaction. "With Petrov gone, no one in Russia will possess the authority or the nerve to launch a counterattack."

The new Vice President inquired, "How can we be sure that Petrov will be present?"

Chang replied, "We have the means to ensure he is in the Kremlin when we strike."

Others had indeed observed that, with dissent brewing, Petrov rarely left the safety of his office, making him an easy target.

The allure of the Satoshi Hoard, the vast fortune in Bitcoin held in the Kremlin's vault, added fuel to the fire. Chen, with his technological acumen, pointed out the tantalizing prospect: "Petrov trusts no one. With his demise, his private keys—and his Bitcoins—will be gone forever. Our remaining Bitcoins will surge in value."

This, as much as the thirst for vengeance, swayed the Central Committee. Greed, as it often does, proved to be the most persuasive argument.

Their decision was unanimous and grim. A ten-megaton ICBM was to be launched on Moscow, set for air burst to minimize nuclear fallout. The Americans would be notified once the missile was airborne, with strict instructions not to intervene or warn Moscow. Full-scale nuclear retaliation was too great a risk to take.

Li Chen volunteered to deliver the message to his old friend and current CIA chief, Tom Michaels. Then the meeting adjourned and the leaders left the chamber, teeming with thoughts of revenge, power, and a dramatic shift in global power.

~

In the clandestine world that Wei and Petrov had inhabited, trust was a rare and fleeting commodity, forged not through words but through actions that echoed across the silent expanses of their respective empires. In the earliest days of their grand machinations, the two despots had sought a means of maintaining a secret chain of communication, a lifeline that would bind them together as they navigated the treacherous waters of their dark alliance.

Thus, in the shadows of the old world, a plan had been conceived: a super-secure, hardwired telephone connection that stretched all the way from Beijing to the Kremlin. This line, a vital artery of secrecy and deceit, was installed with the utmost care and precision, and for years it remained a covert witness to the intricate dance of power between the Dragon and the Bear. Its existence was a closely guarded secret, known only to the two leaders and their most trusted confidants. Each time the phone rang, the solitary chime signaled a new chapter in their sordid tale of intrigue and betrayal.

And, in a twist of fate, this instrument of their bond would ultimately seal the doom of one of the conspirators. In the wake of the destruction of the Zhurihe base, Mao Chang and Li Chen hatched a plan to ensure the demise of Vladimir Petrov. They knew that, to achieve their goal, they would need to exploit the very means by which the two tyrants had once held sway over the world.

As the appointed hour approached, Chang reached for the unassuming device that had bound the Dragon and the Bear together. The moment the unmistakable voice of Vladimir Petrov echoed across the line, Chang issued the order to launch the missile that would spell the end of the Kremlin and the dreams of a Russian Empire.

The skies above Moscow, set ablaze by the fires of retribution, were a haunting reminder of the frailty of human ambition and the inexorable march of time. The Dragon and the Bear, once the architects of a new world order, now both lay dead, testaments of the folly of those who seek to bend the world to their will.

YES, IT CAN GET WORSE

As the missile unleashed by Chang streaked toward its target in the Kremlin, Li Chen prepared to deliver the news to his American counterpart, Tom Michaels, the CIA Director with whom he shared a long and complicated history. The call would be fraught with tension and urgency, with the Chinese leader seeking to assure the United States of good will while imploring them not to intervene or warn Moscow of the impending strike.

In the CIA's headquarters, Tom Michaels heard the voice of his old friend crackle through the secure line. He listened in stunned disbelief as Li Chen recounted the harrowing tale of the Central Committee's decision, the imminent nuclear strike, and the vast Bitcoin fortune that lay in the balance. In that moment, Tom found himself at the crossroads of history, faced with a terrible choice that would test the limits of his loyalty and conscience. With the fate of millions hanging in the balance, he had to decide whether to recommend that President Myers heed the pleas of his old friend or defy the Chinese ultimatum and sound the alarm, potentially plunging the world into an apocalyptic nuclear war.

As the clock ticked down to the moment of truth, Tom Michaels wrestled with the agonizing decision. The course he chose would not only shape the destiny of nations but define his own legacy as a man and a leader.

At last, with a heavy heart, Tom made his choice. The future of the world now rested in the hands of Bob Myers.

~

In the heart of St. Petersburg, amid its storied streets and ancient spires, a man of iron will, and indomitable courage had for years stood poised to challenge the power of the Kremlin. His name was Alexei Nostrov, a figure both revered and reviled\ and a symbol of hope for millions of Russians who yearned for change.

Born to a modest family in a remote corner of the Russian Federation, Nostrov's journey to prominence had been a long and arduous one. His keen intellect and insatiable curiosity had propelled him through the ranks of Russia's legal profession, where he quickly made a name for himself as a crusader against corruption. But it was in the murky depths of the Russian political system that he found his true calling, exposing the venality and duplicity that had become endemic under the rule of Vladimir Petrov.

Nostrov's relentless pursuit of truth and justice had earned him the enmity of the Kremlin, making him a target for assassination and imprisonment. Yet, even in the face of such adversity, he remained unbowed, an embodiment of the Russian spirit. To his supporters, he was a hero, a beacon of hope in an age of darkness, a man who dared to stand against the tyranny of the powerful.

As the years passed and the people's disillusionment with Petrov's regime grew, Nostrov's influence spread across the vast expanse of Russia. Tens of millions rallied to his cause, weary of a stagnant economy, rampant corruption, and a government that cared little for the plight of its citizens. Ordinary Russians, from the humblest farmer to the highest-ranking official, recognized in Nostrov a man who could give voice to their hopes and dreams, a man who believed in a brighter future for their great nation.

In the face of the Kremlin's propaganda machine, Nostrov and his supporters stood firm, resolute in their commitment to the truth. They refused to be swayed by lies that sought to divide and conquer, choosing instead to unite under a banner of freedom and justice.

Now, in the tumultuous world events unfolding around them, these millions of Russians found strength in the figure of Alexei Nostrov, the Lion of Russia. He became the embodiment of their aspirations, fears, and dreams, a man who could lead them out of the darkness and into the light of a new dawn. The people of Russia knew that they too could play a part in shaping the course of history. With Nostrov as their champion, they could rise up to challenge the might of the Kremlin, seizing a brighter future for themselves and generations to come.

Yet, as Moscow's citizens went about their daily routines, they were unaware of the danger lurking in the skies above. The vibrant metropolis, rich with history and culture, bustled with life as its people made their way through the crowded streets, attending to their work, their families, and their dreams—and all the while, hidden from their eyes, a deadly serpent was about to strike from the shadows, wreaking destruction on an unimaginable scale.

~

The dead-hand system, an ominous relic of the Cold War, illustrated the intensity of the nuclear arms race between the United States and the Soviet Union. Designed to ensure Russia's ability to retaliate in the event of a nuclear first strike by the United States, the dead-hand system would detect and respond to a threat only from its most potent rival.

This singular focus on the United States as sole nuclear adversary had long been a cornerstone of Russian strategic thinking. The dead-hand system thus remained blind to potential threats from other nations, even as the world evolved, and new rivals emerged on the global stage.

It was this blind spot that Mao Chang sought to exploit in his daring plan to strike at the heart of Russia. By launching an ICBM on Moscow, Chang hoped to decapitate the Russian command structure, knowing that an attack from China would not trigger the dead-hand system. In his mind, the destruction of Moscow would leave Russia without the centralized leadership needed to mount a devastating nuclear counterstrike. Petrov, continuing Russia's longstanding tradition, had ordered all of Russia's satellite and missile-detection systems to be directed toward the West, leaving the vast Russian Chinese border all but unguarded. And this hidebound decision ultimately contributed greatly to Moscow's undoing.

In the bowels of a hidden Chinese missile silo, a ten-kiloton intercontinental ballistic missile lay in wait. Its deadly payload, a weapon of immense power and destruction, was aimed squarely at the heart of the Russian capital. When Chang ordered the missile to be launched, sending it arcing through the heavens on a collision course with its unsuspecting target, its path went undetected by the Russian surveillance systems, and the people of Moscow remained ignorant of the approaching cataclysm. They continued to sip tea in cozy cafes, to stroll along the banks of the Moskva River, and to marvel at the grandeur of the Kremlin's ancient walls, while the clock ticked inexorably toward their doom.

The impact was as sudden as it was devastating. The warhead, a monstrous force of destruction, struck the heart of Moscow with a blinding flash of light and a deafening roar. In an instant, the city's center was transformed into a hellish inferno, a seething maelstrom of fire and destruction that consumed everything in its path.

The Russian command and control system, carefully designed to withstand the onslaught of just one enemy's attack, was annihilated by the surprise strike. The dead-hand response, a fail-safe mechanism intended to ensure the functioning of the Russian nuclear arsenal in the event of a decapitating strike, lay dormant and untriggered, its sensors blind to the incoming threat.

In the aftermath of the attack, Moscow was left a smoldering ruin, a charred and blackened testament to misplaced trust and miscalculated threats. The once thriving city lay in ashes, its vibrant streets now silent and empty, its people mourning the loss of their loved ones and their shattered dreams.

~

In a secure conference room within the White House, Tom Michaels sat, his heart sinking beneath the burden of responsibility. As Deputy Director of the CIA, he had been entrusted with the unenviable task of advising the American President on responding to the unthinkable: the Chinese ICBM strike that had left Moscow in ruins and the world on the brink of chaos.

President Bob Myers, a man who had always led with a steady hand and a compassionate heart, looked to Tom for guidance in these dark and uncertain times. The atmosphere in the room was thick with the weight of the decisions to be made. The eyes of the nation, and indeed the world, were upon them as they grappled with the situation that had unfolded so suddenly and with such devastating consequences.

Tom could hardly believe the chain of events that had led to this moment. The Zhurihe blast. The destruction of Moscow, the annihilation of Russia's command and control system, and the failure of the dead-hand response had left a power vacuum that threatened to destabilize the entire world. With every moment, the delicate balance of global power slipped further from their grasp.

He took a deep breath, steadying himself against the storm of emotions that threatened to overwhelm him. He had spent his entire career in service to his country, first as a Navy SEAL and then as a member of the CIA, but nothing in his past had prepared him for the task that now lay before him.

"Mr. President," he began, "the situation is dire, and our options are limited. The destruction of Moscow has left Russia reeling, and its nuclear arsenal is now without centralized control. The world is on a knife's edge, and any misstep could plunge us into a conflict that none can win." He paused, his mind racing as he weighed the consequences of each possible course of action. "We must tread carefully, Mr. President," he continued, "and stabilize the situation before it spirals out of control. It is imperative that we open lines of communication with the remaining elements of the Russian government, offering aid and support. We must also engage with China, seeking to understand their motivations and establish a new framework for global stability."

President Myers listened intently, his eyes on Tom as he absorbed the options before him. The silence in the room was deafening as he considered the path that lay ahead, a path fraught with danger and uncertainty, but one that must be taken to ensure the survival of the world as they knew it.

"I understand, Tom," he replied solemnly. "We'll do everything in our power to prevent this crisis from escalating and to restore a sense of order to the world. May God help us all."

And so Tom Michaels and President Myers set to work, guided by a single purpose: to save the world from disaster and secure a future for generations to come.

~

Under the glittering sunlight, the golden spires of the Kremlin were radiant. The royal edifice, standing as the symbol of Russian power and prestige, glittered against the brilliant azure of the Moscow sky. It was a typical day, with bustling life, echoing laughter, and echoing footsteps within the vast expanse of the Kremlin. At the heart of this structure, a meeting of the highest significance was underway.

Vladimir Petrov, accompanied by his closest allies, was engrossed in discussions about the future of Russia after the strike at Zhurihe. Men including Sergei Usnov, Minister of Defense, Alexander Bortnikov, Director of the FSB, and Oleg Melnik, head of cybersecurity, sat around a grand mahogany table, their faces creased with the gravity of their deliberations. The air buzzed with their shared vision of Russia's supremacy, a powerful and resurgent nation standing tall amidst the global powers.

However, unbeknownst to them, a fatal blow was hurtling towards them at breakneck speed. Thousands of kilometers away, a Chinese Intercontinental Ballistic Missile (ICBM), carrying a payload of devastating nuclear weaponry, had been launched towards the heart of Russia. Its target: the Kremlin, the seat of Russian power and home to Petrov and his closest allies.

As the missile pierced the atmosphere, descending towards Moscow, its nuclear payload armed and ready, the azure sky was fractured by an ominous whistling. An unprecedented silence fell over the city, its bustling life paused, as if the very earth held its breath in anticipation of the coming devastation.

The missile struck with an earth-shattering force, the impact instantly transforming the landscape into a hellscape of fire and devastation. The nuclear payload detonated, unleashing a wave of cataclysmic destruction that radiated outwards, consuming everything in its path.

In that terrifying moment, the golden spires of the Kremlin melted like wax, the walls crumbling, and the magnificent edifice crumbling into dust. Petrov and his allies, caught in the blast's epicenter, were obliterated instantly. Men who had once commanded armies, directed national security, and shaped Russia's cyber landscape were reduced to mere particles in a nuclear inferno.

The affluent neighborhoods of Rublyovka and Barvikha, where the country's oligarchs resided in their grand mansions, suffered the same fate. These strongholds of luxury and power were wiped off the face of the earth, their inhabitants evaporated in the nuclear firestorm.

Vladimir Petrov, once a man of supreme power, met his end alongside his dreams of a resurgent Russia, his life snuffed out as swiftly as it had shone. The echoes of his fall, along with his cronies, reverberated through the annals of Russia's history, a grim reminder of the devastating consequences of a nuclear conflict.

In the aftermath of the cataclysm, the world looked on in horror and disbelief, struggling to comprehend the enormity of the catastrophe that had befallen the Russian people. In the face of such unfathomable devastation, old rivalries and long-held grudges faded into insignificance, replaced by a shared sense of loss and a realization that the world would never be the same again.

As the embers of Moscow cooled, the survivors of the apocalypse confronted a future in which all the mighty had fallen. The seeds of change had been sown in the ashes of the old order, heralding an age in which the certainties of the past held no sway.

SO NOW WHAT?

As nations mourned and leaders grappled with the geopolitical implications of the Moscow catastrophe, a subtle shift took place within the realm of cryptocurrency.

With the obliteration of the Kremlin and the digital vault entombed beneath its ruins, a significant portion of the world's Bitcoin supply had vanished, presumably rendered inaccessible and irretrievable. The physical manifestation of the Satoshi Hoard, once a source of endless speculation and intrigue, had been consigned to history, its vast fortune now an eternal enigma. The Bitcoins comprising the Petrov Hoard also appeared to have vanished. And this sudden and irreversible destruction had an unexpected and far-reaching effect: the value of the remaining Bitcoins began to skyrocket.

In the world of cryptocurrency, scarcity is a fundamental principle, with the finite supply of Bitcoin acting as a powerful driver of demand. As the knowledge of the destruction of Russia's Bitcoin wallets became widespread, the realization dawned that the already limited supply of Bitcoin had become even more scarce and, thus, more valuable.

For the surviving Bitcoin holders, this newfound scarcity was akin to a hidden treasure trove. The windfall promised to bestow untold wealth upon those fortunate enough to possess the coveted digital currency. As the value of Bitcoin soared, a new wave of excitement and speculation swept through the cryptocurrency community, fueling dreams of prosperity and financial independence.

So, in the midst of global turmoil and heartache, the Bitcoin market was transformed, its landscape forever altered by the cataclysmic events in Moscow. And as the world struggled to come to terms with the new order, the holders of Bitcoin found themselves facing an uncharted future, their fates bound to the ever-fluctuating fortunes of a digital currency.

~

In the ashes of the fallen Russian empire, the winds of change began to stir, sweeping across the country's vast expanse and fanning the embers of a long-dormant hope. As the cries of a nation in mourning echoed through the air, a figure emerged whose name had become a rallying cry for the oppressed and the downtrodden. Alexei Nostrov, the dissident who had long been a thorn in the side of the Kremlin, now found himself thrust into the limelight, as the last vestiges of Petrov's regime crumbled around him.

Nostrov's journey to power was as unexpected as it was meteoric. Two hundred kilometers from the smoldering ruins of Moscow, the disarray that gripped the Russian military found its resolution in a most unlikely alliance. Tired of being treated as mere pawns in a deadly game, the soldiers and officers who remained loyal to their country rather than to their fallen leader descended upon the prison where Nostrov languished.

In a daring and unprecedented act of defiance, these remnants of Russia's once proud military staged a coup against their own, liberating Nostrov from his dank cell far away from the destruction of Moscow and escorting him to a secure location out of reach of those who would do him harm. All of Petrov's other political prisoners at IK-6, including the Kuznetsov's and Ivanov's, were released as well. Amid the rolling hills and towering forests that had long served as a sanctuary for Russia's beleaguered opposition, Nostrov and his newfound allies set to work on forging a new government.

The establishment of this temporary government, guided by the steady hand of Alexei Nostrov and bolstered by the support of Russia's disillusioned military, marked the beginning of a new chapter in Russian history. No longer shackled by the iron grip of a despot's rule, the people of Russia dreamed of a brighter future in which their voices would be heard, and their destinies shaped by their own hands.

Thus, as the sun set on a world forever changed, the people of Russia stood united, their hearts filled with hope. For in the midst of chaos and despair, a new leader had risen to guide them, his very existence a testament to the spirit of a nation reborn.

NOT QUIET ON THE EASTERN & HOME FRONTS

mid the devastation wrought by the twin nuclear detonations that rocked the world, a silent storm gathered strength off the coast of Guangdong province. The Chinese invasion of Taiwan, long planned and now set in motion, advanced toward its unsuspecting prey. The unthinkable horrors that the world had just witnessed provided the perfect cover for the Chinese fleet as it prepared to strike.

The mighty armada of warships, transports, and aircraft carriers slipped through the South China Sea, their shadows a portent of the coming tempest. At its helm, the remaining Chinese military leaders marshaled their troops, acutely aware of the enormity of their task and the prize that lay within their grasp. The race for the silicon prize had begun.

As dawn broke over the horizon, the unsuspecting residents of Taiwan went about their daily lives, unaware of the menace that lurked just beyond their shores. The bustling streets of Taipei, the verdant fields of the countryside, and the majestic peaks of the Central Mountain Range all stood in stark contrast to the darkness about to descend upon their idyllic island nation.

With a thunderous roar, the Chinese invasion force surged forward, launching a barrage of air and naval strikes that instantly overmastered Taiwan's defenses. The surprise assault was swift and brutal, and the Chinese military's numerical and technological superiority overwhelmed the beleaguered Taiwanese forces. In the skies above, a ballet of dogfights and missile exchanges raged, while on the ground columns of Chinese troops poured ashore, carving a bloody path through the Taiwanese countryside. City after city fell under the crushing weight of the invasion, as the brave defenders of Taiwan fought valiantly to stem the tide of the Chinese onslaught.

As the world awakened to the news of the Chinese invasion, the globe was plunged into a new crisis. Political leaders scrambled to respond, their efforts to avert catastrophe compounded by a massive military confrontation in the Pacific. The once tranquil waters of the South China Sea had been transformed into a churning cauldron of fire and steel as the machinations of a dead madman swept onward, leaving a trail of devastation and heartbreak in their wake.

~

In a world increasingly defined by the marvels of technology, a tiny island nation held the key to an immense and coveted treasure. Taiwan, a vibrant democracy often overshadowed by its powerful neighbor, China, was home to an industry that had become the lifeblood of the digital age: semiconductors.

These tiny, intricate devices, crafted from the element silicon, were the hearts of the world's most advanced machines. From the humblest smartphones to the most sophisticated supercomputers, semiconductors enabled the vast web of interconnected devices that had come to define modern life. Their importance could not be overstated and controlling them had become synonymous with power in the global arena.

Taiwan, through a combination of foresight, ingenuity, and determination, had risen to become the world's preeminent supplier of advanced semiconductors. The island's factories churned out a steady stream of chips, the lifeblood of a technological revolution that showed no signs of slowing.

China, not surprisingly, coveted this prize for itself. The Chinese leaders understood all too well the strategic importance of the semiconductor industry, and they longed to wrest control of it from their smaller neighbor. They dreamed of a future in which China stood at the forefront of the digital age, its technological prowess unchallenged and unrivaled.

As the rituals of diplomacy played out over the years, the tensions between China and Taiwan simmered beneath the surface. The island nation, keenly aware of the covetous gaze of its powerful neighbor, fought to protect its prized semiconductor industry, the crown jewel of its economy. But China was no longer content to sit idly by, watching as Taiwan reaped the rewards of its technological triumphs. A plan had taken shape that would allow China to wrest control of the semiconductor industry from Taiwan's grasp and, with it, the key to the digital kingdom.

~

The waters surrounding Taiwan were now a battlefield, a stormy stage where mighty naval vessels clashed. A series of fierce engagements took place, with both sides enduring heavy losses and displaying exceptional courage.

The Battle of the Taiwan Strait became an epic contest, with US-led coalition forces pitted against the formidable Chinese navy for dominion over the strategic waterway. As the Chinese forces tried to establish a beachhead on Taiwan's shores, they encountered a barrage of resistance from the combined forces of the US Marines, the indomitable Taiwanese military, and other regional allies. Elite airborne and special operations units executed daring raids behind enemy lines, severing the sinews of the Chinese supply chain.

On the water, beneath an ever-threatening sky, the USS Theodore Roosevelt and its accompanying strike group surged through the Taiwan Strait. Every sailor aboard knew that they were venturing into the lion's den, and vigilant eyes scanned the horizon for signs of deadly, incoming missiles. Yet, despite their unwavering focus, the Chinese military, like a skilled predator, caught the carrier group off guard with a devastating hypersonic missile strike. Using a formidable combination of satellite imagery, reconnaissance aircraft, and advanced over-the-horizon radar systems, the Chinese military had been shadowing Roosevelt's movements like a hawk. They patiently awaited the opportune moment to unleash their ambush, when the carrier group was most vulnerable.

The Chinese hypersonic missile, a harbinger of destruction traveling at speeds beyond Mach 5, deftly outmaneuvered the carrier group's defenses and collided with the Roosevelt. The impact, just below the flight deck, sparked a tremendous explosion that tore through the ship's hull, setting it ablaze and hurling debris in all directions. Caught off guard by the sudden attack, Roosevelt's crew scrambled to mitigate the damage and save their ship.

With the roar of flames and the groans of twisted metal as their soundtrack, they doused fires, sealed off damaged compartments, and rescued their trapped shipmates. They knew that every second mattered as the ship's structural integrity decreased and the threat of additional enemy attacks loomed overhead.

Amid this chaos Jason Johns, a valiant damage-control man, rose to the occasion. With smoke stinging his eyes and sweat pouring down his face, he navigated the corridors of the stricken ship, saving the lives of nine sailors who would have otherwise perished in the inferno. Johns' selfless acts of bravery, coupled with the courageous efforts of his comrades, prevented the fires from reaching the ship's critical systems, such as the reactor and munitions storage.

Medical personnel tended to the wounded, while those who had made the ultimate sacrifice were reverently recovered. The missile strike on the Roosevelt offered somber evidence of the vulnerability of even the most formidable naval assets. With the carrier group's flagship crippled, the US Navy was forced to reassess its strategy in the region.

The Roosevelt, though grievously wounded, was not defeated. The ship limped back to a friendly port, where teams of engineers and naval architects labored to restore it to fighting condition.

The incident would later become a rallying cry for the US-led coalition, as they redoubled their efforts to repel the Chinese invasion and secure a future for Taiwan. Roosevelt's tribulation showed the resilience and determination of the US Navy and its allies, proving that even in the face of seemingly insurmountable odds, they would not waver in their mission to protect the free world.

For his heroic efforts, Jason Johns was awarded the Medal of Honor, as one of many fighters who had demonstrated extreme courage. The battles that raged in Taiwan bore witness to exceptional bravery, sacrifice, and determination from all sides.

Meanwhile, in the face of the hypersonic threat, the US-led coalition was forced to adapt its strategies. They increased their reliance on submarine warfare and long-range strike capabilities, deploying stealth bombers and cruise missiles to target Chinese naval and air assets from a safe distance. The coalition also intensified its electronic and cyber warfare efforts, targeting China's communication networks and missile guidance systems to reduce their ability to launch coordinated attacks.

~

Within the United States, the continued machinations of a bitter ex-President and his party brought fresh uncertainty to an already volatile situation. The former administration, openly critical of American intervention in both Ukraine and the defense of Taiwan, stood at odds with the nation's military and diplomatic establishments, who saw the twin conflicts as providing a test of America's resolve and a chance to reassert its dominance on the global stage.

A narcissist with a flair for media manipulation, Harrington, along with his legions of supporters, fought against the United States' actions in world affairs. But as the situation evolved and the value of the US dollar plummeted, Harrington's personal fortune began to suffer. Faced with the prospect of his wealth evaporating, the former President suddenly became a vocal advocate for intervention, claiming as his decision to deploy military forces to both conflict zones.

Harrington's abrupt change of heart was met by skepticism and suspicion even among many of his own supporters, as well as the wider public. They questioned whether his newfound commitment to defending democracy and the international order was driven by a genuine concern for global stability or simply by a desire to protect his own wealth. As the US-led counteroffensives gained momentum, Harrington took every opportunity to position himself as the hero of the hour. He frequently boasted about his decisive leadership, claiming that it was his personal intervention that had turned the tide in both Taiwan and Ukraine.

His actions frustrated Myers' efforts to convince the world that the US could once again be trusted and was no longer as short-sighted as Harrington and his America First doctrine. Harrington's career had long been marred by financial malfeasance. Time and again, he had abused the system of bankruptcy, leaving a trail of broken promises and shattered dreams. Thousands of creditors who had extended loans and credit to Harrington were deprived of the payments they were owed, victims of a man whose ambition far outstripped his integrity.

The consequences of Harrington's actions were felt far and wide, as businesses were forced to close their doors and hardworking individuals struggled to make ends meet. Yet, in spite of the mounting evidence of his questionable dealings, Harrington remained unrepentant. His cavalier attitude was perhaps best exemplified by an incident in which an open microphone caught him suggesting that the United States should "stiff them" rather than repay its creditors.

The potential consequences of such a reckless course were staggering. If the US government were to default on its debt of more than 30 trillion dollars, the repercussions would be felt throughout the global economy. American consumers would face skyrocketing interest rates and a tightening of credit, making it all but impossible for them to secure the loans to buy homes, start businesses, or invest in their futures. The impact would be felt most keenly by the most vulnerable members of society: senior citizens, both in the United States and in countries like Japan, who had invested their hard-earned savings in US debt instruments. For these individuals, a default by the US government would be not just a betrayal of trust but a catastrophe, as they would be left with no means of supporting themselves in their twilight years.

The global economy, already teetering on the brink of disaster, would be thrown into chaos. Countries around the world would scramble to protect their interests, and the spirit of international cooperation that had been the bedrock of the post-war order would give way to an every-nation-for-itself mentality. In this harsh new world, the ideals of peace, prosperity, and mutual support would be cast aside in favor of a ruthless struggle for survival.

As the specter of this grim future loomed over the world, the earth's leaders faced a clear choice. They could succumb to the siren song of men like Harrington, who sought to exploit the fears and anxieties of their citizens for their own selfish ends, or they could stand together in defense of the values that had brought the world progress and prosperity in the past. The fate of the world hung in the balance, and the outcome would be determined not by the machinations of a single man but by the collective resolve of countless individuals who recognized the value of unity, compassion, and a shared commitment to the greater good.

~

Many nations stood together against the threat posed by the Chinese onslaught. And as the US and its allies adjusted their tactics, they began to gain the upper hand in the conflict. The Chinese naval forces, now facing a multi-faceted and increasingly effective enemy, struggled to maintain their momentum in the face of mounting losses. Now on the defensive, some even starting to withdraw from Taiwan to protect the Chinese coast.

The next great challenge, The Battle for the Pacific, proved the resilience and adaptability of the US-led coalition in the face of a determined adversary. The experience also served as a valuable lesson for the international community, highlighting the importance of staying ahead of emerging threats and adapting to new challenges in an ever-evolving geopolitical landscape.

~

Under a cloak of darkness, the entire US complement of B-2 stealth bombers emerged from the inky black skies, soaring silently over the vast expanse of the Pacific. Aboard each of these formidable warbirds was a deadly payload: the world was about to be introduced to Velocity Viper hypersonic missiles. Despite the hard-won victory of the United States and their allies in the Battle of the Taiwan Strait, the formidable Chinese Navy still threatened Taiwan, and so the decision had been made to unleash these fearsome weapons.

Laura Roberts, who played a crucial role in the development of the Vipers, watched anxiously from a control room in Nevada as the stealth bombers approached their targets. Her heart pounded with a mixture of pride and apprehension, knowing that this bold counteroffensive rested on the efficacy of the missiles she had helped to create. As the B-2s approached their launch points, the order was given and Velocity Vipers sprang forth from their metal wombs, streaking across the sky like fiery arrows. Their guidance systems, powered by quantum computing and artificial intelligence, homed in on their targets with unnerving accuracy.

The Chinese fleet, caught off guard by the unexpected attack, scrambled to deploy their defenses. But it was too late: the Velocity Vipers, undetectable by even the most advanced radar systems and traveling at more than seven times the speed of sound, proved unstoppable. In a matter of minutes, the missiles found their marks, striking the Chinese fleet with devastating precision. The once proud warships erupted in flames, their steel hulls shattered by the unstoppable force of the hypersonic projectiles.

Laura watched in awe as the harbingers of destruction she had helped to create exacted their terrible toll on the enemy. The largest navy in the world, the pride of the People's Republic of China, was reduced to a graveyard of twisted metal and charred remains. Over half of the Chinese capital ships lay in ruin, while the survivors limped back to port, their once imposing silhouettes now marred by the scars of defeat.

The Day of Reckoning, as it would come to be known, marked a turning point in the conflict. The United States and its allies, having demonstrated the overwhelming power of their new weapon, had regained the upper hand. In a single, decisive strike, they had crippled the Chinese fleet and shattered its illusion of invincibility.

While the world recovered from the shock of the unprecedented attack, the leaders of the United States and its allies knew that with their newfound power had come a new burden of responsibility. The United States now possessed an unprecedented tool of warfare, and the future of global stability rested on its ability to wield this power with wisdom and restraint.

~

The Battle of the Pacific would go down in history as the moment that changed the course of the war. At the heart of the carnage were China's prized aircraft carriers: the Liaoning and the Shandong. The carriers were similar in size and design, each boasting a crew of 2,600 personnel and each carrying 36 fighter jets, as well as a variety of helicopters. Both also featured the distinctive ski-jump design of

Soviet aircraft carriers; the Liaoning, in fact, had been built using an old Soviet hull retrofitted to meet modern standards. Both carriers relied on conventional diesel-propulsion systems, which, as events soon demonstrated, were their undoing.

Prized targets, the Liaoning and the Shandong found themselves in the crosshairs of the first four Velocity Vipers. Each carrier was targeted by two missiles, one aimed at the ammunition storage area and the other at the diesel-fuel tanks. The Vipers struck with deadly accuracy, their warheads tearing through the Chinese carriers, igniting the ammunition and fuel stores in a conflagration that lit up the night sky. The sea itself seemed to recoil from the blast, and the proud vessels were reduced to smoldering wrecks in mere moments. There was no time for escape, no hope of survival for the thousands of sailors and airmen aboard the doomed carriers. In that terrible instant, the Liaoning and the Shandong were swallowed by the waves, their destruction absolute.

The Battle of the Pacific would be remembered not just for the scale of the devastation but for the stark reminder it offered of the terrible cost of war. The dual loss of the Liaoning and the Shandong was a watershed moment, both militarily and psychologically, for the Chinese forces, and the world looked on in horror as the ugliness of modern warfare was laid bare.

A NEW WORLD ORDER

n the wake of the devastating Velocity Raptor strike, Li Chen, who
had replaced Mao Chang as the leader of China, convened an
emergency meeting of the Central Committee. The grim faces of the
assembled members spoke volumes. Their once mighty nation had
been brought to its knees. With their navy in ruins and their ground
forces decimated, China found itself in a position of unprecedented
vulnerability.

The dire nature of their situation was inescapable. No longer able
to project its power, China had little choice but to cease hostilities
and sue for peace. Li Chen, a pragmatist to his core, understood that
the time for military adventurism had passed and that the survival
of his country now depended on the goodwill of others. As if to
underscore this point, America and her allies extended a gracious
hand, offering to release all prisoners of war and provide much-needed
humanitarian assistance.

The sight of American hospital ships steaming toward the
Taiwan Strait was a potent symbol of the changing tide, and the global
community watched as the once proud Chinese Dragon grudgingly

accepted help from its former adversaries. With so much of their military capability wiped out, China—like the remnants of Russia—could no longer be considered a superpower, leaving the United States as the sole remaining global hegemon. As in conflicts past, America had emerged from the chaos relatively unscathed, her technological prowess and ability to project power unparalleled on the world stage.

For Li Chen, the road ahead was fraught with challenges. He knew that to rebuild his shattered nation he would need the assistance not just of the United States but of the entire global community. Gone were the days of bluster and bravado; now, humbled, and chastened, he must guide his people through adversity to a brighter, more peaceful future.

The world looked on with cautious optimism and a hope that out of the ashes of this terrible conflict might arise a new era of cooperation and understanding. For the people of China, and indeed for all of humanity, the path to peace and reconciliation would be long and arduous. But in the face of such devastation, the only way forward was together, united in a common purpose and a shared commitment to building a better world for all.

~

The peoples of Russia and China now found themselves at the precipice of a new world. The remains of their once mighty armies and navies limped back to port, their shattered vessels and broken spirits illustrating the catastrophic consequences of their leaders' unchecked ambition and insatiable greed. As the full extent of their losses became apparent, a great awakening spread through these ancient and proud nations. The citizens of Russia and China, long subjected to men who sought power and glory above all else, began to question the foundations upon which their societies had been built. The lies and deceit that had held them in thrall for generations began to fade away, revealing the stark truths that lay beneath.

In Russia, the death of the iron-fisted Vladimir Petrov heralded a new era of hope and possibility. Alexei Nostrov, who had long fought for the rights and dignity of the Russian people, rode upon a tide of change that promised to reshape the nation. Across the vast expanse of the Russian Federation, the people rallied behind Nostrov, their voices joining together in a resounding cry for freedom, justice, and a brighter future.

In China, the loss of the ruthless Zhang Wei left a void that begged to be filled by a new kind of leader. Li Chen, the brilliant computer engineer, and respected member of the Chinese Communist Central Committee emerged as the figurehead of a new generation of leaders. His vision of a peaceful and unified China, working hand in hand with its fellow nations, struck a chord with the millions who had suffered under the yoke of tyranny and oppression.

As the world watched in awe, these two great nations began a remarkable transformation, casting off the chains of the past. United in their shared desire for change and driven by the unquenchable fire of human potential, the people of Russia and China rose up, their collective voice a clarion call for a new world order. In the wake of destruction that had threatened to tear the world apart, Li Chen and Alexei Nostrov signaled the dawn of a new era. Their boundless courage and determination would become symbols of hope in a time of darkness.

AMERICA REACTS

The world's axis tilted on the precipice of momentous change. The tectonic plates of global politics and economics were shifting, with Russia and China poised on the cusp of a new era under untested leadership. Still, the specter of hardliners Mao Chang and Ramzan Umarov loomed ominously over their respective countries, both defiant remnants of a time when power was pursued with ruthless ferocity and nationalistic fervor.

Yet, both nations stood ravaged by their pasts, yearning for the healing salve of international aid and cooperation. As their beleaguered economies gasped for breath, the world watched with a mixture of hope and apprehension. How would the titan of the West respond? Would America, the world's remaining superpower, extend a helping hand in their hour of need?

Within the halls of power in Washington D.C., an epic battle was on the horizon. The upcoming presidential election promised to pit the incumbent, Bob Myers, against ex-president Harrington, in a contest that would shape the destiny of the world. Would America revert to an isolationist stance, prioritizing its interests above all else, or would it summon the spirit of the Marshall Plan, offering a lifeline to nations in distress?

The reverberations of these decisions would ripple across the global stage, affecting not just America's reputation but also the global financial architecture. As the dollar continued its seemingly inexorable decline, there were whispers of a new form of economic structure emerging, one that relied less on trust in centralized institutions and more on the immutable logic of decentralized technologies. Bitcoin, the once-fringe asset, was now a colossal force, its value measured in the trillions, and the world was watching closely to see how the next American president would navigate this new terrain.

Harrington, a seasoned politician, clung to the doctrine of America First, seeking to prioritize the nation's interests above all else. His detractors argued that his isolationist policies had weakened the United States' influence on the world stage, leaving a vacuum that less benevolent actors had filled.

Bob Myers, on the other hand, represented a new vision for America. He advocated for a more collaborative and compassionate approach to international relations, recognizing that the challenges of the 21st century could not be addressed by any single nation acting alone. He believed in the importance of global cooperation and sought to rebuild America's alliances while promoting human rights, democracy, and sustainable development.

In the lead-up to the election, Myers again sought the counsel of Tom Michaels. Michaels had a deep understanding of the shifting geopolitical landscape, and he believed that the United States had a unique opportunity to help guide Russia and China toward a more democratic and peaceful path. He argued that by engaging with these nations and supporting their efforts to reform and rebuild, the United States could help create a more stable and prosperous world order.

Michaels urged Myers to seize this moment, emphasizing the need for a strong and principled American leadership that could navigate the complexities of international diplomacy. He advised Myers to work closely with allies and partners, using both soft power and hard power, when necessary, to promote a global system based on the rule of law, human rights, and democratic principles.

As the campaign season wore on, the two candidates presented their contrasting visions of America's role in the world. Harrington's vision of a self-reliant and insular nation resonated with those who felt that the United States had been stretched too thin, sacrificing its own well-being in the name of global security.

Myers' vision, however, found support among those who believed that the challenges of the modern era – climate change, Artificial Intelligence, Bitcoin, nuclear proliferation, terrorism, and economic inequality – could only be addressed through concerted international cooperation. His message of unity and shared responsibility struck a chord with a nation weary of conflict and seeking a brighter, more hopeful future.

But questions loomed like gathering storm clouds. Would the world continue to underwrite American deficit spending? Or would they seek solace in the decentralized promise of Bitcoin and its brethren? The world needed a leader of substance, a beacon of trust, someone who would wield the power of the office with the measured sagacity and principled courage befitting the role.

The eyes of the world turned towards the White House, where the victor of the upcoming election would set the tone for the future. Would it be a leader of integrity, one who respected the delicacies of international relations, or would it be someone whose self-centered ambition and disregard for global harmony threatened to further fray the fragile fabric of international cooperation?

In the volatile crucible of world affairs, the fate of nations hung precariously in the balance. The world watched with bated breath, yearning for a leader with a strong moral compass, someone who could restore faith in American diplomacy and navigate the uncharted terrain of a world increasingly influenced by the disruptive power of Bitcoin.

As nations braced for the storm, the winds of change carried an echo of the past, a stark reminder that the future was not yet written.

The stage was set for a seismic shift in global power dynamics, a crucible of change that would decide the course of history. In this arena of high stakes, trust would be the most precious currency, a beacon guiding nations through the tumultuous currents of geopolitical and economic uncertainty. The world waited, poised on the precipice of an epoch-defining moment, yearning for a new dawn, a beacon of hope in the gathering storm.

~

In the Oval Office, President Bob Myers sat with furrowed brow, his gaze fixed on a report detailing the current state of the world in the aftermath of what was now being called "The Bitcoin Wars." The responsibility of steering the United States through these digital waters weighed heavily upon him, and he found solace in the counsel of his most trusted advisor, Tom Michaels. Tom had become Myers' sounding board, providing honest and politically neutral suggestions about the myriad of issues that plagued the nation.

Myers looked up from the report, his gaze meeting Tom's. "We've still got the Bitcoin issue to deal with," he said wearily.

Tom leaned back in his chair, rubbing his chin. "I haven't any idea how to deal with that," he admitted, "but I know someone who would."

Intrigued, Myers raised an eyebrow. "Who's that?"

"My fiancé, Laura Roberts," Tom replied. "She's brilliant, Mr. President. She led the Velocity Viper project, and she is one of our foremost experts in cryptocurrency and financial regulation. I believe she's exactly the person we need to help untangle this mess."

Myers considered Tom's recommendation carefully. The Bitcoin conundrum was a complex one. Both China and Russia still possessed vast amounts of the digital currency, acquired through a mix of direct purchasing and less honorable means. It was crucial to find a solution that would ensure the stability of the millions of Bitcoins held by ordinary citizens while preventing either of those two nations from profiting from the scheme.

After a moment of contemplation, Myers nodded. "Let's bring her in. I want her to chair a Presidential commission on what to do about the remaining Chinese and Russian Bitcoins."

So, with a decisive stroke of his pen, President Myers signed an executive order establishing the Commission on Bitcoin and Financial Stability, with Laura Roberts as its chair. In the months that followed, Laura and her team strove to unravel the complexities of the Bitcoin issue, consulting with experts from around the globe. As the commission's findings developed, it became clear that the path to a just and equitable solution would be fraught with challenges and risks.

Yet, under Laura's steady guidance and with constant support from President Myers, the commission pressed onward. Determined to bring closure to a chapter of history marked by greed and deception, they charted a new course for the future—one defined by transparency, collaboration, and a shared commitment to the greater good.

~

Laura found herself in a precarious position as she took on the role of chair for the newly formed Presidential Commission on Bitcoin and Financial Stability. President Myers, a pragmatic leader, had chosen her for her expertise and her discretion. Now, she was tasked with navigating the uncertain waters of this new frontier.

Their first order of business was to better understand the power of Bitcoin and to determine the fate of the Satoshi horde. Should this wealth stay buried in the now obliterated Kremlin Vault, a lost treasure consigned to the annals of history? Or should they reveal to the world that the Satoshi horde was not only intact but also within the control of the United States government?

The commission was meticulously curated to represent a balanced cross-section of political ideologies and professional backgrounds. There was a delicate equilibrium to maintain, a careful calibration of voices and perspectives, where radical extremes on either end of the political spectrum were consciously excluded. The objective was to encourage constructive dialogue, foster mutual understanding, and ultimately reach a consensus.

Representing the America First Party was Senator Franklin Moore, a seasoned politician with a reputation for his pragmatic approach to policymaking. His in-depth understanding of domestic affairs, coupled with his experience as the former Chair of the Senate Banking Committee, made him a valuable asset to the commission.

From the Democrats, Professor Amelia Zhao was invited to join the commission. A renowned economist from Stanford University, Zhao was known for her seminal work on digital currencies and their impact on global financial systems. Her deep understanding of cryptocurrencies and their potential to revolutionize financial markets brought a much-needed academic perspective to the commission's work.

Bethany Keller, the former CEO of a leading multinational bank, represented moderate Republicans. Keller's vast experience in the world of finance, along with her nuanced understanding of the complex interplay between financial markets and public policy, provided a unique vantage point.

Completing the commission was Dr. Rajesh Nair, a technologist, and a thought leader in the field of blockchain and cryptography. A non-partisan, Nair's expertise was vital in decoding the intricacies of Bitcoin and its underlying technology. His comprehensive knowledge of the technological side of cryptocurrencies ensured that the commission's discussions and decisions were grounded in a thorough understanding of the system's capabilities and limitations.

This diverse group of individuals was tasked with the monumental responsibility of deciding America's future Bitcoin and financial policy. They were not only deciding the fate of immense wealth but also charting the course for potentially a new global financial order. Their decisions, guided by their collective wisdom and expertise, would not only impact the United States but also ripple out to affect the entire world.

The task before them was daunting. Yet, as they convened, there was a shared sense of purpose, a collective resolve to rise to the challenge. After all, they were not just deciding on the future of Bitcoin; they were shaping the future of the global economy. It was a responsibility they did not take lightly, and they were prepared to do their utmost to ensure a stable and prosperous future.

As the chair of the commission, Laura stood at the head of the large mahogany table. To her right, Bethany Keller was assembling her notes, her face reflecting the gravity of the meeting. Both women were acutely aware of the vast responsibility they had been entrusted with.

Clearing her throat, Laura began, her voice steady, resonating with conviction. "Our discussion today revolves around the intrinsic genius of the Bitcoin blockchain," she started, her gaze sweeping over the room, meeting the curious eyes of the other commission members. "The underlying strength of this system is that it has created what is currently the most secure network in the world."

A murmur echoed through the room. Senator Moore, sitting across from Laura, furrowed his brows, the unfamiliar concept visibly daunting. Laura acknowledged his confusion with a gentle nod and decided to simplify the concept.

"I see you're struggling with this, Franklin," she said to Moore. "Let's try a different approach. Consider Bitcoin like a gold mine."

Laura paused, letting the image settle in the minds of her listeners. "In our grand tapestry of human civilization, gold mines have always been the center of attraction, a symbol of immense wealth. But with Bitcoin, we are talking about a different kind of mine."

Bethany Keller, former CEO of a multinational bank and representing the Republicans, stepped in to support Laura's analogy. "Indeed," she added, "this is a gold mine that is not beneath the earth, hidden away in a remote location but right in the heart of a bustling city. A network of computers, each one a miner, working relentlessly to extract Bitcoin. Much like how traditional miners dig for gold."

Moore's face showed the first traces of understanding. Laura continued, "And like any valuable mine, the more valuable the gold, the more miners will want to participate in its extraction. Similarly, as the value of Bitcoin increases, more people set up their computers to mine, thus increasing the security of the Bitcoin network."

Laura picked up a gold coin from the table, catching the sunlight streaming in through the tall windows. "As a thief, breaking into this gold mine would be no easy feat," she said, her eyes reflecting the glint of the coin. "The more miners or security guards there are, the harder it is for the thief to succeed."

Bethany chimed in, "And in this context, the thieves could be hackers or fraudsters. The more miners there are in the Bitcoin network, the harder it is for these nefarious actors to execute fraudulent transactions."

Dr. Nair then added his thoughts to the discussion, "The value of having the most secure network in the world cannot be understated. In a digital age where cyber threats are a significant concern, a secure network can provide a high degree of confidence for users. It becomes a safe place to store and transact value (like a highly secure bank), reducing the risk of theft and fraud. This can be especially important for large transactions or for people in countries with unstable financial systems.

Laura then added two final thoughts "Additionally, as the most secure network in the world, Bitcoin can become a foundation for other financial services and applications, much like the Internet is the foundation for countless apps and websites. This could potentially revolutionize the global financial system, making it more open, inclusive, and efficient. "In summary, as the value of Bitcoin increases, so does the security of the Bitcoin network, attracting more users and use cases, creating a virtuous cycle of increasing value and security. This is one of the key reasons why Bitcoin has garnered so much interest and investment over the years."

The room was silent, everyone immersed in the analogy. Laura gently placed the coin back on the table, breaking the spell. "In essence, Bitcoin is like a fortified gold mine in the middle of a city, constantly guarded by miners. It's a network built on trust in mathematical laws and secured by a decentralized network of computers. In a world where cybersecurity threats are an increasing concern, Bitcoin presents the most secure network ever developed, a veritable fortress in the digital world."

Laura's analogy of the gold mine had made the complex concept of Bitcoin mining and security more tangible to the members of the commission. As the meeting ended, they left with a new understanding of Bitcoin's power and potential, setting the stage for the monumental decision that lay ahead.

Now that they had established the value of the Bitcoin network itself, Laura prepared to discuss the status of the Satoshi Horde. President Myers had already advised her that he would prefer to leave this decision until after the upcoming election. It seemed prudent to leave this decision to the next president, even if that wasn't to be Bob Myers himself. Laura assured the other members of the commission that the Bitcoins were safe until a decision could be made as to whether they reappeared under the control of the US government or remained buried in the radioactive Kremlin vault forever.

~

An air of gravity pervaded the Roosevelt Room as members of the Presidential Commission on Bitcoin and Financial Stability reconvened for the second time. The midday sun painted the room in a solemn golden hue, casting long, somber shadows that danced upon the grand mahogany table. Laura, once again taking her place at the helm of the commission, felt the weight of the world on her shoulders. In her possession lay a secret of such magnitude that it could shift the global economic balance, forever altering the course of financial history.

The formidable portraits of presidents past seemed to scrutinize the assembly with spectral gazes, silent witnesses to their deliberations. Laura exhaled softly, her gaze sweeping across the room before settling on the faces of those before her.

First, she reminded the commission members of President Myers' preference for deferring the decision regarding the horde till after the upcoming election. Laura understood the wisdom behind his prudence. Very few were aware of the existence of these dormant bitcoins, and fewer still knew that the U.S. government had the means to access them. It was Pandora's box of sorts, one whose lid was best kept shut until the country's political future was determined.

With measured words, Laura began to address the room. She told them about the existence of another key holder - a man whose identity must remain a veiled secret. A man who was undoubtedly, one of the world's foremost experts on cryptocurrency. His role in the government was not to be disclosed, but Laura reassured them that the keys to the treasure trove could not be accessed without her direct participation. The bitcoins, she once again assured them, were safe until a decision could be made - whether they would be reanimated under the aegis of the U.S. government or left to slumber in the depths of the radioactive Kremlin vault.

As Laura concluded her discourse, a silence hung in the room - a silence that resonated with the gravity of the information revealed. Each member of the commission was grappling with the enormity of the secret they now bore.

Laura's voice once again broke the silence, her words a solemn reminder of the oath they had taken upon accepting membership in the commission. The mandate was clear - all deliberations and information disclosed within the confines of the Roosevelt Room were to remain secret. Apart from President Myers, no one else was to know of their proceedings. The oath was a crucible of trust, a bond that united them in their shared responsibility.

As the second meeting of the commission drew to a close, each member left with the burden of the secret they now held, the knowledge of the Satoshi Horde seared into their consciousness. And so, the stage was set for the next act in this grand historical drama, the future of the Satoshi Horde resting in the hands of the commission and the impending election.

A STARK CHOICE; THE AMERICAN ELECTION

Senator Franklin Moore's move was as predictable as the setting sun in the annals of political maneuvering. Moore was not an evil man but was loyal almost to a fault. Compelled by this loyalty and a misguided sense of duty, he raced to divulge the secret of the Satoshi Hoard to his confidant, former President Harrington. The ripple of this betrayal reached Laura through her intricate network of government insiders. She received it with an air of resigned anticipation, having been prepared for such a scenario. However, Laura had held onto the most crucial information - the identity of the second key holder, the new Satoshi Nakamoto.

A deep sense of foreboding, a dread that made her stomach churn, gripped Laura. If Harrington managed to claw his way back to the presidency, she knew she would have to yield the final secret. The thought of revealing the new Satoshi's identity was a daunting prospect. Nevertheless, she was determined to safeguard this secret until it became absolutely necessary to disclose it.

Inside his opulent study, Harrington received the news with explosive rage. His furious roar echoed off the high ceilings, a predatory beast in his concrete savannah. "Who the fuck has the other key?" He thundered, his gaze burning with ferocious intensity. The audacity of someone daring to withhold such an immense secret from him was unthinkable. "Get me a name, Franklin! Those keys will be under my control before I step foot back into the Oval Office."

The insatiable hunger for power and control glowed in Harrington's eyes. The prospect of laying claim to a trillion dollars in bitcoins was impossible for him to resist. His orders to Franklin didn't stop there. "We need control over the Russian and Chinese Bitcoins too!" His words echoed with unrestrained greed and a ruthless gleam in his eyes.

But Harrington's thirst wasn't merely for financial gain. He craved a legacy, a permanent and indelible mark on history. "Myers has this vision of a second Marshall Plan, and if anyone's going to be hailed as the world's savior, it's going to be me!" His words rang with a proclamation of his boundless ambition.

His cold-hearted sentiment was clear: "We should have just let the Russians and Chinese wipe each other out; it would've solved our problems." Such a chilling outlook was telling of the man that Harrington was—relentless, unyielding, and ruthless in his pursuit of power.

Moore stood in shock, feeling a sting of regret for having revealed the secret. The intensity of Harrington's response was a stark reminder of the man's relentless ambition, a facet of his character Moore had previously overlooked in his misplaced loyalty. The realization filled him with a heavy sense of remorse.

Meanwhile, Laura braced herself for the impending storm. The stage was set for a clash that could potentially reshape the world order. But for now, the identity of the new Satoshi Nakamoto was safe, nestled securely within the shadows, awaiting the right moment to emerge.

~

In the months following the cataclysmic bombings in China and Russia, the full scale of the devastation began to reveal itself. From the farthest corners of the Earth, people watched in horror as images of the shattered landscapes and ruined cities were broadcast, the grim reality of the consequences of unchecked power and ambition displayed for all to see.

But as the initial shock and outrage at the actions of the Russian and Chinese governments subsided, a new sentiment took hold in the hearts and minds of people across the globe: compassion for the suffering of the innocent citizens of both nations, as the world recognized that the despots who had triggered the nuclear disaster were gone, and that in their place now stood new leaders who sought to heal the wounds of the past and embrace a brighter, more peaceful future.

In China, Li Chen's swift ascension to the role of General Secretary signaled a dramatic shift in the nation's political landscape. The system of corruption and greed that had held the country in its grip for so long dissipated in the light of Li Chen's vision of unity, progress, and peaceful coexistence. The people of China, long oppressed and downtrodden, looked to their new leader with hope and a renewed sense of purpose, daring to dream of a better tomorrow.

In Russia's vast and rugged expanse, Alexei Nostrov offered himself as the voice of a people hungry for change and desperate for a new path forward. With an election hastily scheduled for the coming months, Nostrov's rise to power seemed all but assured, for the citizens of Russia rallied behind him in an unprecedented wave of support. The promise of a future free from Petrov's iron grip had ignited a passionate fire in the hearts of the Russian people.

In the halls of power and the homes of ordinary citizens alike, the message was clear: it was time to set aside the animosities of the past and to work together toward a common goal—the betterment of the human race. The scars of the past would not heal overnight, but with the leadership of Li Chen and Alexei Nostrov, the two nations embarked on their new journey.

~

In the wake of what was now called the Bitcoin Wars, the balance of power in the world shifted dramatically. The United States, now the unchallenged global leader, found itself entrusted with the immense responsibility of guiding the world into a new era of peace and prosperity. Its leaders faced unimaginable obligations, including the ethical development of AI, rebuilding a world devastated by two nuclear explosions, managing the potential and danger of Bitcoin, and controlling weapons of unprecedented power like the Velocity Viper. Many wondered whether American hegemony would prove to be a force for good or if the world would once again be plunged into a trough of unchecked ambition and greed.

In academia, scholars debated the merits and drawbacks of American hegemony. Some argued that the United States' dominant position on the world stage had created a zero-sum game in which the success of one nation came at the expense of others. Others maintained that American hegemony had not been an entirely negative force. For decades, they said, the Pax Americana had provided the stability necessary for international trade and economic growth to flourish. The United States had also championed human rights and democratic values, helping to lift millions out of poverty and oppression. Moreover, its role as the world's policeman had deterred aggression and maintained a semblance of order in an often-chaotic world.

As the debate raged on, a consensus emerged among the more thoughtful observers of the global stage. They posited that the true danger lay not in American hegemony itself but in the potential for those who wielded such power to lose their moral compass. When leaders' decisions were driven by self-interest and personal ambition rather than a genuine concern for the well-being of all, the world was put at risk.

President Myers, mindful of the responsibility that rested upon his shoulders, was determined to ensure that the United States would be a force for good in this new era. His advisors assured him that the Bitcoin Hordes alone would pay most of the costs of recovery and that very little would fall on American taxpayers. Still, he sought the counsel of other wise and experienced advisors, including Laura Roberts and her Commission members, who shared his commitment to a more just and equitable world. But he knew the task before him was monumental and the road ahead would be fraught with challenges. After all, tens of millions of American voters would be presented with the extraordinary dilemma of putting someone who could be a convicted felon back into the Oval Office and entrusting him with the nation's most vital secrets, national security, and democracy.

As he addressed the nation in a speech remembered for generations to come, President Myers spoke of the importance of humility, empathy, and compassion in exercising power. "We must never forget that our actions reverberate across the globe," he said, "and that the decisions we make today will shape the world our children inherit. Let us strive to be guided not by fear, greed, or ambition but by a shared commitment to the betterment of all mankind."

In the wake of the Bitcoin Wars, the world stood at a crossroads, poised to embark on a journey into uncharted territory. The challenges ahead were daunting, but the wisdom of those who understood the true nature of power and the importance of moral leadership offered a glimmer of hope. With a renewed sense of purpose, the United States and the world prepared to face the future together, united in their determination to build a better world for all.

~

In Washington, DC, politicians and economists gathered to discuss a matter of great importance: the United States' ability to finance its deficit spending at attractive interest rates.

The world looked to America as a bastion of stability and security, and its faith in the nation's financial strength was reflected in the willingness of other countries to invest in US treasuries, effectively subsidizing the nation's IOUs at rates far lower than those offered to any other country or entity.

However, this preferential treatment came with a price, and it was incumbent upon the United States to pay it willingly. The nation was expected to promote global stability and act with a strong moral compass, acting to benefit not only its citizens but the entire world. This unwritten agreement underpinned the global financial system, and the United States had long been a willing participant, embracing its role as a global leader.

US treasuries were widely regarded as the most secure debt in the world, thanks to the nation's unparalleled ability to repay its obligations. In more than two hundred years, the United States had never defaulted on its debt, earning it a reputation for reliability that other countries could only envy. The faith that investors placed in the US government was reflected in the vast holdings of US treasuries, which formed the bedrock of the global financial system.

Yet, despite the strength of this arrangement, there were those who sought to disrupt it. The remnants of Harrington's America First party, clinging to the belief that their country should prioritize its own interests above all else, floated the possibility of default as a means to achieve their goals. They were either ignorant or willfully blind to the consequences of their actions, which threatened to upend the delicate balance that had sustained the world for generations.

If the United States were to default on its debt, the global financial system would be plunged into chaos. Confidence in the nation's ability to repay its obligations would be shattered, and the attractive interest rates that had long been a cornerstone of the US economy would evaporate. The resulting instability and turbulence would reverberate across the globe, affecting not only the United States but countless other nations as well.

As the world stood at the precipice of this potential catastrophe, the wise and far-sighted leaders who still controlled the United States government understood the importance of the delicate balance upon which their nation's prosperity depended. They recognized the value of the world's trust. They were determined to ensure that America continued to meet its obligations as a global leader, acting with strength and compassion to promote the well-being of all people, not just its own citizens.

~

America's responsibility for the greater good extended to a force that had only recently emerged and would reshape the contours of power and influence: artificial intelligence. This technology, as subtle as it was formidable, had the potential to redefine the boundaries of American hegemony.

The tendrils of AI reached deep into the economic fabric of the United States, promising a revolution that would reshape entire industries and usher in unparalleled productivity. American companies, long the harbingers of progress and prosperity, found themselves in a unique position to harness this newfound power and assert their dominance over the global market. With each technological leap, the foundations of the American economy grow stronger, buttressing the nation's influence and authority.

In warfare, the utility of AI was readily apparent. The United States' military prowess, long the cornerstone of its hegemony, would be unquestionably bolstered by the integration of AI into its arsenal. The promise of enhanced capabilities in every arena, from the depths of the ocean to the vastness of space, carried with it the assurance of America's continued ability to protect its interests in an increasingly complex world. But this newfound strength would come with a high price: the military-industrial complex constantly expanded its reach and influence, feeding the machinery of war and cementing the nation's position as the global security arbiter while ensuring its own power.

The United States had long held sway in innovation, boasting a roster of technology companies that stood as titans in their field. American leadership, development, and the proliferation of AI solidified this advantage, granting America the ability to establish global standards and norms for the use of this groundbreaking technology. In the years to come, the winds of change would blow strong, carrying the potential for a new era of American hegemony in which the power of AI would elevate the nation to unprecedented heights.

Yet, for all its promise and potential, the deployment of AI demanded careful stewardship, lest the unintended consequences of this new technology sow the seeds of discord and strife. With the dawn of a new age came the responsibility to ensure that AI was wielded judiciously and with foresight, guided by a steadfast commitment to the common good.

And so, as the world stood poised on the brink of a new epoch, responsibility for the course of American hegemony was compounded by the indomitable force and undeniable burden of artificial intelligence. In this delicate balance of power and progress, the fate of nations was at stake, their destinies entwined in a dance as old as time itself.

~

My Fellow Americans,

I stand before you today from the hallowed confines of the Oval Office, began Bob Myers, *a place that has seen countless decisions, each shaping the course of our great nation and the world beyond our borders. Today, I wish to address a moment in history that shaped our world and the stark alternate reality that could have unfolded.*

In the smoky aftermath of the Second World War, Europe was a continent brought to its knees. The vibrant cities of culture and civilization were little more than charred ruins. The German nation, which had lit the fuse of this horrific conflict, was a desolate landscape of loss and despair. With no helping hand extended, Germany and the whole of Europe faced a daunting, perhaps insurmountable path to recovery.

On our shores, voices urged isolationism, a retreat within our borders while Europe teetered on the edge. Yet, in a bold affirmation of our shared humanity, we enacted the Economic Cooperation Act of 1948, or as it is more commonly known, the Marshall Plan. By today's measures, we committed the staggering sum of 130 billion dollars to mend the scars of war, not as conquerors but as compassionate human beings.

Now, let us tread the path not taken. What if we, as a nation, had decided to turn a blind eye to the suffering beyond our shores post-World War II?

In this alternate history, the wounds of war would deepen in Europe. Bereft of hope and aid, Germany would remain a desolate landscape of despair. The recovery of Europe would have been a slow and agonizing journey. The vibrant continent would be mired in economic stagnation, its cities mere skeletal reminders of their past grandeur.

A Europe left to its own devices could have been swept under the ever-looming shadow of Soviet Communism. The delicate balance of power during the Cold War could have tilted alarmingly. The world as we know it could have been a landscape riddled with heightened tensions and increased instability.

Without the Marshall Plan, the transatlantic bonds we cherish could have been strained, perhaps even severed. The spirit of cooperation and mutual respect fostered by the aid could be replaced with resentment and discord. A world divided, not united, could be our reality.

In essence, the Marshall Plan was not just an act of aid; it was a strategic, compassionate move that stabilized Europe, halted the spread of communism, and furthered our position as a force for good. Extending our hand across the Atlantic helped shape a world of cooperation and relative peace.

Today, as we face the challenge of rebuilding two continents ravaged by the horrifying specter of war and nuclear destruction, we look back at the lessons of the Marshall Plan. We remember the world that could have been and vow to make a difference again.

Thank you, God bless you, and God bless the United States of America.

~

The United States found itself on the precipice of historical change, caught in the throes of a presidential election that bore the weight of its future. The stage was set for a faceoff between two ideologically disparate contenders; former President Harrington, bearing the stains of numerous criminal indictments and adverse civil judgments, and President Bob Myers, a beacon of hope in uncertain times.

Harrington's resilience was perplexing. Despite his tarnished reputation, he had somehow continued as the standard-bearer for his party, doggedly clawing his way into the primaries, threatening to unravel the progress that had been painstakingly achieved since his previous loss. His American First doctrine, underpinned by isolationist policies, had seen America's global influence wane, allowing less benevolent forces to creep into the void. Harrington's first term wreaked havoc on America's global standing, and another term could reduce America to an international pariah, an entity bereft of the respect it had commanded for decades.

Myers, however, presented a stark contrast. A visionary leader, he saw a world where the challenges of the 21st century could not be met by a single nation. He championed global cooperation, aiming to restore America's alliances while advocating for human rights, democracy, and sustainable development. He envisioned an America that was an active participant in a globally collaborative system rather than a self-serving outlier.

As the electoral campaign gathered momentum, Myers again sought advice from Tom Michaels, a pragmatist who believed that America had a golden opportunity to steer Russia and China toward democratic reform and peace. He counseled Myers to seize the moment, urging a robust American leadership that could adroitly navigate the international diplomacy labyrinth.

The primary season was brutal. In a grotesque spectacle of

mudslinging and character assassination, Harrington locked horns with another Ultranationalist contender, ripping each other apart with ruthless aggression. And, as the primaries progressed, a perceptible shift occurred. The tide began to turn against extremism, signaling a collective weariness of their autocratic stance.

Meanwhile, the Myers campaign radiated positivity. His vision resonated with those who recognized the global nature of contemporary challenges - climate change, nuclear proliferation, terrorism, artificial intelligence, and economic inequality. His message of unity and shared responsibility kindled a spark of hope in a nation scarred by conflict and yearning for change.

As the election drew closer, the American public wrestled with their choice, acutely aware of the repercussions. The election result would echo far beyond America's borders, influencing the trajectory of global history. Their vote would either shepherd an era of peace, prosperity, and global unity or plunge the world further into extremism, chaos, and isolation.

Finally, on election day, the American people, with bated breath, cast their votes. As the results trickled in, it became evident that the winds of change were blowing. The extremist order was being swept away, ushering in a new era led by a renewed America, striving to be a beacon of hope and progress in a complex world.

EPILOGUE

I n the vast tapestry of human history, the American experiment stands as a beacon of hope and progress, a testament to the indomitable human spirit that has propelled the nation to great heights. The United States, for all its flaws and imperfections, remains a powerful force for good in the world, and countless individuals dream of joining its ranks, eager to partake in the opportunities it offers. The ingenuity and innovation that have long been the hallmarks of America continue to flourish, and the country's technological prowess remains unrivaled. As the world looks back at the monumental efforts of the United States to rebuild the world after the devastation of two global conflicts, it becomes apparent that the American spirit is one of resilience and determination, capable of rising to challenge time and time again.

And yet, the winds of change are ever-present, and the passing of the Greatest Generation raises questions about the path that lies ahead. Can America once more rise to the occasion, as it did in the past, to guide the world through the turbulence of an uncertain future? Under the faltering leadership of President Harrington, the answer may appear uncertain. But hope endures, as it always does, and figures like Bob Myers stand as a testament to the potential for greatness that exists within the American people.

~

In an imperfect world, the existence of a superpower with a strong moral compass and a willingness to shoulder the burden of debt in the pursuit of the greater good is invaluable. The United States, guided by principles that reach beyond the realm of mere self-interest, has the potential to continue shaping the world in a positive manner, provided it never loses sight of the values upon which it was founded.

The US dollar, that symbol of American economic might, will continue to thrive as long as the country's moral compass remains true. And with it, American hegemony will endure, safeguarding the promise of a brighter future for generations to come. In the end, the imperfect world needs the United States, now more than ever, to remain a beacon of hope, guiding humanity through the darkness and into the light.

Picture a starry sky where countless celestial bodies sparkle against the dark expanse, each with its own unique brightness and purpose. In the cosmic dance of global finance, two stars stand out: Bitcoin and the US dollar. Though they might seem to be on a collision course, they're destined to shine together, illuminating the world with their combined brilliance.

Bitcoin, the digital marvel, represents a revolutionary shift in the way we perceive and handle money. Its decentralized essence and the security provided by blockchain technology make it a guiding light for those yearning for an alternative to conventional financial systems. With its finite supply, Bitcoin is viewed as a bastion of value, immune to manipulation and debasement, offering a safeguard against inflation and economic uncertainty.

The US dollar, meanwhile, symbolizes a more adaptable form of currency. As the world's primary reserve currency, it fuels international trade and finance, drawing strength from America's stable and powerful economy. Although the dollar's value might ebb and flow, it remains an indispensable tool in global economic policy, especially in addressing crises and promoting growth.

When the earth trembles and storms rage, a superpower like the United States can harness its monetary might to marshal the resources needed to face and conquer adversity. In these moments, the US dollar assumes the mantle of an economic catalyst and savior, enabling swift and resolute action.

Bitcoin and the US dollar can not only coexist but also thrive in harmony, enriching the global economy. Each possesses unique strengths and serves different purposes within the financial ecosystem. Bitcoin acts as a digital fortress of value, offering stability in a fluctuating world, while the US dollar continues to be a potent force in economic policy and the anchor of global commerce.

United, these two luminaries can reinforce the world's financial infrastructure, ensuring that the global economy remains strong, flexible, and primed for the challenges ahead. Together, Bitcoin and the US dollar can form a celestial alliance, guaranteeing prosperity and progress for generations to come. The stars have aligned, and the future is brighter with this dynamic duo shining in unison.

Made in the USA
Thornton, CO
11/01/23 11:01:11

8aeafe83-b591-41fe-819f-3edf4b9ab05fR01